Ideology

Key Concepts Series

Barbara Adam, *Time*
Alan Aldridge, *Consumption*
Alan Aldridge, *The Market*
Jakob Arnoldi, *Risk*
Will Atkinson, *Class*
Colin Barnes and Geof Mercer, *Disability*
Darin Barney, *The Network Society*
Mildred Blaxter, *Health 2nd edition*
Harriet Bradley, *Gender 2nd edition*
Harry Brighouse, *Justice*
Mónica Brito Vieira and David Runciman, *Representation*
Steve Bruce, *Fundamentalism 2nd edition*
Joan Busfield, *Mental Illness*
Damien Cahill and Martijn Konings, *Neoliberalism*
Margaret Canovan, *The People*
Andrew Jason Cohen, *Toleration*
Alejandro Colás, *Empire*
Patricia Hill Collins and Sirma Bilge, *Intersectionality 2nd edition*
Mary Daly, *Welfare*
Anthony Elliott, *Concepts of the Self 4th edition*
Steve Fenton, *Ethnicity 2nd edition*
Katrin Flikschuh, *Freedom*
Michael Freeman, *Human Rights 4th edition*
Russell Hardin, *Trust*
Geoffrey Ingham, *Capitalism*
Fred Inglis, *Culture*
Robert H. Jackson, *Sovereignty*
Jennifer Jackson Preece, *Minority Rights*
Gill Jones, *Youth*
Paul Kelly, *Liberalism*
Anne Mette Kjær, *Governance*
Ruth Lister, *Poverty 2nd edition*
Cillian McBride, *Recognition*
Jon Mandle, *Global Justice*
Marius S. Ostrowski, *Ideology*
Anthony Payne and Nicola Phillips, *Development*
Judith Phillips, *Care*
Chris Phillipson, *Ageing*
Robert Reiner, *Crime*
Michael Saward, *Democracy*
William E. Scheuerman, *Civil Disobedience*
John Scott, *Power*
Timothy J. Sinclair, *Global Governance*
Anthony D. Smith, *Nationalism 2nd edition*
Joonmo Son, *Social Capital*
Deborah Stevenson, *The City*
Leslie Paul Thiele, *Sustainability 2nd edition*
Steven Peter Vallas, *Work*
Stuart White, *Equality*
Michael Wyness, *Childhood*

Ideology

Marius S. Ostrowski

polity

Copyright © Marius S. Ostrowski 2022

The right of Marius S. Ostrowski to be identified as Author of this Work has been asserted in accordance with the UK Copyright, Designs and Patents Act 1988.

First published in 2022 by Polity Press

Polity Press
65 Bridge Street
Cambridge CB2 1UR, UK

Polity Press
101 Station Landing
Suite 300
Medford, MA 02155, USA

All rights reserved. Except for the quotation of short passages for the purpose of criticism and review, no part of this publication may be reproduced, stored in a retrieval system or transmitted, in any form or by any means, electronic, mechanical, photocopying, recording or otherwise, without the prior permission of the publisher.

ISBN-13: 978-1-5095-4072-3
ISBN-13: 978-1-5095-4073-0 (pb)

A catalogue record for this book is available from the British Library.

Library of Congress Control Number: 2021948304

Typeset in 10.5 on 12pt Sabon
by Fakenham Prepress Solutions, Fakenham, Norfolk NR21 8NL
Printed and bound in Great Britain by CPI Group (UK) Ltd, Croydon

The publisher has used its best endeavours to ensure that the URLs for external websites referred to in this book are correct and active at the time of going to press. However, the publisher has no responsibility for the websites and can make no guarantee that a site will remain live or that the content is or will remain appropriate.

Every effort has been made to trace all copyright holders, but if any have been overlooked the publisher will be pleased to include any necessary credits in any subsequent reprint or edition.

For further information on Polity, visit our website:
politybooks.com

Contents

Figures and Tables vi
Preface vii

1 Introduction 1

2 The evolution of ideology theory 17

3 What is ideology? 42

4 Ideology and ideologies 70

5 The experience of ideology 109

6 The dimensions of ideology studies 141

7 Conclusion 164

References 168
Index 187

Figures and Tables

Figures

1	The history of ideology theory	21
2	An overview of ideologies' historical development	88
3	The ideological compass	106
4	Ideological apparatuses' operations over the life cycle	120
5	Sources of ideological influence	124
6	The ideology studies compass	162

Tables

1	The criteria of ideological characterisation	65
2	Social domains	74
3	Overview of ideologies' social morphologies	95
4	Ideological apparatuses across social domains	118

Preface

In 1967, in his essay 'Negative and Positive Freedom', the philosopher Gerald MacCallum put forward a deceptively simple but at the time profoundly radical claim: that the idea of freedom referred to a single concept. To understand the radicalism of MacCallum's proposition, we have to recall its intellectual context. Under the shadow of recent and ongoing conflicts between liberal democracy and fascist and communist totalitarianism, the philosophical study of freedom had settled on the view, developed by Erich Fromm in 1941 and popularised by Isaiah Berlin in 1958, that there was an irreducible bifurcated distinction between two supposedly incompatible concepts of freedom, each with their own lengthy intellectual traditions. One was 'negative' freedom, x is (is not) free from y, defined as the absence of any external interference or constraint; the other, 'positive' freedom, x is (is not) free to y, the capacity to enact one's will and achieve one's aims and potential. With his intervention, MacCallum sought to upend this established consensus. He suggested a formulation that could unite these two understandings, which he termed the 'triadic relation': x is (is not) free from y to do (not do, become, not become) z. The term 'freedom', he concluded, was in fact a single concept; and its 'negative' and 'positive' interpretations were not mutually unintelligible concepts or traditions but merely two *conceptions*, two ways of looking at the same concept from different angles. MacCallum's essay has become a staple presence on Anglo-American political philosophy syllabi. Every year, legions of students are invited to consider whether the various defenders and detractors of 'negative' and 'positive' freedom – and of its recently recovered sibling 'republican' freedom – are representatives of colossal worldviews talking blindly past one another or indulging the narcissism of the tiniest differences by exaggerating tweaks of perspective into grandiose existential feuds.

It is a similar situation with the concept of 'ideology'. One of the first choices you have to make when writing about 'ideology' – under pressure from representatives of different methodological perspectives, from Marxism to poststructuralism, from comparative politics to social psychology – is whether to run with the idea that there are many incommensurable meanings of the term or insist on staking out a patch of analytical common ground with a concept of 'ideology' on which the various different 'sides' can put their unique 'spin'. There are persuasive defences by eminent names within ideology theory arrayed on either side: to name only a few, Raymond Boudon, Terry Eagleton, and John Thompson for the former approach, David Manning and Martin Seliger for the latter. In very broad terms, the first camp takes the view that 'ideology' is used to refer (correctly or incorrectly, sincerely as well as insincerely) to a host of social phenomena that have only a loose connection with one another – or even contradict one another outright – and that only some should be included in the formal study of ideology, others excluded from it, but all kept rigorously analytically distinct. The second camp, meanwhile, insists that such diversity of phenomena illustrates above all the social pervasiveness and complexity of ideology but does not eliminate the possibility – or obviate the need – to find a way of bringing all of them theoretically 'under the same roof', precisely to reflect the fact that ideology is 'implicated' in all of them, no matter how differently or (seemingly) incompatibly. In this book, I side with the second camp. The upshot is an account of ideology that acknowledges the cumulative wisdom of different ways of analysing it but carves a path towards a definition that is of interest, and of use, to all the areas of social life and social research in which 'ideology' appears.

Neither the fall of Babel of Genesis narrative, then, nor the angels dancing on a pinhead of anti-scholastic polemic, but a judicious ecumenism.

All that remains is for me to acknowledge the help and support of all those who have contributed to making this project come to fruition. Special thanks go to George Owers and Julia Davies at Polity, as well as the anonymous reviewers appointed to read my proposal and my manuscript; the same to my colleagues at the *Journal of Political Ideologies*, especially Michael Freeden and Mathew Humphrey; to all my friends and colleagues who have allowed me to benefit from their invaluable feedback; and to Esther Brown, who has had to listen to me talk excitedly about ideology more than anyone else.

Marius S. Ostrowski
King's Lynn, September 2021

1
Introduction

Among the concepts that colour social life and permeate social research, few carry as many and as diverse connotations as 'ideology'. In essence, 'ideology' signifies a worldview or overarching philosophy, constituted by an integrated body of individual or collective characteristic claims, aims, principles, beliefs, and manners of thinking. Yet, in our vernacular usage, we also inflect the term with a series of highly specific and loaded overtones. We call 'ideological' ideas and arguments that we consider wrong and misleading, that we find lacking in evidence, limited and 'broad-brush' as opposed to nuanced and comprehensive. We use the word to dismiss implausible, abstract theorising when it crowds out sensible pragmatism, idealism versus a solid grip on reality, and fanciful 'visionary' speculation when we want 'cold hard facts'. 'Ideology' means something dangerous and risky, weird and abnormal rather than mainstream, radical as opposed to moderate, synonymous with 'taking things too far'. The term sometimes takes on religious associations: the doctrinal formality of a credo, dogma, or gospel; the zealotry and fanaticism of the 'true believer'. Similarly, we think of ideology as ossifying or freezing discussion and debate, trapping us in a state of opinionated, unreflective mindlessness. This often overlaps with advocacy and propaganda (especially from official or pre-eminent sources), grandstanding, 'playing to the gallery', bias, and blind partisanship rather than impartiality. 'Ideology' becomes tied up in the material and cultural self-interest of (especially powerful) social groups, who pursue a hidden, nefarious agenda for society with crusading militancy. Meanwhile, we use the most iconic signifier of ideology, the 'ism', to casually and indiscriminately refer to almost any 'way of thinking' (or 'being') or collection of ideas: transnationalism, postmodernism, neoliberalism, Peronism, secularism, of course, but also truism, witticism, neologism, alcoholism, ageism, and so on.

At the same time, in its original historical form, 'ideology' denotes the '*study* of ideas', in the same sense as the (often scientific) acquisition of knowledge associated with constructs such as 'biology', 'criminology', or 'sociology'. Paring the concept down to its semantic roots reveals the rich penumbra of allusive meaning that surrounds it. The 'ideo-' morpheme stems from the ancient Greek word *ιδέα*: a form or shape, a kind or class of 'element' with a certain inherent nature or quality, a particular outward semblance or appearance, expressing a clear archetypical style, mode, or fashion, all encapsulated in terms such as 'principle', 'notion', and ultimately 'idea'. In turn, *ιδέα* connotes *εἶδος*, which shares the meanings of 'form', 'kind', 'quality', and 'appearance' but expands on them to incorporate physical figural 'looks', a typical habit, exemplifying or constitutive pattern, state or situation, policy or plan of action, even designated province or department of referential meaning, thus covering the gamut from 'core essence' to 'visible likeness'. Meanwhile, the 'logy' suffix derives from the notoriously multifarious word *λόγος*: fundamentally, it refers to a word or utterance and the process of thought or reflection; yet these meanings are both stretched to cover wider language and spoken expression, phrases and even full sentences, argumentative reasoning, deliberation, and explanation, which together shape debate, discussion, and dialogue. In turn, these inform a vast range of further meanings, from computational reckoning and measurement to reputation, value, and esteem; relations of correspondence to regulative laws; statements of case and cause to formulated hypotheses; mentions of rumour and hearsay to narrative histories or legendary tales; proverbial maxims, proposed resolutions, assertive commands, eloquent literature, and all other senses of purposive discourse. Perhaps the most accurate way to distil these all into a single definition is to describe 'ideology' as literally an 'account' or 'telling' (i.e., both enumeration and narration) of ideas. Through metonymy, 'ideology' has shifted from referring to a *field* of study to naming the *object* of study itself, as with 'geology', 'pathology', or 'technology'; but the sense of a deliberate, meaningful arrangement of ideas has remained.

These two alternative ways of parsing the concept of 'ideology' speak to rival understandings of the role that ideas and their patterned groupings play in society (Boudon 1989, 23; Geuss 1981, 4–25; Thompson 1990, 5–7). The first casts ideology in a pejorative or negative light: as a source or instrument of dissimulation and manipulation, which fosters equally fictitious unity and disunity among us where neither need exist. The second understanding adopts a non-pejorative if not strictly positive view of ideology: as a way to understand and describe the nature and meaning of the world around us. While there is scope for overlap and compatibility between their claims about 'what ideology is and does', these two understandings have engaged in a long-running struggle for epistemic primacy. Over the two centuries that have elapsed since the term 'ideology' entered the lexicon of social research, their relative balance has continually oscillated, propelled by many crucial developments and 'watershed' events that punctuated society's historical trajectory. Mass enfranchisement, economic collapse, total war and genocide, colonialism and decolonisation, religious revival, and the proliferation of countercultures all left their mark on our conceptions of ideology, tying it to an ever-expanding range of views covering everything from personal identity and behaviour to models of social order. Meanwhile, the analytical study of ideology and ideologies ('ideologology'!) has at various times fostered, resisted, aligned with, and cross-cut these trends. Some approaches have understood their essential task as being to expose and undo the damage ideology causes, from the first Marxists and later the first critical theorists to 'end of ideology' and 'end of history' approaches. Others favour the more equivocal role of seeking to accurately determine ideology's 'laws of motion', from the original *idéologues* and subsequently the first political scientists to the social theorists, intellectual historians, and social psychologists working on ideology today.

§1 The central questions in the study of ideology

Despite often strongly divergent inclinations towards pejorative or non-pejorative understandings of ideology, the various approaches to ideology analysis consistently feature a core roster of essential debates, which can be framed as a series of contrasting pairs. The most fundamental of these concerns whether ideology is *true* or *false*. This debate hinges on whether ideologies as integrated bodies and 'tellings' of ideas correspond closely and demonstrably with reality, or whether they act as 'alternative realities' that obscure, deflect from, or contrast with reality 'as it actually is'. On the former side, ideology is presented as a set of claims about reality, either as it is or as it should be. Ideologies and their constituent ideas are themselves real, acting as generalised 'placeholders' for everything from personal mindsets to societal institutions; they are also true in that we 'hold' ideas, which influence us into actions and reactions that are likewise real. Moreover, since our encounters with reality in our social existence and actions are always ultimately through (our own and others') subjective experiences, to all intents and purposes the reality 'that matters' is our ideological construction of it, so that ideology is 'true as far as we are concerned'. Meanwhile, the latter side instead sees ideology as an attempt to portray reality as something other than it is: a 'mask' placed over the actual facts, a misdescription of 'how things *really* work' or 'why things *really* are the way they are', a superficial explication and justification that (often deliberately) does not capture the deep societal forces at play. It distracts from other, more important motive influences on our existence and behaviour, such as our interests, drives, or contextual incentives. Above all, ideology creates and maintains a tension between our perception and our experience of society, since there is still a reality 'out there' beyond our capacity to 'name' it.

A closely related question is whether ideology is a *necessary* or *unnecessary* factor in our engagement with reality. The core consideration here is whether all humans rely unavoidably on (in)formal ideological frameworks of meaning, knowledge, and value to understand the world and their place within it, or whether some at least can – and should – transcend ideologies' convenient, insufficiently considered hermeneutic and epistemic 'shortcuts' to reach a 'higher', clearer, and direct form of understanding. One approach argues that our 'access' to reality is only possible via some form of ideology – even if it does not call itself by that name – in the sense that some 'account' of ideas is required to make *any* claims about reality at all. Ineradicable societal division and disagreement over how to engage with reality engenders several viable alternative ways of 'telling' ideas and manifesting them in society (via factions, movements, parties, etc.), laying the foundations for ideological disputes. Moreover, since reality is itself inherently changeable and indeterminate, ideas and their meanings can always be challenged and revised. By contrast, the opposing line is that it is both possible and highly desirable to attain a stance towards reality that lies 'outside' or 'beyond' ideology, typically through applying scientific and critical methods of enquiry. It finds that all divisions can be bridged or overcome, and that compatibilising different 'tellings' provides permanent resolutions to ideological disputes, leading in effect to ideology's elimination. Similarly, it is possible to 'settle' how ideas should be 'recounted' and integrated, and a healthy dose of logical reasoning and empirical testing can mostly remove reality from ideology's 'reach'.

The next dispute is over whether ideology represents a *temporary* or a *permanent* fixture in society. This concerns whether ideology is uniquely a feature of certain forms, phases, or time-periods of human society's developmental trajectory, with an identifiable beginning and end, or a constant presence wherever human society exists, with at most marginal qualitative changes in its essential character. The former position identifies modernity as the 'starting point' of ideology, characterised by increasingly dense, urbanised populations, the shift to mass production in agriculture and manufacturing, innovations in communication and transport, and an increase in the purview and complexity of state and legal functions. Ideology, on this account, is the fortuitous product of intersections between industrial capitalism and class conflict among bourgeois business owners and proletarian wage-workers, constitutional parliamentary democracy and electoral competition among parties, and contingent Western European geoeconomic–geopolitical–geocultural primacy. It likewise has an identifiable 'end point' through the transition to a new societal form or phase (e.g., 'final communism', globalised liberal democracy). The latter view, meanwhile, denies that ideology can have a definite beginning and, instead, points to clear milestones of qualitative ideological transformation from its long premodern history, tied to theological disputes, feudal rivalries, or personalist courtly factionalism. It observes that ideology is not only present but has often pursued parallel, entirely unrelated trajectories in different societies that are (at least partly) independent of capitalist, democratic, or Eurocentric developments. Accordingly, it is sceptical that there can ever be an 'end of ideology' and, instead, conceives of large-scale societal transition as a change in the dynamics of ideological 'dominance' or 'hegemony', expecting ever new social divisions around which future ideologies can take shape.

Another dimension of debate is over whether ideology is best conceived as a *singular* or a *plural* phenomenon: as ideology or ideolog*ies*. The key question here is whether it should be grasped as a totality alongside other powerful social forces, without becoming distracted by petty internal differences that do not alter its overall effects, or whether treating it monolithically prevents detailed analysis of how complex interpersonal and intergroup social dynamics play out through inter-ideological encounters. One side insists that ideology must be understood, first and foremost, as a discrete social domain with dedicated functions, ranked alongside (and sometimes subordinated to) the economic and political domains and sometimes elided with 'discourse' or 'culture'. On this conception, ideas and how they are 'recounted' or 'told' are epiphenomenal to ideology's social functions, and differences between ideologies are inconsequential compared to the gulf between them and society's economic and political 'drivers'. Insofar as ideology is significantly internally differentiated, it can be modelled as a single spectrum along which people's positions can be ranked (e.g., liberal–conservative, left–right, radical–reactionary), often using scalar numerical quantifications. The other side argues for a more refined breakdown of ideology that incorporates its extensive range of different social manifestations: its legal, religious, media, and educational aspects as well as its economic and political forms. Likewise, it holds that the precise hierarchy, ordering, juxtaposition, and deployment of ideas is vital to charting simultaneous and intertemporal differences within and between ideologies and their effects on the shape of society. On this granular account, ideology is a collection of many different partly overlapping bodies of ideas – older or newer, larger or smaller, more or less complex and stable – which can be meaningfully sketched out only in multidimensional space.

A further question concerns whether ideology is primarily an *individual* or a *collective* phenomenon. This debate is about whether the locus at which ideology's social effects should be evaluated is human beings' personal mental and bodily status and behaviours, or whether it is more promising to treat ideology as the expression of various societal group dynamics. One view frames ideology in terms of identity, as a mechanism to impose social salience on our personal biological and demographic features, and to create, recognise, and/or push back against our positions in hierarchies of privilege and discrimination. It sees ideology as a social force operating on our personal psyches – mobilising our unconscious and subconscious, crafting correlations with our personality-traits, fostering certain emotions and forms of reasoning, and influencing our evaluative and epistemological judgments. Moreover, it shapes our social behaviours, from voting and consumption preferences to labour decisions and choices over 'personal growth' and self-development (e.g., sport, fitness, leisure pursuits). The alternative view examines ideology as an articulation of social group solidarity based on posited commonalities of contextual situation and experience, motive drives and interests, and social aims and plans. For it, ideology chiefly affects and manifests in the mass psyche, steering the substantive content, direction, and intensity of social attitudes (i.e., public opinion) and collective sentiments (e.g., 'moral panics', 'group feelings', 'national moods') and affecting our conduct in public debate. It defines parameters of toxicity versus acceptability and taboo versus encouraged behaviour in (interpersonal) social interactions, especially where these bridge identity or group divides, and either perpetuates or counteracts power relationships between their participants.

Lastly, ideology analysis divides over whether ideology is principally an *explicit* or *implicit* social phenomenon. Here, the substantial issue is whether ideology takes the form of overt and conscious articulations of its constitutive ideas, which are openly and unambiguously ideological in nature, or whether it is (also/instead) to be found in forms that are not consciously ideological – or even specifically claim to be *non-ideological* – that nonetheless 'deliver' ideological content in a subtle, unwitting, even disguised way. The former approach treats ideology as primarily linguistic and textual, found above all in print, digital, online, and broadcast media, where ideas are directly rendered and where their content and delivery can be subjected to lexical, logical, subtextual–contextual–intertextual, or rhetorical analysis. On this account, ideology appears mainly as self-aware programmatic statements and (discursive) behaviour expressly designed to deliver, frame, and thematise specific ideas in a particular 'telling' (e.g., manifestos, statements of principle, op-eds, demonstrations, scholarly interventions). By inference, ideological analysis is empirical, measuring ideology's social effects through observable, (usually) quantifiable data and involving historical and comparative assessments of social phenomena and events according to their frequency of incidence, scale, and popularity. By contrast, the latter approach highlights how ideology can also be symbolic and 'applied', non-linguistically embedded or summarised, with sensory (especially audiovisual) cues acting as a 'shorthand' for ideas and for the social behaviours and institutions that 'instantiate' them. This approach focuses on 'what is left unsaid', 'everyday' behaviour that reveals unstated, underlying ideological commitments, often presented as 'natural', 'apolitical', 'neutral', or 'common sense'. Its ideological analysis is correlatively more interpretative, evaluating ideology's effects using theoretical models that depict various 'deep-structure' social forces and generalised trends that are not always immediately discernible from surface-level empirics but require reasoned extrapolation.

Different traditions and approaches within the study of ideologies have different views on each of these six debates. Some of these views are well known within and even beyond social research: orthodox Marxism's assessment of ideology as false (an illusion), temporary (a feature of the capitalist present), and singular (the total assemblage of pro-capitalist values and institutions); or the assumption that it is plural (divided into rival families), collective (held by groups of voters and legislators), and explicit (expressed in manifestos and opinion polls) in comparative-political party systems studies. Of course, these differences are a major part of what delineates such traditions from one another, partly because of and partly in parallel to deeper divergences in their methodological assumptions. Yet even where they happen to agree, they may do so for entirely unrelated reasons: for example, a view of ideology as individual may stem from an atomistic conception of the structure of society or a focus on the priority of subjective experience. What makes these questions *central*, however, is the fact that every tradition finds itself in the position of having to take a stance – whether one-sidedly 'committed' or equivocally 'compatibilist' – within each one of these debates. This means that these six 'contrasting pairs' are best conceived as binary poles at the extremes of six 'ideologological' spectrums, with ideology-theoretical approaches falling somewhere in between them on each one: for instance, seeing ideology as 'more false than true', 'largely necessary', 'definitely plural', 'both explicit and implicit', and so on. It is thus possible to 'map out' traditions of ideology analysis in terms of the constellation of points they occupy on all of these spectrums: for example, social psychology's view of ideology as (roughly) true–(fairly) necessary–permanent–plural–(mainly) individual–explicit, or critical discourse analysis's reading of it as false–(reluctantly) necessary–permanent–(more) plural–individual *and* collective–explicit *and* implicit, and so on. By the same token, as a heuristic exercise, we may find it useful to 'map out' our own views on each of these questions to see whether we find ourselves more sympathetic to some traditions than others, to a hybrid combination of their positions, or to a whole new 'ideologological' conception entirely.

§2 From the study of ideology to ideology studies

Aspects of these questions have formed part of the standard material of philosophy and social theory since at least the Renaissance. Epistemology and philosophy of mind, language, science, and religion, and branches of early ethnography and cultural studies have long considered the relationship of abstract ideas to reality as either 'inner essences' or mediated representations, whether we can acquire reliable knowledge about the world, whether morality is real or synthetic and absolute or relative, the nature and sources of popular opinions, and so on. But, since around 1800, these questions have been increasingly corralled together under the rubric of addressing a specific social phenomenon. The first to use the term 'ideology' for this phenomenon were a group of late Enlightenment philosophers in post-Revolutionary France, who saw in it the promise of a new science of ideas, mental perceptions, and thought processes. But its rise to prominence (and its metonymic shift) came with the Marxist transformation of social thought from post-Hegelian philosophical materialism into the embryonic outlines of sociology, which tied 'ideology' explicitly to the cultural manifestations of capitalist, classist society. At the turn of the 1900s, sociology's crystallisation as a discipline with many parallel traditions (positivist, anti-positivist, conflict-theoretic, functionalist, etc.) introduced new focuses on the collective and individual dynamics of crowd psychology and the role of propaganda and the media, as well as non-classist explanations for ideological support. Meanwhile, the growing prominence of scientific and statistical research methods enabled new approaches to studying ideology via polling, quantitative survey research, and breakdowns of electoral results. By the mid-1900s, the ascendancy of social science pushed the study of ideology heavily towards comparative empirical assessments of voters' and legislators' policy preferences and the demographics of pro- and anti-system movements. At the same time, new challenges and modifications to classical social theory (especially the rise of structuralism and poststructuralism) found 'ideology' increasingly inflexible and outmoded as an analytic tool, spurring the development of new lexicons to explain the conditions and impulses for human thinking, expression, and other social actions.

Parallel to these developments, the same period saw the emergence and consolidation of a growing number of 'schools of thought' that fit the description of integrated bodies or 'tellings' of ideas – which are increasingly defined as (and accept the label of) 'ideologies'. From the early 1800s, the amorphous strands of post-Enlightenment political, economic, religious, and legal thought coalesced into a 'Big Four' of increasingly distinct 'families' (conservatism, liberalism, socialism, anarchism), the inaugural forms of their respective ideological traditions. In the late 1800s and early 1900s, these 'Big Four' underwent major transformations in response to four new ideological arrivals (social democracy, communism, Christian democracy, fascism), the results of split-offs from the conservative and socialist traditions. The mid- to late 1900s saw further transformations and shifting fortunes among all eight of these ideological families and, thanks to seismic shifts in the economic, political, and cultural constellations of global power that have continued into the 2000s, the ascendancy of two more (libertarianism, green ideology). All the while, developments in these ten ideological traditions were accompanied by a cumulative succession of narrower ideological currents that coursed within and between the 'Big Four' and their rivals – from nationalism and republicanism in the 1800s to feminism, religious ideologies, and ideologies of race in the 1900s, and finally to queer ideologies, populism, and ideologies of (dis)ability at the turn of the 2000s. This proliferation of rival intellectual movements led to competing 'canons' of symbolic, literary, and media outputs tied to the rising importance of various (often cross-cutting) social groups – including groupings by geography, language, occupation, wealth and income, age and health, sex, gender, and sexuality, religion, race and ethnicity – which together fostered alternative accounts of 'which ideas matter'.

For much of this time, the 'study of ideology' and the 'study of ideolog*ies*' operated with considerable mutual autonomy and internal diffuseness. But by the turn of the 1980s, and accelerating prodigiously since the 1990s, a major wave of new appreciations of ideology and ideologies have emerged that seek to unite the study of both in a systematic, holistic way. They do so from a wide range of disciplinary angles: social and political theory, intellectual history, philosophical hermeneutics, sociolinguistics, communication studies, social psychology, and political science. Their shared aim is to elevate 'ideology' from an instrumental factor in analysing other social phenomena and a tool in other subfields' arsenals into a dedicated 'subject' and subdiscipline in its own right. Early markers of the emergence of 'ideology studies' and its multiple theoretical approaches were laid down by a spate of books that explicitly tackled the concept's definition and social function and offered the first syncretic overviews of the history and 'state of play' of ideology studies. These ranged from conceptual histories of ideology theory by Hans Barth (1977) and Jorge Larraín (1979) to evaluations of its latest developments by David Manning (1980), Howard Williams (1988), and David McLellan (1995), along with a mixture of both by Terry Eagleton (1991); from the critique of 'thinking in ideology terms' by Kenneth Minogue (1985) to the defence of ideology analysis as a tool of critique by Raymond Geuss (1981); from refinements of existing traditions by Göran Therborn (1980) and John B. Thompson (1984) to wholly novel accounts by John Plamenatz (1970), Martin Seliger (1976), and Raymond Boudon (1989). At the same time, academic journals were founded that made explicit space for ideological analysis, including *Rethinking Marxism* (1988–), *Constellations* (1994–), and *Historical Materialism* (1997–) in the Marxist tradition, *Philosophy and Social Criticism* (1973–) and *Theory, Culture & Society* (1982–) in a more ecumenical vein, and the *Journal of Political Ideologies* (1996–) as the first dedicated ideology studies journal, alongside the formation of university centres dedicated partly or fully to the study of ideologies, at Essex (1982–), Boston (1988–2010), Cambridge (1994–), Oxford (2002–11), Queen Mary (2007–), Nottingham (2013–), St Andrews (2013–), and Helsinki (2016–).

This development has been accompanied by an increasing percolation of 'ideology' terminology into the conduct and self-conception of popular discourse. Individual and collective exponents of social thinking describe themselves and others more and more using ideological labels alongside their occupational credentials. Formally impartial academic or civil-society bodies are increasingly described as 'left-wing' or 'right-wing' activists or advisers; cable and online news outlets and talk radio present as 'conservative' or 'progressive/radical', sometimes featuring partisan 'paid contributors' and framing issues as 'both-sides' debates; and voters' ideological self-identification in attitudes surveys is becoming more label-explicit and polarised. Meanwhile, in vernacular language, we increasingly deploy ideological labels as terms of insult – neoliberalism, racism, sexism, Eurocentrism – or distinction – antifascism, multiculturalism, constitutionalism, patriotism. This trend both reflects and supports the current long-term rise in ideological polarisation, which originated in the 1970s to 1980s but has distinctly accelerated since the 1990s. The proliferation of ideological traditions has widened the range of salient issues on which we can take a stance: forms and levels of taxation, public healthcare, abortion, military intervention, gay marriage, and so on. The views we hold about these issues are grouped into binaries or stretched out along several spectrums; where these binaries/spectrums extensively align rather than cross-cut, and our views on one issue correlate strongly with certain views on the others, we become clustered into a small number of camps with few overlaps. In recent decades, ideological polarisation has manifested as intensifying 'us-versus-them' divisions, marked by mutual distrust between different camps, questioning one another's moral legitimacy, and viewing one another as existential threats (to themselves and their way of life or to society as a whole). Society, in short, has become more ideologically self-conscious and more self-consciously ideological – more aware that there are multiple ways to 'recount' or 'tell' ideas, and more prepared to take a clear position on which 'account' or 'telling' to commit to.

§3 Plan of the book

For at least two centuries, ideology has been vitally important to shaping society in many complex ways. Yet over the last three or four decades, ideology has achieved hitherto unmatched prominence in social research and social life: it has recaptured scholarly attention, and it has risen to the forefront of popular consciousness. In doing so, it has brought the central questions about the concept back into focus, prompting new developments in the study of ideology on both sides of the pejorative/non-pejorative divide. This book is intended as a waymarker along the path of consolidation of ideology studies: an opportunity to take stock of how ideological (and 'ideologological') understandings have evolved since the 1970s to 1990s, which centres the discussion on ideology rather than using it to preface elucidations of (political) ideolog*ies*. It draws on historical and contemporary approaches to ideology analysis, emphasising areas of overlap and disjunction and illustrating how to profitably combine them to illuminate ideology's personal and social impact. A book of this size cannot hope to provide an exhaustive account of every aspect of ideology and its study. But it can act as a point of orientation for those searching for a way into ideology's complex societal role.

The remainder of this book is divided into five chapters. Chapter 2 traces how the theory of ideology has evolved over the last two centuries. It begins by analysing the problems of ideology theory historiography and argues that ideology theory's evolutionary trajectory has been marked by a mixture of shifts and accumulations in concerns and approaches. The chapter traces the connection between ideology and illusion, science, class, and capitalism during the 'classical' period of ideology analysis (1800–90), followed by new concerns about the role of intellectuals and mass opinion, party politics, and ideological diversity (1890–1945). It overviews the subsequent shift to associating ideology with extremism and totalitarianism, along with the rise of alternative objects of analysis such as culture and discourse (1945–80), and ends by examining new focuses on identity and 'ordinary' thinking and expression that have accompanied the rise of ideology studies (1980–*now*).

The next three chapters form the book's theoretical core, offering a syncretic, compatibilist statement of what ideology is and how it works that integrates and builds on the trajectory of ideology theory presented in chapter 2. Chapter

3 defines the concept of ideology, summarised as *a specific combination and arrangement of ideas*. These ideas are abstract or generalised representations of a set of perspectives, dispositions, norms, practices, structures, and systems: tools to help us 'make sense' of fundamentally chaotic and confusing (social) reality. How an ideology combines and arranges this set of elements constitutes its 'morphology', which can vary in thickness and robustness depending on the overall number, relative distribution, individual specificity, and mutual coherence of these elements. Of course, not every group of ideas is automatically an ideology, and the chapter closes with some criteria to distinguish what ideology *is* and what it is *not*: specifically, ideology's claim to provide a comprehensive, complete, and correct 'picture' of reality.

Chapter 4 explores the relationship between ideology and ideolog*ies*. It starts by outlining the historical trends that have led to ideological differentiation, then outlines the social preconditions that typically must be met for ideological traditions to emerge: the existence of hierarchical social differences, factionalism, and a specific context on which ideologies can draw. It surveys the global history of ideologies, especially the last two centuries of intensive consolidation and evolution, and offers a morphology of different ideologies according to the perspectives, dispositions, norms, practices, structures, and systems they embrace. Finally, it addresses the question of ideological categorisation, including the origins of the left–centre–right spectrum and alternative dimensions of ideological comparison.

Chapter 5 turns to how we experience ideology in society. It examines the place of individuals as the basic units of ideology and the processes of ideological socialisation by which we are formed into social 'subjects' over the course of our lifetimes. It also considers how these 'subjectification' processes can fail, how ideology's 'grasp' on us can be limited and incomplete, and the consequences this can have for our societal experience.

Finally, chapter 6 outlines the different approaches that characterise ideology studies today. It opens by describing its steady coalescence into an independent subdiscipline, then summarises twelve approaches to ideology analysis developed by different fields. It divides these approaches into an 'epicentre' rooted within social and political theory, along with a 'penumbra' of input from the humanities and social sciences, arguing that they can be categorised along two cross-cutting dimensions: the surface-level or deep-level focus of their engagement with ideology and the theoretical or empirical methodology they use to do so.

2
The evolution of ideology theory

A cardinal feature of the renaissance in ideology studies has been a steady effort to stipulate a definite cast list of its canonical theorists and traditions. Early on, constructing a history of ideology theory was born of the simple need to systematically clarify what was then still largely historiographical *terra nullius*, flecked with only partial, outdated precursors (Mannheim 1936, 53–74). But, over recent decades, repeated attempts to offer a comprehensive history of ideology theory have revealed two problems. First, the history of ideology theory is often difficult to prise apart from the overarching history of social research. This cuts two ways: (1) there is not always a consensus between or even within different analytical traditions on what authors mean by 'ideology'; (2) authors sometimes refer to aspects of our experience that we would recognise as (and bracket under) 'ideology' using different terminology, either because 'ideology' was not *de rigueur* or because they were deliberately avoiding it. The issue is where the cut-off point falls. *Substantively*, we have to balance inclusivity with exclusivity: we cannot lose ideology's distinctive focus and meaning, or we simply end up giving a 'potted history' of social research that is diffusely uninformative about the concept or its study; nor can we prioritise particular aspects of ideology's definition and functions over providing a full picture, or we lose its social richness and diversity, as well as potential insights from different disciplines and methodological traditions. *Intertemporally*, we need to decide 'when ideology theory starts': going too far back makes the account ahistorical, losing important differences between contexts and drawing analogies and applying modern terms and frameworks to a context for which they are inappropriate; but remaining too contemporary makes it excessively presentist, losing continuities between contexts and arbitrarily ruling out prototypical forms of what we understand as ideology today.

Second, the history of ideology theory faces a difficult choice between prioritising individual authors or intellectual traditions. It is often summarised through a 'mighty handful' of core authors who significantly advanced the understanding of ideology in social research: Antoine Destutt de Tracy, Karl Marx and Friedrich Engels, Karl Mannheim, Antonio Gramsci, and Louis Althusser (Billig 1991, 3–13; Freeden 2003, 4–30; Stråth 2013). Certainly, each of these men made a major contribution to the study of ideology. Destutt de Tracy is credited with inventing the term 'ideology' and laying the foundations for its non-pejorative meaning; Marx and Engels did likewise for its pejorative reading by tying ideology to class structures of exploitation and domination. Mannheim pioneered a 'sociology of knowledge' that addressed the relationship between thought and societal context; Gramsci explored who leads the production of ideology and how ideas 'prevail' in society; and Althusser advanced our understanding of the institutions that disseminate ideology to us. But this parsimonious list comes with several caveats. It is heavily skewed towards Marxisant social theory, omitting contributions from parallel, countervailing traditions with differing views on ideology. It overemphasises the implied continuity between these 'big' names, downplaying the extensive dissensus within the Marxian tradition. It leaves out other theorists who should otherwise 'slot' chronologically in between them and stays silent on 'what happens after Althusser'. Lastly, and most glaringly, it centres individuals at the expense of looking at wider traditions of ideological analysis.

One way of rectifying this is to extend the list of 'honourable mentions' to include, for instance, György Lukács, Michel

The evolution of ideology theory 19

Foucault, Jürgen Habermas, or Clifford Geertz (Barrett 1992; Freeden 1996, 14–22; Thompson 1990, 29–52; van Dijk 1998, ix). But this does little to improve on the 'mighty handful' – not least because most of these further additions are still Marxist or Marxism-adjacent in their theoretical orientations. Another way is simply to accept that there is not just one history of ideology theory but rather several histories, which exhibit mutual continuities, discontinuities, and temporal overlaps (Eagleton 1991; Larraín 1979). This produces alternative 'ideologological' continuities, grouped around common 'threads' of analysis: one based on science and illusion, running from Destutt de Tracy via Marx and Engels to the socialists of the Second International, with Émile Durkheim as a point of contrast; a second on psychology, reaching from Arthur Schopenhauer via Georges Sorel and Vilfredo Pareto to Sigmund Freud; a third group of historicists and contextualists, including Lukács, Mannheim, Gramsci, and Lucien Goldmann; and, finally, a structuralist tendency, starting with the Frankfurt School, Roland Barthes, and Claude Lévi-Strauss and ending with Althusser, Nicos Poulantzas, and Pierre Bourdieu. While this certainly gives a better sense of ideology theory's rich tradition, it risks 'lifting' authors out of their social and intellectual contexts and inserting them fictitiously into synthetic continuities. Moreover, it still centres individual authors over traditions and overemphasises the continuity between the figures in each 'thread'.

To solve both problems, especially for a concise overview, we can prioritise looking at specific themes that have become associated with ideology analysis. In doing so, we can acknowledge that not every 'ideologological' author or tradition laid equal weight on every theme, but we must include them all to provide a suitably summative history of ideology theory. This means indulging a modicum of ahistoricism to incorporate cases where our overarching narrative 'retcons' a given theme as having implicitly started chronologically before any explicit association with ideology. To soften this slightly, we can contextualise each of these themes and how they emerged within deeper background developments in society and their intellectual underpinnings. This lets us focus more closely on shifts and accumulations in ideology theory's concerns over time: some have retained a central place, while others have fallen out of fashion or been transformed. Not everything from the early days of ideology analysis is outdated, and we must acknowledge the legacies that debates from any given period have left on later developments in ideology theory. Ultimately, what a thematic overview captures best is that ideology theory is constantly changing and growing as it becomes established as a mainstay of social research.

§1 1800–1890: the classical period of ideology analysis

The early years of ideology theory saw an unusually swift definition of its leading frames, raising themes and developing approaches that laid the foundations for many central questions and debates that still persist today. Right from the start, this period featured both pejorative and non-pejorative understandings of ideology: its initial positive formulation as a promising new addition to social analysis was soon overshadowed by its long-lasting interpretation as a pathological, epiphenomenal by-product of other social forces in need of critique and eradication.

One of the earliest themes of this classical period still arguably remains the fundamental question exercising ideology analysis: ideology's relationship with *illusion and reality*. How our ideas and the 'accounts' we weave them into relate to the world around us played a central role in several attempts to logically extend or overturn different strands of Enlightenment epistemology. Their essential difference turned on the causal priority they assigned to reality versus how we form ideas about it. The *idéologues*, empiricists in the Lockean tradition influenced by the *philosophes* and *encyclopédistes*, held that our ideas emerge out of the sensations we experience when we interact with reality and acquire a reality of their own as objects on which our 'intellectual faculties' work and which we externalise through our actions. For them, ideas and their interrelations reflect reality as closely as our minds can, making the study of ideas

The evolution of ideology theory 21

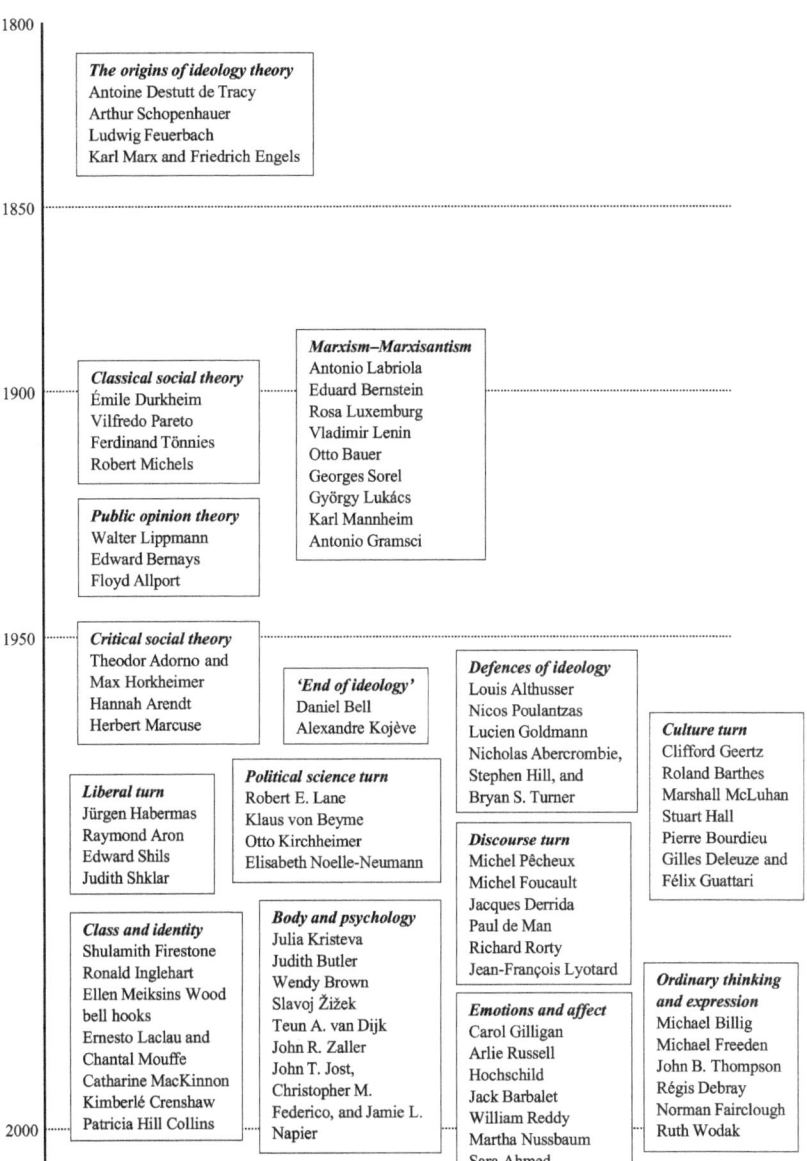

Figure 1 The history of ideology theory

and their organising philosophies an important part of the wider study of society, nature, and our place within them (Destutt de Tracy 1804). At the other extreme, Schopenhauer (1819) argued that we do not experience reality as such but a 'representation' our cognitive processes create of it, and that our ideas are projections that superimpose onto reality conceptions of space, time, and causality. Reality's essential character is inaccessible to us except through our self-consciousness as embodied beings driven by wants, urges, and strivings – our own manifestations of the 'will', the universal innermost 'kernel' of nature and society. Occupying an intermediary position, Ludwig Feuerbach (1841) saw the disjunct between ideas and reality as more narrowly circumscribed. He suggested that religious attempts to frame reality in terms of divinely ordained morality are merely our externally idolised fantasies of how the world (and we) should be: idealised antitheses of its (and our) flaws and shortcomings. Marx and Engels (1976 [1845]) expanded Feuerbach's anti-theological position to a general criticism of all abstract philosophical reflection, whose 'accounts' of ideas they saw as capable only of distorting and inverting reality, similar to the images captured by a *camera obscura*.

These various strands' stances on illusion and reality proximately determined their views on ideology's relationship with *science*. The legacy of the scientific revolution in natural philosophy, with its demonstrable successes in mathematics, physics, engineering, and industrial technology, provoked a late Enlightenment surge of enthusiasm for applying its insights of systematic knowledge, prescription, and prediction to societal questions. Accordingly, both the *idéologues* and Marxists sought to overturn the primacy of metaphysical depictions of ideas' formation and connection to reality by establishing laws of tendencies generated by scientific observation, taking advantage of the massive expansion of social statistics and increasingly sophisticated mathematical modelling. But they differed over where to introduce scientific methodology and whether they saw it as compatible with ideology – a refinement and improvement to previous philosophy of mind and social theory – or as the way to overcome it, to free us from ideology's hold over the ideas we use to represent reality.

The *idéologues* targeted their efforts at personal psychology. True to their empiricist origins, they hoped to make ideology a *'science* of ideas': a 'gnosiology' (i.e., epistemology) of knowledge gained through sensory perception applied to the formation of ideas. Their focus lay on the physiological factors of human spirituality, and they considered in almost zoological terms how our physical make-up and pathologies influence our passions, intelligence, and character. But they were interested less in formulating a universal theory of ideas than in empirical observation of our perception and cognition and detailing their probable changes, recurrence, and importance in response to societal developments. To definitively remove ideas from the rhetoric and speculation of social philosophy, the *idéologues* advocated careful ethnographic study (e.g., travel accounts, field surveys) and placed the emergent sciences of geography and anthropology at the heart of positive knowledge about ideology's connection to reality. Marx and Engels, meanwhile, turned their scientific attention to social analysis. For them, even a more scientific treatment of our ideas and psychology is still too superficial, as it simply offers a more systematic version of the philosophical *camera obscura*. Specifically, it does not explain the root cause of our own and others' ideas and psychological tendencies – i.e., why the way reality is constituted provokes particular ideas in our minds. To understand this, they argue, we must be sensitive to the causal effects of social contexts: specifically, our worldly material conditions, brought about by their (re)production through our own creative labour, and the social relations that arise alongside particular states or changes in these conditions. Consequently, Marx and Engels reoriented social explanation away from preoccupations with thought, the intellect, and the mind and towards the economy as the domain of human activity concerned with production. For them, the economic 'base' has primacy in determining the contours of reality, with other domains – politics, law, religion, art, and philosophy, i.e., ideology – forming a 'superstructure' that is ultimately conditioned by it. Our ideas, our 'social consciousness', can only correspond to 'what is there' in our economic conditions of existence. Scientific social analysis of ideas, then, relies on detailed study of historical trends based on economic statistics and anthropology of social production relations (e.g., landownership, slavery, family and kinship units) to determine the economic reasons for their emergence and prevalence.

With Marxism's 'economic turn', by the mid-1800s, ideology became ever more closely linked to the division of societies into economic *classes*, tied specifically to *capitalism* as a mode of production resting on private ownership of land, tools, and capital and fabricating goods for market exchange. The rise of agrarian, mercantile, and industrial capitalism dramatically reconfigured societal stratification according to levels and sources of wealth, income, and occupation. It eroded the feudal aristocracy and latifundist landowners in favour of a new class of large-, medium-, and small-scale business owners, merchants, and bankers, collectively termed the *bourgeoisie*. The class struggle for power between the essentially opposed interests of aristocracy/landowners and bourgeoisie within the economic base metastasised into political and ideological conflicts in the superstructure over their competing visions of society. These struggles gave rise to new ideas related to capitalist production – private property, voluntary exchange, competition, economic freedom, rights, parliamentary democracy, etc. – and the more the bourgeoisie managed to 'win' its class struggle, the more prevalent the ideas associated with its 'class consciousness' became within society.

However, in Marxist analysis, the capitalist transformation of society brought about another 'remainder', which bourgeois ideology leaves out of its 'account'. Urbanisation, the shift to factory production, and later flexible specialisation converted a growing share of the displaced peasantry, artisans, craftspeople, and other petty manufacturers into a working class: the *proletariat* of manual workers, then also managerial and service workers. Shut out of the aristocratic–bourgeois struggle between owners of land, tools, and capital, they instead entered a separate class struggle against the owners as a whole due to their position as resources in the capitalist production process, which exploits their labour to produce goods for profit in exchange for a wage-income. Marx and Engels saw this status as proletarian wage-labourers as the real social experience of a growing tranche of the population. But prevailing bourgeois ideology does not show this reality: proletarians do not benefit from private property, since they own no land, tools, or capital, and their equal rights and democratic citizenship are meaningless given the sheer class imbalances in wealth, income, and occupation. In this light, abstract philosophy that speaks of rights, freedom, democracy, property, etc., merely 'masks' how far reality is arranged to the benefit and in the interest of the bourgeoisie. Worse, through its painstaking appeals to reason, divinity, or (human) nature, it generates the 'false consciousness' that the proletariat must endorse its representation as 'the' natural, inevitable, best, and most just way that reality can (and should) be. The connection of ideology to capitalist class power is Marxism's single most lasting contribution to ideology theory: ideology's prevailing ideas not only fail to accurately represent reality; they are an explicit instrument which the powerful use to misrepresent reality to deceive and dominate the powerless.

§2 1890–1945: new concerns and approaches

The significant hiatus between Marx and Engels's decisive intervention in ideology theory and the next major contribution reflects a long period of dominance for their reading of ideology. But a mixture of Euro-American economic, political, and cultural trends during the 1870s to 1890s – the rise of large monopoly business enterprises, financialisation and credit expansion, the growth of state policy functions and expenditure, the 'new imperialism', religious revival and new social teaching, and philosophical/artistic turns to existentialism, nihilism, scientism, and modernism – led to an eruption of new perspectives at the turn of the 1900s. Ideology became increasingly perceived as an active, powerful, quasi-independent societal force worthy of serious investigation – prompting a gradual thawing of attitudes towards 'ideology' and a resurgence of its non-pejorative understandings after prolonged dormancy. The study of ideology itself also started to become decoupled from some of the (implicit and explicit) ideological assumptions of the classical period, especially the commitments to revolutionary overthrow of either monarchical or capitalist societal orders.

This period was marked by increasingly deep evaluation of the dynamics of ideological circulation, including new interest in the processes of knowledge-production. Rapid developments in publishing and telecommunications technology, coupled with growing state and private investment in school and university education, led to the significant expansion and professionalisation of teaching, academia, journalism, and the media. A new occupational group of 'knowledge workers' emerged, typically referred to as *intellectuals* or the 'intelligentsia', and ideology theory was confronted with the question of what role they play in the analysis of ideology and in its dissemination to *mass public opinion*. Some theorists straightforwardly argued that intellectuals are there to ensure that certain 'right' ideas become prevailing ideas within society, spreading them to a fundamentally intellectually passive population. Pareto (1935 [1916]) defined intellectuals' task as interpreting and steering unchanging human 'sentiments' and pseudo-logical (customary, traditional) 'derivations' among the popular mass, manipulating them in the desired direction – a task Walter Lippmann (1922) later allotted to the 'public philosopher' and Edward Bernays (2011 [1923]) to the 'public relations counsel'. Sorel (1912) similarly advocated embracing ideology's illusory nature: the intellectual's purpose was to encapsulate desirable ideas as epic mythical imagery, by nature immune to scientific evaluation or critique, to guide the population's actions by aesthetically mobilising their deeper sentiments. Gramsci (2011 [1929–35]), meanwhile, located intellectuals in 'civil society' – a distinct part of the superstructure from the 'state' – as cultural formulators consciously producing coherent social philosophies that integrate society's prevailing ideas. These philosophies percolate into wider culture and then popular religion and opinion, becoming ever more unconscious, embryonic, and fragmented as they reach mass ideological consumers, among whom ideological producers 'manufacture consent' for the political-economic *status quo*. This theme of mass beliefs as an unconscious, quasi-religious mirror of society's prevailing ideas was echoed by Ferdinand Tönnies (1922), who saw such construction of public opinion as a vital prerequisite for maintaining social unity in increasingly diffcrentiated *Gesellschaft*-type social formations.

But Gramsci's account also lent itself to a countervailing position, where intellectuals do not just monologically steer public opinion but also give voice to it. This dual possibility is rooted in ideology theory's changing understanding of how society's economic conditions affect its prevailing ideas. Departing from the orthodox Marxist understanding that a society's ideology expresses solely the ideas of its dominant economic class – under capitalism, those of the bourgeoisie – several theorists proposed that it instead represents a site of conflict between the ideas of its struggling classes – in capitalist society, those of bourgeoisie *and* proletariat. Lukács (1923) saw the ideas of any social group as conditioned by their societal context – their status position in societal stratifications, the time-period in which they were living – which Mannheim expanded into a 'total' conception of ideology as the unconscious/irrational partial worldviews of rival classes. Thus, bourgeois ideas were capitalist because conditioned by the bourgeoisie's ownership of land, tools, and capital; proletarian ideas were anti-capitalist because likewise conditioned by the proletariat's ownership of only its exploited labour power; and both coexisted simultaneously in the ideology of capitalist society. Intellectuals, meanwhile, occupied an intermediary 'middle-class' category in the capitalist hierarchy. In their wealth, income, and occupational situation, Eduard Bernstein (1911) argued, they fell between bourgeoisie and proletariat, alongside other marginal cases such as 'upper' managerial workers and 'petty'-bourgeois small-business owners. Exposed to the opposite pulls of contradictory class tendencies, they were equally capable of allying with either bourgeoisie or proletariat, and hence of representing either capitalist or socialist ideas (Lenin 1961 [1902]). For Gramsci, the outcome of ideological conflict and compromise led by such class-aligned intellectuals determined the contours of society's ideological 'hegemony'.

The shift from scientific 'unmasking' to ideological contestation of capitalist illusions did not, however, betoken the wholesale abandonment of critique; Antonio Labriola (1907), Bernstein (1901), and Lenin all emphasised that scientific critique of (one) ideology was not only compatible with holding a (different) positive ideology but that the success of both was intimately intertwined. Their view prefigures Mannheim's distinction between 'utopian' visions of perfect alternatives and the conscious distortions and calculated lies of ideological 'myth'. The latter had to be dispelled by an intelligentsia that could 'transcend' its conditioning to provide enlightened world-interpretations to society. Yet, *pace* Lukács, Mannheim recognised that even intellectuals' 'transcendent' insights could not escape their context – stopping short of Durkheim's (1895) insistence that sociology as a discipline dedicated to dispassionate study of 'social facts' could free itself of the ideological biases afflicting 'ordinary' thinking.

Recognising the divisions among intellectuals went hand in hand with a growing tendency to view ideology as heterogeneous rather than monolithic and to stress the differences between separate *ideologies*. The steady democratisation of many major European countries brought profound changes in the basis of political authority and the locus of legislative, administrative, and policy accountability and control. It eroded the supremacy of absolute monarchy, theocracy, or military dictatorship by asserting a constitutional role for mass popular participation in the governing process, above all by extending the electoral franchise, turning passive subjects into active citizens. Groups of 'like-minded' citizens-as-voters clustered together based on shared policy preferences, aided by increasingly sophisticated networks of communication, transforming political 'clubs' and societies into consolidated mass parties, which vied for popular support using rival programmatic manifestos summarising the ideas they stood for. The rise of mass parties posed a vital challenge to the Marxist conception of ideology as ultimately rooted in economic conditions. It implied a degree of quasi-autonomy between base and superstructure – or, rather, between economics and politics conceived as 'neighbouring' domains – with the political domain also increasingly defining ideological content. Bernstein and Lenin embraced this shift from (otherwise diametrically opposed) perspectives, modifying the Marxist reading of ideology to reflect the fact that 'party struggle' was increasingly the main channel through which the underlying class struggle was fought. Mediating economic class consciousness through political partisan consciousness made overcoming 'false consciousness' and fostering a 'true' alternative a more concrete task: parties were mass organisations with tangible structures, legal forms, and a definite size that could efficiently systematise and propagate the ideas 'belonging' to the conditions of an otherwise amorphous and diffuse social group.

With successive franchise expansions, parties competed for the votes of ever greater shares of the population. The ideas and ideologies they represented became increasingly detached from economic class divisions – which Michels (1911) saw as the start of a self-reinforcing tendency towards partisan self-interest and bureaucratic oligarchy. Several simultaneous trends combined to challenge the 'primacy of class'. First, the rising salience of non-class identities, which rapidly coalesced into new or resurgent ideologies: the resounding electoral success of national appeals in the lead up to the First World War, the proliferation of movements influenced by political religion, growing pressures for women's rights and enfranchisement, and early movements for decolonisation. Second, the emergence of ideologies that deliberately cross-cut and sought to bridge opposing class aims and interests – above all fascism and Christian democracy, which respectively elevated ethnicity and religion over class allegiances. Last, intensified intra-class factionalism within both bourgeoisie and proletariat: conservatism and liberalism shifted from interclass aristocratic–bourgeois struggle to an internal divide within the bourgeoisie, while the proletariat was riven by successive splits between anarchism and socialism, then later between communism and social democracy. The question for ideology theory was how far to accommodate these trends into its understanding of the social underpinnings of ideology. Orthodox Marxists such as Rosa Luxemburg (1976 [1909]) resisted the intrusion of non-class, cross-class, and intra-class formations into the core logic of ideological analysis, but some, most notably Otto Bauer (1907) and Sorel, looked for ways to compatibilise them with classist approaches. Ultimately, the 'electoral turn' in ideology analysis became further established with the rise of scientific public opinion research and statistical polling methods, which rapidly elided ideology with partisan affiliation or voting intention – and reduced class to a subordinate variable, equivalent to gender, ethnicity, age, or regional location (Allport 1937).

§3 1945–1980: terminological and methodological challenges

The advent of a plethora of approaches that challenged Marxism's prominent status in social enquiry, as well as the primacy of class politics framed largely in a socialist idiom, promised to open up ideology to innovative new readings, measurements, and assessments. Yet they were overtaken by the cataclysmic events of the 1920s to 1940s – mass discrimination and genocide against religious and ethnic minorities, wholesale societal mobilisation under total war, a global division into capitalist and communist political-economic blocs, innovations in medical and engineering technology, and a cultural backlash by realism and postmodernism against modernism and by scientistic behaviouralism against formalism and interpretative theory – which severely curtailed these promising avenues, instead fostering perspectives on ideology that were often explicitly framed as counter-reactions. Social research turned vehemently against 'ideology' as both a societal phenomenon and an analytical term, with a sharp swing back to pejorative understandings and a consequent forced 'reshuffle' of non-pejorative understandings into alternative (often carefully circumscribed) objects of analysis.

The most significant change in ideology's treatment was its abrupt association with extremism. Ideology analysis became synonymised with critiques of *totalitarianism* – specifically, the legacies of Nazism and the Holocaust, but also of Stalinism and the famines and purges of the 1930s – and often attached itself to substantive ideological assumptions that had become neglected during the era of fascist and communist ascendancy. This debate hinged on whether ideology necessarily lent itself to collapsing into fanaticism, dogmatism, wanton destruction, and disregard for human life, and that consequently any attempt at positive ideological thinking had to be abandoned, or whether some ideological thinking could still be retained as long as it was safely domesticated within pluralist-democratic norms and institutions (Halle 1972; Sartori 1969). Representing the first view, Daniel Bell (1960) confidently predicted the 'end of ideology' as a social phenomenon, on the grounds that the 'grand humanistic' ideologies of the 1800s and early 1900s had 'exhausted' their potential to attract widespread mass support. With the advent of welfare-state institutions and intergroup bargaining in post-Second World War capitalist society, revolutionary extremism's appeal was effectively neutralised, so that all future prevailing ideas would be 'parochial' ideologies geared towards technocratic tweaks of societal arrangements. Alexandre Kojève (1947) suggested that the 'end of history' had arrived even earlier, with the French Revolution's articulation of the 'rational supremacy' of individual rights and equal recognition – which reduced ideological competition to a process of gradual approximation towards a capitalist–socialist synthesis.

But also on this 'anti-ideological' side were numerous authors who had suffered first-hand under the Nazi terror, and who sought to recalibrate more or less Marxisant 'ideology critique' to account for these new threatening ideological forms. Hannah Arendt (1976 [1951]) articulated a classic account of totalitarianism as essentially total domination through terror, fed by social dislocation and isolation. Ideologies, for her, exhibit totalitarian tendencies when they resent, persecute, and replace intellectual, spiritual, and artistic initiative and talent with dull mass compliance and engage in explicit, elaborate esoteric deception about their social aims through a complex system of propaganda. The critical theorists of the Frankfurt School, chief among them Max Horkheimer and Theodor Adorno (1972 [1947]), sought to explain the social–psychological conditions that gave rise to the new totalitarian forms of social domination – in place of the emancipatory revolution that Marxist theory expected to occur once state intervention and centralised planning had resolved class exploitation. They saw in totalitarianism the failed Enlightenment promise of historical progress and a regression of reason into the myth and superstition from which it had emerged. Like them, Herbert Marcuse

(1964) saw totalitarian tendencies in ostensibly democratic society as well, through its hegemonic bureaucratic–technocratic rationality and its reliance on a homogenising culture industry to manipulate the population into passive mass docility. Affluent consumerist society controls and co-opts us and disguises our exploitation by cultivating 'false needs' to pursue material comforts; these lead us to commodify our pursuit of happiness and social connection and to ignore the psychological and environmental damage society causes, limiting our aptitude for critical thought and our opportunities for revolution and contributing to our ultimate loss of humanity.

Various approaches on the other side of this debate advocated to varying degrees for an explicit 'ideologological' rapprochement with a substantive ideological commitment to liberalism. Habermas (1975, 1984, 1987), a 'second-generation' Frankfurt School member, echoed his precursors' critique of the ideological character of scientific-technical expertise, which masks the prevailing values that align elite decision-making with maintaining the capitalist societal structure. But, in a compatibilist move, he argued that critical reflection on societal values is best conducted via public discussion under strictures of 'communicative rationality' – an 'ideal speech situation' that relies on a modified version of the deliberative institutions that post-Second World War democratic society claims it alone can foster. Other voices, however, were less sympathetic to retaining any link to Marxism. Far from offering critical scientific insight into the illusions of capitalist society, Raymond Aron (1955) argued, Marxism had become a flawed, sectarian, partial social perspective, an 'opium of the intellectuals' that blinded ideology theory to the failings of anti-capitalist (i.e., communist) systems – a view generalised by Edward Shils (1968), who saw elite ideologies as sitting always at a stage of remove from societal reality. If the aim was to secure individual rights and equal recognition, then in the wake of the totalitarian experience this had to be pursued within and through liberal (capitalist) democracy – motivated by the fear, in Judith Shklar's (1964) view, of the injustices, vices, and abuses that a renewed departure from pluralist constitutionalism would resurrect in society.

These social-theoretical approaches were joined *en masse* by the burgeoning political-science literature on ideology, which had essentially hived off ideological analysis into the study of party systems and public opinion. Robert E. Lane (1962), a leading representative of 'behaviouralist' social research, epitomised the new scientific view of ideologies as conscious, explicit, emotionally and rationally justified moral belief-systems, which can be analysed by means of observable conduct (voting, roll-call data) without needing to theorise underlying social conditions. Moreover, following Klaus von Beyme (1985), ideologies are integrally tied to electoral competition and should be viewed primarily in terms of the *'famille spirituelle'* ('spiritual family') to which the parties that represent them commit themselves. But substantive differences between these electoral ideologies, as Otto Kirchheimer (1969) argued, were far more reduced than the full range exhibited by pre-Second World War ideologies. The parties that endorsed them after the war all aspired to *Volkspartei* ('people's party') status, bidding for popular support across class or any other social 'cleavages'; in parallel, their policy programmes were becoming technocratic and 'de-ideologised', pushing them steadily towards the paradigm of the *Allerweltspartei* ('catch-all party'). Applying new statistical methods to attitudes surveys and public opinion field research allowed for increasingly granular appreciation of the aggregate distribution and variations of popular beliefs. Ideology's individuation to the level of personal opinion decoupled it from any sense of its social group origins – leading Elisabeth Noelle-Neumann (1993 [1980]) to invoke a model of self-reinforcing interpersonal 'spirals of silence' to explain shifting majority–minority dynamics of conformity and dissidence towards society's prevailing ideas.

The success of these new positions in discrediting ideology meant that, by the 1960s, social researchers who hoped to build on the insights of previous ideology theorists were obliged to switch to alternative (but substantially overlapping) terms and areas of study. To aid in this, they applied a plethora of new research methods to the specific economic, political, and cultural objects of social enquiry – drawing on linguistics (Ferdinand de Saussure, Roman Jakobson), anthropology (Claude Lévi-Strauss), phenomenology (Martin Heidegger), and psychoanalysis (Freud, Jacques Lacan). The insights from these new encounters and injections into ideology theory spiralled off into a vast array of (often mutually critical) directions; but their common thread was a sharpened focus on understanding individual people and their social agency as 'bearers' of ideology. Some authors, many associated with the 'structural Marxist' tendency, resisted the trend against ideology and its co-option by Cold War liberalism. Althusser (2014 [1970]) and Poulantzas (1975 [1968]) continued the trend started by Lenin, Gramsci, and Lukács of recognising the quasi-autonomy between base and superstructure and the differentiation within the superstructure and characterised more precisely society's specifically ideological structures and institutions – which they considered an inevitable, 'eternal' part of society no matter its underlying economic arrangements. Althusser argued that ideology operates through several 'ideological state apparatuses' across various societal domains (e.g., law, religion, the media, education, the family), which determine the circulation of values and information to maintain the 'subjection' of the subordinate to the ruling classes. These apparatuses 'interpellate' (call, 'hail') us individually as ideological subjects, shaping how we think and act by imbuing us with imaginary, distorted representations designed to accommodate us to our social conditions (specifically, exploitation and state repression).

Others tried to shore up the link between ideology and class from a historicist perspective. Goldmann (1964 [1955]), drawing on Lukács, argued for a 'genetic' account of ideologies as the 'mental structures' of particular classes conceived as 'collective subjects'. These mental structures exist at two levels: 'worldviews', revealed in literature, philosophy, and art, expressing the class's aspirations in a 'pure', elevated, 'ideal' global form, which are 'true' to actual historical conditions when the class is in the ascendancy; and the partial, distorting, deceptive rationalisations that exist as 'dominant ideology' when the class is in decline. By contrast, Nicholas Abercrombie, Stephen Hill, and Bryan S. Turner (1980) sharply criticised the view that society's prevailing ideas, reflecting those of its dominant class, are primarily responsible for maintaining and reproducing class society. Such a 'dominant ideology' is typically poorly defined and at most binds together this dominant class; its effects on the societal structure are eclipsed by political factors (repression, partisan factionalism, legal property relations) and the brute 'dull compulsion' of its economic arrangements.

The majority of the new approaches, however, fell in line with the rejection of 'ideology', turning their attention to one of two substitutes. One group cloaked ideology analysis in the garb of analysing *discourse*. Michel Pêcheux (1969) emphasised the historical and linguistic material reality of discourse as not just a reflection of economics (i.e., class struggle) but a quasi-autonomous, irreducible domain with its own way of functioning. He proposed a 'semantics of discourse' focused on language as an instrument of ideological communication, 'ankylosed' (fused, stiffened) to 'sutured' (stitched-together) rules of grammar and syntax, which related the meaning of discursive expressions to the class positions of those using them at a given societal 'conjuncture' (set of circumstances at a point in time). This analysis of how ideology determines 'what can/should be said' tallied with Foucault's (1977, 1982a [1969], 1988 [1961], 1994 [1966], 1996 [1963], 2007) efforts to uncover the 'genealogical' origins of socially (ab)normal and (un)acceptable expression. Pursuing an 'archaeology of knowledge' geared towards uncovering 'subjugated' ideas and discourses led Foucault to examine the role of disciplinary mechanisms such as hospitals, schools, and prisons in cultivating certain psychological and behavioural norms. Discourses not only take a 'biopolitical' approach to managing our activity as objective living bodies but also foster in us a 'governmentality' that aligns our subjective self-conceptions with society's dominant *raison d'état* – which can be resisted only by 'parrhesiastic' challenges to its 'regimes of truth' and a transgressive, spontaneous, 'carnivalesque' 'ethics of the self'.

The social construction and conditionality of language is a central theme in the project of 'deconstruction' associated with the anti-structuralist turn. Jacques Derrida (1973 [1967], 2001 [1967]) argued that the meaning of words as discursive units depends on their 'synchrony' with other words in their language and the 'diachrony' between their contemporary and historical definitions; discourse analysis must unpick the constant 'differentiation' and 'deferral' (together, '*différance*') that prevent 'complete' or 'total' meaning from ever being definitively determined. Paul de Man (1982) and Richard Rorty (1984) mirrored this approach, focusing on the subversive ideological content revealed by tensions between coexisting 'accidental' features and apparent 'essential' messages of discursive expressions. Jean-François Lyotard (1988), meanwhile, extended the deconstructionist impulse to our discursive attempts to grasp a sense of reality itself, stressing both the inadequacy and indeterminacy of language in generating agreement about its meaning and the frequent inability of 'sublime' reality to be neatly captured by the 'finitude' of linguistic concepts.

The other cognate topic that absorbed ideology theory's surplus energy was the analysis of *culture*, specifically of symbols and symbolism. Geertz (1973) described ideology as the ordering of multifaceted, multi-layered symbols with cultural meanings attached to them, which selectively represent and efficiently organise social space and (historical) time. These symbolic orderings act as 'maps' or narratives that help us orient ourselves within society – not exhaustive catalogues of everything it contains, but a carefully filtered, simplified record of essential information about it. Cultural semioticians such as Barthes (1957, 1964) and Marshall McLuhan (1951) examined how specific cultural objects embody prevailing collective ideas and their narrative organisation. Barthes focused on the role of ideological myths as symbols operating in a second-order system of 'metalanguage', which take the literal, explicit meanings of existing symbols that are already established as 'language-objects' in our first-order linguistic systems and add connotations that transmit further implicit meanings representing ('signifying') other social objects. Building on Barthes and Gramsci, Stuart Hall (1973, 1980) argued that whether symbols deliver their intended ideological meaning relies on reciprocity between the 'encoding' of meaning by their producers and its 'decoding' by their consumers. When we receive symbolic messages, we do not have to passively accept the 'dominant' ideological meanings they encode but, rather, have scope to 'negotiate' (make situational exceptions to) and 'oppose' (offer contrary alternatives to) these meanings, and thereby subvert ideological hegemony – which McLuhan (1964) argued would require different amounts of effortful participation from us depending on whether the media through which symbols are transmitted are 'hot' (high-definition) or 'cool' (low-definition).

Other cultural theorists examined ideology's unconscious manifestations. Bourdieu (1977, 2010 [1979]) characterised ideology as generating cultural *doxa*: deep-founded unconscious beliefs perceived as universally self-evident, which favour existing societal arrangements by 'naturalising' them and presenting socially constructed narratives about them as common-sensical, a process Barthes described as the 'exnomination' (denying the need to name) of dominant ideas. *Doxa* informs part-rational, part-intuitive 'dispositions' that condition our responses in different 'fields' of societal activity, which combine into a *'habitus'* comprising durable unconscious schemes and strategies of perception, thought, and action. Our *habitus* typifies our social (class) position, making us tend to accept and reproduce our *status quo*, and shapes our mannerisms, tastes, and opinions, which become markers of our position and hence sources of social 'distinction'. By contrast, Gilles Deleuze and Félix Guattari (2004 [1972, 1980]) turned to psychoanalytic treatments of the unconscious to explore the 'investments' of libidinal desire generated by our social (class) positions – ranging from 'paranoiac' (reactionary) to 'schizoid' (revolutionary) – which lie even deeper than preconscious social (class) interests, let alone conscious ideological opinions.

§4 1980 to now: the emergence of 'ideology studies'

The two sides of the 'turn against ideology' looked set to bring ideology analysis to a definitive close outside a few comparatively narrow branches of social (especially political) research. But successive economic, political, and cultural developments in the 1960s to 1980s – decolonisation and the rise of ethnoreligious multiculturalism, sexual and racial emancipation and civil rights movements, a new salience of ecology and sustainability, the fragmentation, decline, and disintegration of the communist bloc, extensive privatisation and deregulation of state functions alongside programmes of public expenditure 'austerity', and the deindustrialisation and *embourgeoisement* of Euro-America through its shift to tertiary, quaternary, and quinary sectoral specialisations and the relocation of manufacturing and gradual proletarianisation of the global South – highlighted an analytical 'gap' where ideology was needed and where it used to be, prompting its gradual reintroduction into social enquiry. This has been led by several 'pro-ideological' elaborations of the previous period's insights into ideology-as-*realised*-ideas (culture) and ideology-as-*communicated*-ideas (discourse), leading to another far-reaching thawing of attitudes and a swing back towards non-pejorative understandings of the term.

Ideology theory inherited from the cultural turn a broadened understanding of how ideas can be materialised in society, manifesting in an apotheosis of concern with questions of *identity*. Continuing the focus on individuals as 'bearers' of ideology, the contemporary debate turns on whether identity, conceived as commitment to a certain outlook or set of interests and priorities, is primarily mediated via collective solidarities with groups in similar social positions or via personal attributes shared with other individuals who self-identify in a similar way. Central to the former view has been a definitive 'retreat from class' as the basis for ideological affiliation, especially under pressure from feminism, postcolonialism/antiracism, and queer ideology. Ellen Meiksins Wood (1986) reads this as a logical consequence of Poulantzas's 'autonomisation' of ideology and politics from economics, while Ronald Inglehart (1977, 1990, 2018) sees in it evidence of a massive intergenerational shift towards the primacy of 'post-material' cultural values. The emergence of rival ideological pulls due to drastically expanded understandings of (e.g.) sexual/gendered or racialised forms of social domination have informed vehement debates about how to compatibilise the ideologies and identities that attach to them. Some theorists have articulated 'hybrid' accounts that fuse specific identities, as Shulamith Firestone (1970) and Catharine A. MacKinnon (1989) have done for class and gender, or Patricia Hill Collins (1990) and bell hooks

(1981) have done for gender and race. Altogether, these have become bracketed under the theme of finding what Kimberlé Crenshaw (1989, 2017) calls 'intersectionality' between the ways these identities and their associated ideas reflect societal power asymmetries – which, in Ernesto Laclau and Chantal Mouffe's (1985) terms, can underpin 'chains of equivalence' between social movements that seek to represent them.

The 'individual attributes' side has focused primarily on which aspect of our person ideology influences. In the Foucauldian tradition, Judith Butler (1988, 1990, 1993, 2004) has expanded theoretical appreciation of how ideology shapes the characteristics, uses, and treatment of our bodies, arguing that we follow an ideological 'script' that guides our presence and actions in society – which they call the 'performativity' of identity. Similarly, Wendy Brown (1995) emphasises the 'wounded attachments' that underpin our identities, based on the concrete injuries and suffering our bodies have endured at the hands of ideologically motivated violence. Some theorists, following in the psychoanalytic footsteps of Lacan and Deleuze and Guattari, have further analysed ideology's effects on our unconscious and subconscious – such as Slavoj Žižek's (1989, 2006, 2010) portrayal of ideology as an unconscious 'fantasy' of justifications and symbolic rituals underpinning hegemonic representations of disordered, inconsistent reality or Julia Kristeva's (1980) evaluation of tensions between 'semiotic' instinctive emotion and 'symbolic' shared cultural meaning alongside individual psychic and sexual experience in driving identity-formation. This, in turn, is mirrored in the resurgence of social-psychological interest in ideology – such as, for instance, Teun A. van Dijk (1998) and John R. Zaller's (1992) studies of the 'mental models' and 'schemata' by which ideology shapes our perception of reality, or John T. Jost, Christopher M. Federico, and Jamie L. Napier's (2009, 2013) examination of correlations between specific ideologies and personality-traits.

Meanwhile, the discursive turn has moved ideology theory decisively away from the rationalism–irrationalism binary towards including the diverse ideological content found in everyday, vernacular *'ordinary' thinking and expression*. A common theme has been a desire to abandon unjustified preconceptions that privilege reasoned, logical argument in theoretical texts as the only ideological language worth studying. One pronounced tendency has been the concerted effort to restore the ideological centrality of emotions such as joy, sadness, anger, fear, love, resentment, despair, shame, or disgust, often to counter what Carol Gilligan (1982) portrayed as the 'patriarchal', androcentric normalisation of rationality to mark 'mature' social thinking. Drawing on the sociology of emotions, Jack Barbalet (1998) and Arlie Russell Hochschild (1983) stress the social contexts and institutions that facilitate and constrain, affirm and repress, certain emotions through 'feeling rules' that determine our routine interactions as well as ideologically (un)acceptable emotional displays – to which William Reddy (2001) adds a historical perspective, tracing how the social origins and effects of our emotional lives change over time. A special case of this is ideological mobilisation of unconscious, uncontrolled emotional projection in social (moral, legal) appraisals – particularly disgust or revulsion, which Martha Nussbaum (2004) argues plays a central role in justifying the subordination of social groups (especially women, ethnoreligious minorities, and homosexuals). In turn, Sara Ahmed (2004) extends this to the physical experience of emotionality in discourse, emphasising its basis in our relationships with others and with objects in our social environments.

Meanwhile, other authors have challenged reductive philosophical criteria of what is considered 'good argumentation' for obscuring many of ideology's most widespread forms and effects. Michael Freeden (1996, 2015) has returned attention to the variations in sophistication, rigour, and nuance between (e.g.) formal ideological 'outputs' by professional academics and journalists versus more nebulous, protean idea-formations in the wider public – arguing for an expansion of 'what counts as' ideological thinking to capture the powerful social effects of *un*reason and *il*logic in forming the maps through which we 'read' reality. Michael Billig (1991) shares Freeden's attentiveness to the inconsistencies of 'common-sense' ideological forms, advocating a reappraisal of their constitutive social attitudes not as topic-specific substantive views but, rather, as discursive stances for conducting social arguments and conversations – which he suggests are best assessed via the analytical categories of classical rhetoric.

Finally, ideology theory has also seen continued emphasis on the media through which ideological symbols are disseminated – ranging from Régis Debray's (1996) distinction between 'iconic', 'idolatrous', and 'visionary' forms of ideological symbolism to John B. Thompson's (1990) critique of how symbolic commodification and exchange helps propagate or reproduce ideologies and Norman Fairclough's (1995b) and Ruth Wodak's (1996) explorations of ideological symbolism in advertising, marketing, and political programmes.

All in all, the developments during the most recent period of ideology theory's evolution have left its methodological terrain richer, more diverse, and more fragmented, above all in two ways. First, the recent period has definitively weakened the 'Cold War'-reminiscent binary between Marxist–Marxisant (and often socialist- or communist-committed) and political-science-led (likewise often liberal-inflected) approaches to the study of ideology. Certainly, ideological and 'ideologological' commitments remain intertwined in a variety of subtle ways, and many of the protagonists in the nascent subfield of 'ideology studies' have pursued more or less intense parallel careers as normative theorists, journalists and public intellectuals, party activists and strategists, and other exponents of ideological content. But, at the same time, they have parted company with the hard oppositional boundaries of earlier periods and define themselves to a decreasing degree in terms of the restrictive parameters of 'Marxism' or 'political science'. Second, and related to this, the recent period has picked up where the 'turn against ideology' left off in terms of opening up ideology analysis to a far greater range of disciplinary foci and approaches. Gone is the shifting oligopolistic primacy of 'philosophy of history', political economy, or empirical social science; instead, ideology studies as it has taken shape tends strongly towards 'broad-church' methodological diversity and syncretism, drawing on the study of ideas and language, media and literature, social behaviour and psychology, and ranging from the pure humanities to the 'hardcore' social sciences. The upshot is a subfield marked by a plethora of parallel approaches from across social research broadly construed, the twelve primary categories of which are explored in more detail later on (see chapter 6).

3
What is ideology?

The development of ideology theory since its classical foundations has bequeathed the concept of ideology a multitude of meanings and analytical associations, which lend themselves to a variety of social applications. To offer a view of ideology that is accessible and relatively universalisable to all the areas of social life and research where the concept is used, we need to establish some definitional common ground between its various conceptions – a locus of consensus based on the cumulative insights of both historical and more recent theoretical contributions. Despite areas of considerable disagreement about the concept's other connotations, both pejorative (vernacular) and non-pejorative (semantic) understandings of ideology are united in seeing it as concerned fundamentally with *combinations and arrangements of ideas*. The emphasis in this fundamental concern is twofold. First, it is above all *ideas* that ideology combines and arranges. Whatever other forms ideology operates in or manifests as, the core stock-in-trade in which it deals – the 'common language' into which all other forms can be translated – are abstract ideas. In other words, when ideology analysis is looking at the 'ideological content' of social phenomena, its focus is on naming and interrogating the underlying principles, motivating ideals, and descriptive terminology of these phenomena, expressed in conceptual form. Second, the ideas that ideology contains are combin*ed* and arrang*ed*.

What is ideology? 43

There is more to ideology than just the presence of multiple ideas, and there is a considerable significance in several meta-level questions about the 'logic' of this 'presence': how and why it came about, when and where it did so, and who and what is accountable for it. That is to say: when ideology analysis treats ideas as 'ideological', it is looking at the grouping of ideas not as random or accidental but as subject to deliberate ordering in relation to one another, with a clear chain of causality and justification, with clear temporal and spatial points of origin and trajectories of development, and above all as the result of (un)conscious human or supra-human agency responsible for the decisions over their combination and arrangement.

The internal construction of an ideology – its *morphology* – is determined by *which* ideas it incorporates and *how* it combines and arranges them (Freeden 1996, 75–91, 124–7; 2013). The purpose of creating such an ideological 'cast list' of ideas and 'roster' of combinations and arrangements is to provide a mental *representation* of reality, in particular social reality, usually *as it is* or *as it used to be*, but also *as it is not*, *as it will be*, or *as it should be*. The reason for this is a fundamental, irreducible dualism that lies at the heart of our existence as conscious beings in the world. 'Raw' or 'pure' reality is made up of an immense number of materials: physical, earthly substances that constitute the world, matter and 'stuff' that is concretely present, which includes human beings and other living things, and resources that can be used as tools, equipment, means, or materiel. These materials are imbricated in a similarly vast number of relations with one another: linkages that connect them, forms of comparison and involvement based on the existence of mutual contact, whether contrast or correspondence, clashing or alignment, independence or association. In and by themselves, how these materials are distributed and these relations are arranged is deeply chaotic: a formless mass and jumbled mixture of phenomena alongside seemingly random, unpredictable events (including changes and the lack thereof). It is also profoundly (self-)contradictory and often features the simultaneous coexistence of opposites and diametrically inverse pressures and tendencies. Reality thus lacks any transcendent unity; its seemingly manifold nature is a reflection not of any prior 'wholeness' that has become fragmented but, rather, of its inherent, eternal qualitative and quantitative 'multiplicity' (Deleuze 1988, 13–14; 1991 [1966], 38–47; Deleuze and Guattari 2004).

Because we are 'embodied' beings – i.e., because we 'occupy' flesh-and-blood bodies – we are ourselves material 'stuff', and we are put ineluctably in relations with other 'stuff'. The part of reality within which we are physically and temporally present, and which we thus directly experience, is our 'environment': the circumstances, factors, or conditions by which we are surrounded (Heidegger 1962 [1927], 83–5, 94–123, 134–48; Zaller 1992, 21). Our encounters with the materials and relations in our environment can be more or less soft and gentle or abrupt and violent, giving us experience of sensual pleasure, help, comfort, and palliative healing, as well as inflicting on us sensual pain, harm, hurt, and traumatic stress and injury. But our mental 'processing' of this experience, the way we think and feel about it, necessarily always happens indirectly, at one stage removed. Reality is not immediately accessible to human cognition; instead, it is mediated by our bodily perceptual faculties – senses of sight, hearing, touch, and so on. What we think of as our conscious experience of the world is not of reality itself – 'the real real' (Lacan 2006; Žižek 2002) – but of the neural results of sensory stimulation. We convert the sensory information we gather from external stimuli into an internal replica of our environment: a more or less integrated collection of virtual constructs based on provisional selections 'captured' from our sensory perceptions, which Lippmann (1922, 15, 20, 25–8) calls our 'pseudo-environment'. What we 'access' when we think and feel 'about the world' is in fact only how it is mirrored in this pseudo-environment – the 'imaginary' likeness of reality we have derived from the intermediary information that our perceptual faculties have provided us about it (Lacan 2006). Thanks to our embodiment, our mental 'processing' of reality is also at the mercy of the physical and temporal limits of our perception: even if our perceptual faculties are not seriously impaired in any way, they are already restricted to an outer 'horizon' beyond which we are unable to experience reality, because they (we) are irrevocably bound to the context in which our bodies are

What is ideology? 45

situated (Fairclough 1989; Gadamer 2013 [1960], 313–17; Raftopoulos 2007; Wright and Ward 2008).

Moreover, reality *as a whole* is far too large and complex to be something we are even able to experience or process fully, (self-)consciously, or for an extended period of time; instead, we only ever do so partially, momentarily, and in dim awareness, typically when something happens to us that we do not expect. It is 'sublime', in that its sheer massiveness and powerful impact on us and our surroundings places it 'beyond' our faculties of perception or our cognition, even while we have an inkling that 'there is more to it' than might appear on the surface (Lyotard 1988, 1994; Žižek 1989). In our attempt to 'process' our material and relational encounters, including the topography of their distribution and the contours of their arrangement in our environments, our experience of reality proves overwhelming and incomprehensible. It is confusingly disruptive and unpredictable, getting in the way of our attempts to distinguish or discriminate between different phenomena and events – to 'sort' reality ontologically into discrete singular objects ('persons', 'things') with describable dimensions and other attributes (Badiou 2005 [1988]). A lot happens in it at once: too much to process in one go, and rather a sensory onslaught to the point of overload that prevents us from working out what is going on, never mind what really matters (McLuhan 1964). Reality offers us no spatial or temporal points of reference, leaving us lost and disoriented, with no idea where to turn or how to locate ourselves in relation to its phenomena and events (Schopenhauer 1819). It is unexplained and unreasoned, shocking and horrifying but also 'random' and banal, with no basis to draw inferences about it and no sources on which to pin 'how it all got here' (Žižek 1999). Lastly, worst of all, reality identifies no clear agency to which to attribute it all (to praise or blame for it); at most, it permits us a vague notion that human agency (by an unknown number and character of human agents, immediate or mediated through other social entities) has some part to play in its creation.

In this light, the function of ideology is in the first instance one of intercession. It aims to make reality palatable and viable, to overcome the problems it poses for our inherently limited mental and physical faculties, by creating 'mental pictures' that 'abridge' reality as a whole until it becomes intelligible to us (Bennett and Hacker 2003; Brant 2013; Engels 1987 [1878]; Lippmann 1922, 4, 11–13, 29–32). Ideology imposes meaning on the meaninglessness of reality and 'makes sense' of its inherent 'non-sense', by formulating and applying symbolic frameworks of understanding that make reality 'manageable' for human psychology and human behaviour (Lacan 2006). In this way, it acts as a kind of map that 'charts' the features of reality by conceptualising them in a way we can grasp (Freeden 1996), as a type of analgesic therapy that numbs the intensity of our experience of reality so we can (mentally and physically) function within it (cf. Marx 1975 [1843], 175), and – bridging the two – as a form of 'counselling' that empowers us to 'do the work' needed to overcome reality's capacity to swamp and devastate us. All three together aim to enable us to confront reality confidently and capably and escape the anxiety and cluelessness that accompanies our unmediated experience of it.

The ideas ideology contains are intended to capture the phenomena in reality, the encounters between them, and the events that affect them – both those 'present' and those 'absent' (defined with reference to those present) (Lacan 2006). Ideology defines phenomena, assigns them their significance, describes their associations and implications, delineates and groups them by criteria of similarity and difference, and explicates their existence in terms of an 'order', 'process', 'sequence', 'context', or other 'frame of reference'. It makes reality 'our reality' by sketching out for us a way in which we can grasp both its macroscopic enormity and its microscopic details. Ultimately, there always remains a 'gap' between conceptual representation and reality. Of course, ideological combinations and arrangements of ideas are themselves 'real', in the sense that they exist neurologically as internal thoughts and often also as external expressions. But ideas and their combinations and arrangements fundamentally *are not the same as* the phenomena they represent; and the materials and relations that make up reality do not necessarily correspond to any representations we make of them (Baudrillard 1983, 1; McLuhan 1964). As will become clear later, this 'ideology–reality gap' is the basis for many of the most fundamental problems of ideology and its study.

A set of ideas and the representations they provide of reality becomes established as 'an' ideology by giving the set a collective label as a 'shorthand', typically in the form of a pre-existing or newly created term built on a chosen 'root' word ('X'). While this label sometimes takes the form of 'X ideology' (e.g., green ideology, queer ideology), it appears most familiarly as 'X-ism', to the extent that the suffix 'ism' is often (albeit not always quite accurately) used more or less interchangeably and synonymously with '(an) ideology' in a vernacular sense. This ideological labelling imposes the set of ideas, 'told' or 'recounted' in a certain way – i.e., in the morphological construction into which they have been combined and arranged – onto the chosen term. Naming an ideology by calling a particular combination and arrangement of ideas an 'ism' and 'claiming' the chosen term as its label is thus a further layer of representation: using a single abstract idea (and its cognates) to 'code for' an entire way of making reality make sense to us. Such ideologisation of the 'root' word has a reciprocal effect both on its meaning and on that of the ideas it stands for. It expands, modifies, and sometimes even overrides the word's accepted vernacular meaning by (re)orienting it towards the specific series of ideas to which it is now ideologically 'attached'. At the same time, it also adds the word's familiar connotations of meaning to the overall 'aura' of its associated arrangement and combination of ideas. The idea of companionship or fellowship connoted by the word 'social' gives 'socialism' its collective, solidaristic overtones; 'liberal' as unrestrained permissiveness or generous abundance has turned into the free openness of 'liberalism'; and the protective retention implied by 'conservative' has lent 'conservatism' its sceptical resistance to societal change. Ideological labelling thus creates space for a whole family of cognate terminology, either by 'ideologising' other pre-existing words or by inventing wholly new ones. The suffix '-ism' has given rise to a number of derivatives to describe different aspects of ideology's social presence: '-ist' or '-istic', 'ise(d)' and '-ising', '-iser', '-isation', and '-isant' to depict the ideology's bearer(s) or agent(s), its (increasing) social influence or implementation, and its social tendencies or approximations.

§1 Making sense of reality

Before continuing with the analysis, it is worth providing a working definition of the concept of ideology: an ideology, or an 'ism', is *a combination and arrangement of ideas that determines how we understand reality.* Yet when we engage with our surroundings, we have to bridge this gap between reality as ideology represents it and reality as it 'actually' is (i.e., in its chaotic, contradictory form). Both, in different senses, are 'our reality' – reality as we (inter) subjectively understand it and the reality in which we are objectively present. In engaging with our surroundings, we use ideological maps as 'guides' – not only to help us 'navigate' reality but also to help us 'steer' it. We do not just 'pass through' reality passively as yet more material 'stuff', but we play a crucial role (individually and collectively) in *impacting* it through our willed, purposive action – either perpetuating reality *as it is* or transforming it into an *alternative* reality. When we use ideological representations to 'guide' our psychology and behaviour (how we think, feel, and act) we are also 'realising', in the sense of 'making real', these representations within our environments; in other words, ideology both 'captures' *for* us and 'crafts' *through* us *'what is* the case' in the world around us, and it is as a result of our action that ideological representations of reality are *'made* the case'. The ideological combinations and arrangements of ideas form a 'common thread' that unites all the ways in which we engage psychologically and behaviourally with reality: the shared basis or fundamental underlying position from which all our engagement derives, which informs it, and which it always 'falls back on'. Ideology, then, covers not just the combinations and arrangements of 'pure' ideas but also the combinations and arrangements of a series of other 'applied' elements that shape human action which these ideas 'stand for' in generalised abstraction, and which put these ideas 'into effect'. If we stay true to the view that the study of *'ideology'* covers εἶδος as well as ἰδέα, a full account of the morphology of ideology becomes incomplete without also looking at the different forms in which

What is ideology? 49

the 'fundamental underlying position' of combined/arranged ideas can manifest.

Ideology shapes the starting point for our psychological and behavioural engagement, namely the outlooks or attitudes with which we 'approach' the reality we experience. It affects the stance we take towards what our ideological map tells us is happening around us: what we see, what we think or feel about it, what 'gut reactions' or 'instincts' it provokes in us. It decides whether we are (e.g.) deeply touched by shows of kindness or piety, outraged at rudeness or profanity, or snidely satisfied with cruelty or bigotry. On its own, reality offers no basis for us to make epistemological or evaluative judgments, i.e., to form cognitive convictions or prescriptive estimations about what is in it; materials and relations do not by themselves 'encode' any 'clues' that can help us gauge how we are supposed to assess them. But merely experiencing a social phenomenon instantly and automatically 'triggers' a cluster of meaning and connotations associated with its abstract representation as an idea (in its combination and arrangement with other ideas), so that we in effect experience the two in tandem. This is the result of ideological *dispositions*: 'durable, transposable' frames of mind and 'schemata', prevailing tendencies to behave in a certain manner, and propensities for certain moods and attitudes towards our surroundings (Boudon 1989, 71–81, 94–8, 103–8; Bourdieu 1990, 52–3; van Dijk 1998, 56–8; Zaller 1992, 37, 274–80). These dispositions give reality a certain 'gloss' that can inform the distinctions and preferences we formulate between social phenomena, providing us with a 'nudge' that makes us susceptible, and willingly inclined, to assessments that align with our ideological map.

This manifestation of ideology is perhaps best conceptualised as a *lens* that colours and clarifies how we 'view' reality as we engage with it. The ideological lens brings (certain) phenomena 'into focus' when we cast our highly calibrated 'gaze' (Butler 1990; Foucault 1977; hooks 2003), highlighting them and making them stand out, drawing our attention and raising our awareness, and fine-tuning our sensibility and sensitivity to their existence. It makes us regard other people and objects as triggers of arousal or revulsion, motivates us to help or commit violence against them, deifies or dehumanises them. It allows us to register and recognise materials and relations in terms of how our ideological maps represent them and thus to 'grasp' that (and 'how') they are 'there' in our vicinity *at all*. Without it, reality would seem blurred and out of focus, uniform in emphasis, and devoid of features noticeable enough to 'draw the eye', with our attention caught only contingently by random collisions and 'close encounters' with our surroundings. Our lens makes reality 'manageable' by ensuring that the phenomena that matter (in the ideological map) come prominently 'into view' – albeit always at the potential cost of 'smudging', 'greying out', or distorting other phenomena that our 'vision' would include with a different lens. It 'grafts' ideas inseparably onto the social phenomena they represent, superimposing a 'photographic filter' of ideological saturation onto reality, but at the same time letting it appear 'natural' (Barthes 1957).

Lenses are relatively 'passive' manifestations of ideology, in the sense that they operate regardless of whether, or how, we choose to engage with (navigate, steer) reality. Moving now onto human action, ideology also sets the rules that govern our psychological and behavioural demeanour. It determines how we translate what our ideological dispositions incline us to think or do into concrete instances of action: by what criteria we judge specific circumstances, how we proceed or respond in them, what 'move' we make or 'step' we take. It tells us (e.g.) how we should signal our 'strength' or 'legitimacy', what a 'just' or 'cheap' thing to do would be, how we should 'keep fit and healthy' or 'get woke'. There are no 'pointers' in reality that show us the likely impact or consequences of the choices we make towards what is in it; social materials and relations do not 'carry' any indications to help us decide how, and even whether, we are meant to interact with them. Again, simply experiencing a social phenomenon immediately prompts a 'know-how' (*savoir*) of the 'best' (most moral, efficacious, etc.) way to prefigure or affirm certain abstract ideas about this phenomenon, so we go straightaway from experience to (re)action (Foucault 1982a). Ideology achieves this by presenting us with certain *norms*: binding, regulative prescriptions of 'right/wrong' action, authoritative standards to adhere to regarding what is desired, expected, or required of us in our given contexts,

What is ideology? 51

and 'stereotypes' about what constitutes healthy, sound, or non-defective social functioning. Norms define what we acknowledge as our 'average' permitted or prohibited engagement with social phenomena, creating a common source of control that makes us prone to conform to conventions that tally with our ideological map.

A useful analogy to understand how ideology works here is the image of a *primer*, a book we can consult that outlines the rudiments of 'good' usage and style (e.g., for reading, grammar and punctuation, or etiquette) and which points out the 'right' or 'best' way to engage with reality. The ideological primer outlines elementary rules that link certain phenomena to certain psychological and behavioural decisions, bringing 'ready-to-hand' an abridged 'reference work' or introductory booklet of 'how-to' information as a rolodex of first principles that we can consult when we need concrete guidance (Heidegger 1962, 98–122, 135–47). It indicates how we can carry out a logical or emotionally intelligent appraisal of our situation, how we should greet someone in the street or complete a classroom assignment, how to 'be on our best behaviour' at a christening or a job interview. By using it, we can 'treat' social materials and relations in line with what our ideological maps tell us about them and thus (re)act 'appropriately' as they appear in front of us. Without it, reality would leave us 'at a loss' and vulnerable, 'on the back foot' out of ignorance and hesitancy, and (re)acting erratically and sporadically to whatever happens to be in our surroundings. The primer ensures that the 'proper' course of action towards social phenomena comes unmistakably to mind – although by doing so it 'crowds out', discourages, or prevents other courses of action that we might pursue if we used a different primer. It 'condenses' ideas into simple task-specific instructions regarding the phenomena they are 'about', designed to give us the full ideological preparation we need to 'deal with' reality and 'normalising' our response to it.

Of course, we do not just engage with reality via isolated actions, nor do we apply ideology mechanically in every separate situation. Instead, ideology also engineers a shift from the quantitative aggregation of norm-governed actions to a qualitative 'character profile' that comprises consistent psychological and behavioural traits (i.e., tendencies of thought and action). The emphasis here is on how we internalise what our ideological norms require of us into how we typically think or what we ordinarily do as we go about our lives: what everyday habits and routines we stick to, which 'rules of thumb' we abide by, what our usual *modus operandi* looks like. Ideology tells us (e.g.) 'how to be a good' parent or team manager, what 'following orders' looks like for a sous-chef compared to a paratrooper, what makes for a diligent retail worker or an accomplished pianist. Reality itself is devoid of any 'hints' that our active choices within it are repeatable or replicable at different times and in different spaces; materials and relations do not betray the extent or limits of their mutual similarity and predictability, which could help us pick what tactics or strategies of action we should deploy. But when we experience a social phenomenon, we respond to it not just with a succession of individual, newly (re)considered actions that reflect certain ideas but with an integrated set of default psychological and behavioural (re)actions. This happens due to our particular ideological *practices*: aggregations of usual or customary 'good' or 'right' actions, repeatedly observed duties and habitually obeyed commands to foster familiarity and proficiency, and an ongoing crafting to optimise our decision-making (Bourdieu 1977, 1990; Giddens 1984). In essence, these practices combine and arrange the separate instances of our engagement with our surroundings into a regular pattern, developing ingrained memories that make us liable to continue carrying out pursuits that fit with our ideological map.

At this level, we can compare ideology to a *script*, a compilation of carefully specified instructions that stipulate far more precisely than a primer 'the' (i.e., the only right) way(s) for us to engage with reality (Butler 1988, 1990; Tomkins 1987). The ideological script stipulates detailed psychological and behavioural procedures for us to follow towards (certain) phenomena, a '*hexis*' that leads us to hold and use our bodies in particular ways (Bourdieu 1977, 82, 87; 1990, 69, 74), a directed sequence of carefully choreographed scenes or highly considered scenarios, *in extremis* in the form of a list of commands or prescribed drills to execute.

What is ideology? 53

It lets us know what postures exude confidence or elicit sympathy, how to play a winning 'dating game' or outmanoeuvre political rivals, the steps to securing a promotion or persuading someone else of our arguments. As long as we 'know our lines' in the form it 'gives' them to us, we can 'act with' the materials and relations around us in accordance with how our ideological maps depict them. In its absence, reality would leave us undertaking a slow and disjointed process of case-by-case normative evaluations, susceptible to going wilfully off-piste and improvising new and inefficacious directions, and forced constantly to revisit and reconsider the basis on which we (re)act towards our surroundings. The script always reminds us of the 'part' we are 'meant' to be playing towards our surroundings – which entails 'rejecting', 'passing up', or 'failing to audition for' other 'parts' that a different script might give us. It 'inscribes' ideas into our physical embodiment among the phenomena they represent, giving us a well-developed ideological 'role' to inhabit within reality and making our performance of it become 'routine'.

So far, the focus has been on how ideology influences us as agents confronted with reality, treated as a kind of 'background' enormity. But one of the most important and furthest-reaching effects of ideology lies in how it tries to replicate and establish the deliberate ordering it imposes on ideas in the phenomena these ideas represent – in effect, to close the 'ideology–reality gap' and make its likeness of reality 'come true' – *by means of* human behaviour. What matters here is how the various intentions and many infinitesimal effects of ideological practices 'add up' to things changing or staying the same: what 'mark' we leave, what results we achieve, and above all how successfully we alter materials and relations to 'match' how they are represented by ideology. Ideology gives us (e.g.) the language to understand 'money', 'weaponry', or 'territory', a conception of what it means to 'make a difference' or 'have it our way', and a sense of what urgently needs fixing or what we should not touch with a bargepole. Beyond the point that reality is chaotic and self-contradictory – i.e., that it does not have an 'inner logic' or order that ideology merely has to 'discover' – there is also the problem that it offers us no sign of how amenable or resistant it is to our choices of action; materials and relations are not 'marked' in a way that can help us work out to what uses they lend themselves and what enabling or limiting effects they impose on us. Nevertheless, as we experience social phenomena, we instantly recognise whether, and how far, they constitute instruments or constraints for 'realising' certain combinations and arrangements of ideas. Ideology presents them to us as *structures*: aggregations of distinct material and relational elements into cohesive entities, the assembly and adjustment of separate parts into a definite underlying form, often patterned as lattice-like or cage-like frameworks that incorporate, regiment, and envelop us (Bourdieu 1977, 72–95; 1990, 52–65; Giddens 1984; Poulantzas 1975; Sewell 1992; Thompson 1984, 148–72). Just as practices combine and arrange our actions, structures impose a similar kind of 'organisation' on reality by combining and arranging its constitutive phenomena and events, building the conditions that we encounter into a close mimicry of our ideological map.

Ideology thus provides a kind of architectural *design plan*, a projection of the edifice that 'houses' us and which we 'construct' through our psychological and behavioural engagement with reality. The ideological design plan works out a thorough schematic into which (certain) phenomena are 'slotted', an oblique axonometric diagram intended to 'capture' their layout in the form of illustrative patterns and symbols. It shows us what 'generation', 'income bracket', or 'faith' we belong to, which 'bosses' we answer to and who our 'dependants' are, and what everyday worries, constraints, or pressures we face as a result. By following it, we can 'fit' the materials and relations with which our environment confronts us into a coherent shape, modelled after how our ideological maps represent them. Without it, reality would remain for us an indistinguishable mass, and we would have no conception of the scale and extent of our surroundings, the mutual distance and distribution of elements within them, or the dynamics and duration of their motive events. The design plan contains only the desirable or essential phenomena of interest for our engagement – which may mean that it 'omits', 'erases', or 'misrepresents' other phenomena that an alternative design plan might feature more prominently. It 'renders' ideas into our environments, providing us with a refined ideological blueprint of reality, and making our subordination to it an 'integral' part of our existence.

At the 'highest' level, ideology 'manages' the whole overarching complex of psychological and behavioural processes by which we interact with external phenomena, defining the specific occasions and points of contact between our actions and reality. Here, the main question is how what ideological practices accustom us to think, feel, and do marries with how ideological structures organise our surroundings to create an intricate composite: how its 'moving parts' join together and, ultimately, quite simply how reality works and what our purpose is within it. Ideology fills us in with 'big picture' clues about (e.g.) whether we are living in a 'parliamentary democracy' or a 'mixed market economy', whether society's 'operating logic' is one of dutiful service to a higher good or total licence for self-expression, and what vehicles or channels are available for us to 'do our thing' for ourselves and for others. By itself, reality does not identify when and where our activity intersects with it; materials and relations are not 'tagged' if at any given moment they are imbricated in our tactical or strategic choices in a way that would help us establish whether or not we can (enabling) or have to (limiting) take them into account. All the same, whenever we experience a social phenomenon or event (or a series of either), we immediately 'visualise' the constellation of default psychological or behavioural *savoirs*, instruments, and constraints we are operating with (or within) – i.e., which situational instantiation of the combinations and arrangements of ideas we hold we 'have to do with'. Ideology frames each of them for us in terms of *systems*: 'closed', bounded institutions or networks that link together social action, phenomena, and events into a more or less harmonious set-up, spread-out bodies of interactions and mutually influencing forces characterised by particular 'autopoietic' (self-recreating) operations and shared purposes, offering taxonomic classifications for joined-up sets of neighbouring and simultaneous devices and 'takings-place' (Bateson 1991; Luhmann 1995 [1984], 2012–13 [1997]; Parsons 1951, 15). Systems effectively 'fuse' the familiar patternings defined by practices with the organisation imposed by structures to establish an 'order' within reality, creating an 'organism' that reveals our interdependence with our surroundings as our ideological map envisages it.

Uniting both its operations as a script and a design plan, ideology here provides us with a *simulation*, a more or less fully 'guided tour' of the motions we have to go through to carry out our ideologically specified tasks within the confines of the edifice in which we find ourselves (Baudrillard 1983; Therborn 1980, 32ff.). The ideological simulation creates a fleshed-out *mise-en-scène* that integrates both us and (certain) phenomena in our environment, an audit or thoroughgoing explanation as if for an ideological 'novice', a 'storyboard' or 'walkthrough' that sets parameters for our psychological and behavioural engagement. It determines what our opportunities and obligations are as a 'citizen', an 'immigrant', an 'ex-con', or a 'dropout', what a decent career path or 'proper' family set-up looks like, or when we should stop 'fighting the machine' and 'make ourselves useful' to society. It allows us to 'array' the materials and relations around us and follow 'step-by-step paths' through them in a way that imitates the 'mental picture' our ideological maps give of them. Without it, we would be continually 'in the dark' about how we fit psychologically and behaviourally into our context, specifically about when we are perpetuating or transforming the muddled *mélange* of phenomena and events around us through our purposive action. The simulation places at our constant disposal a 'demonstration' of the specific 'playbook' we are supposed to be following towards reality – which, as ever, means 'redrafting', 'cutting', or rejecting the other variants that a different simulation might present to us. It 'traces' ideas into the processes that run our lives and inserts us into an intricate ideological 'stage production' in which we participate within reality, making our everyday involvement in it an 'organic' part of who we are.

There is one final way in which ideology influences how we engage with reality. To understand this, we need to grasp a vital ideological 'spiral' of recursivity that characterises our engagement. As we have seen above, ideology relies on human action (governed by norms, combined and arranged into practices) to steer (perpetuate or transform) reality. This means that reality is – at least partly – the product of *previous* iterations of ideological 'steering' by myriad previous human agents, and this cycle is kept going by present and future action that steers reality further. In other words, it is not only how we engage with reality that is ideological; reality as the environment in (or with) which we engage is ideological as well. Crucially, this also includes us ourselves, as by virtue of the fact that we are beings with a physical, embodied form we have also been 'architected' into reality in accordance with (other people's) past 'design plans' and 'simulations'. As the most elementary precondition of engagement, then, ideology determines how, and indeed whether, we encounter and experience reality *at all*.

In a purely mechanical sense, we engage with reality when our bodies tangibly and contingently 'come up against' or 'connect with' materials and relations, 'prompting' us to respond psychologically and behaviourally to these environmental phenomena as they 'appear' within our physical and temporal perceptual horizon. Ideology shapes (e.g.) whether we interpret our affective responses to these encounters as caused by 'women's solidarity', 'xenophobia', or 'gay panic', whether we meet them 'in a professional setting' or 'by coincidence', and whether we are only experiencing them at all because of 'who we are', 'what we look like', or 'where we come from'. By itself, reality does not 'keep track' of the changes it undergoes (what kind, by whom, for what purpose, with what implications, etc.) due to the cyclical iterations of action impacting on it; materials and relations do not 'embed' any 'traces' of their origin or development that can help us determine what encounters we will have as a result, with which parts of them, or what these will 'look like'. Yet when we experience a social phenomenon, we also simultaneously perceive it as the product of past attempts to 'realise' certain ideas, combined and arranged in a specific way – as a kind of 'frozen image' of (past) ideology. This happens thanks to our ideological *perspectives*: angles or points of view from which to detect, consider, and form acute insights about materials and relations, accurately measure and codify the spatial and temporal factors affecting their appearance to us (and disappearance from us), and judge their social significance by their 'visibility' and 'optics'. These perspectives 'situate' us into a particular place within reality, fixing how immediate and remote social phenomena are, giving us a 'vista' that prompts us to discern social facts that corroborate our ideological map.

Here, ideology operates by giving us a worldview – in the literal sense of a specific 'parallax' view-of-the-world or a *vantage-point* onto (or, rather, within) reality (Žižek 2006). The ideological vantage-point pinpoints a 'station' from which we 'survey' our environment, a basis for (self-) orientation and favourable overview of our local scene, which makes certain phenomena and events loom larger and others seem more distant. It decides if we come at a situation from a position of (e.g.) 'white/straight/male/cis privilege' or through the correlative dimensions of disprivilege, whether it reflects a society riven by (class, interreligious, partisan, etc.) conflict, including what sides are involved and which one we are on, and overall whether our society is the 'envy of the world' or fetidly corrupted by 'moral decay'. From it, we can 'locate' materials and relations based on the 'mental picture' offered by our ideological maps and 'triangulate' where our own 'position' lies within and among them. Without it, we would have no grasp of where we are within the spatial and temporal dimensions of our surroundings, i.e., of our comparative 'standing' towards (and also as part of) the constitutive elements of reality (Therborn 1980, 23–5). The vantage-point discloses primarily the 'nearer' or more 'prominent' social phenomena that we are likely to engage with – and, in turn, 'obscures', 'downplays', or 'ignores' other phenomena that different vantage-points might reveal instead. It 'situates' ideas by defining the precise 'juncture' of our insertion into our environments, giving us a geography- and time-period-specific understanding of reality that it presents to us as the 'entire' way of 'accessing' the world.

§2 Criteria of ideological characterisation

These six elements derived from the ideas that make up our 'mental picture' of reality – our ideological perspectives, dispositions, norms, practices, structures, and systems – are, in effect, six possible 'entry points' at which the 'pure' ideas that ideology combines and arranges intervene in how we

What is ideology? 59

interact with our surroundings. When we engage with reality, we do so from an ideological vantage-point, seeing reality through an ideological lens, adhering to an ideological primer and following an ideological script, sticking to an ideological design plan and 'running' an ideological simulation. These six forms of 'applied ideology' constitute what Bourdieu (1977, 52–65; 1990, 78–86) calls a *habitus*, following Norbert Elias (1939) and Marcel Mauss (1934), and what Giddens (1984, 4–5, 24) refers to as 'practical consciousness': a single complex of ways in which ideology shapes how we 'go through' our environments, psychologically and behaviourally acting on it and reacting to it. Different branches of ideology analysis may lay weight on different components of an ideology – more on its 'pure' form as ideas, on how it influences our dispositions and norms, or on the structures and systems with which it surrounds us. But however disparate the elements of this complex may appear at first blush, they all ultimately derive from the same foundation and share the same underlying purpose: to help us 'navigate' and 'steer' a reality that otherwise threatens to overwhelm us. In this light, we can modify our working definition of ideology from above: an ideology, or an 'ism', is a combination and arrangement of (1) ideas that determines how we understand reality and (2) *a set of derived elements (a habitus) that determines how we engage with it.*

An ideology's ideas together with the six elements of its *habitus* constitute what we can call the ideology's *social morphology*. Of course, the relationship between these constitutive ideological elements is neither uniform nor static: it can be more or less smooth or fraught, simple or complicated, and it can bring together psychologies and behaviours with a longer or shorter pedigree which can conflict as much as align, and which may enjoy greater or lesser social relevance and impact. Instead, the essential features of an ideology's social morphology can be characterised and compared according to four criteria, defined with reference to the double emphasis in the definition of ideology noted at the start of this chapter.

The first, which relates to *what* ideologies include in their morphology, is the question of sheer ideological *size*: the total number of 'pure' ideas and 'applied' elements that each one's particular combination brings together. At its simplest, we can mark this by how many different associated elements come to mind when a given ideology is named. This complexity ranges from outright monism, where the ideology is effectively a single idea that has been 'built up' into a full construct, to far-reaching pluralism, where it is characterised by a rich tableau of elements that inform a sophisticated model of our engagement with reality: e.g., 'secularism' as a singularly anti-religious ideology, or 'republicanism' as opposition to monarchy, contrasted with Christian democracy as a blend of faith-informed welfarism, federalised political authority, labour–capital 'social market' compromises, and support for European integration. Ideological size is also determined by the level of incidence an element needs to satisfy for it to 'count' as constitutive for an ideology rather than just an incidental tool used to 'join up' other ideas. Here, approaches to incorporation vary from maximalist, where the ideology errs on the side of generosity in judging 'margin calls' over the inclusion of different elements, to minimalist, where it jealously gatekeeps which elements it is prepared to accept or endorse: e.g., 'Peronism' as a political-economic 'catch-all' ideology that simultaneously bridges popular national identity, labour union interests, state economic involvement, and market privatisation, versus 'Leninism', whose 'faithful' continuations and 'deviationist' interpretations have been hotly contested among global 'left' ideologies. An ideology's size is also affected by how assiduously it maintains conceptual separations between its respective elements. The spectrum of differentiation stretches from stringent division, where the ideology inserts clear boundaries of distinguishing treatment between elements in order to resist their mutual permeabilities of (logical, cultural) meaning, to encouraging elision, where it exploits these permeabilities in order to build and amplify 'inevitable' continuities between elements in the way it formulates them: e.g., libertarianism's circumscription of 'freedom' to denote solely economic concerns of ownership, production, exchange, and consumption, compared with liberalism's use of its political connotations to facilitate a 'social' move towards civic and welfare rights.

The second criterion, which focuses on specifically *how* ideologies assemble their constitutive elements into a morphological construct, is ideological *density*: the contours of the distribution into which 'pure' ideas and 'applied' elements are arranged relative to one another within their given morphology. Central to this is how (far) an ideology relies on the (logical, cultural) relationships of *différance* between clusters of elements, maintained discursively by ties of syntax and grammar, to 'pin down' its definition of each of them (Derrida 1973). Such use of proximity can take the form of either close adjacency, which imposes semantic restrictions on how diverse a set of meanings any of its elements can entail, or far distance, which leaves room for elements to manifest their semantic capacity to a fuller extent: e.g., in liberalism, 'democracy' is usually placed in close proximity to 'rights', 'separation of powers', and 'parliamentarism', which casts it in electoral–constitutional terms; in communism, its conceptual neighbours are far more inconsistent, ranging from '*soviet* (council)' and 'plebiscite' to 'centralism' and 'the party', and frequently challenged by 'dictatorship (of the proletariat)'. A closely related factor is how high a level of focus an ideology gives any one of its constitutive elements, in the sense of its salience within its wider morphology and its critical importance to the ideology's 'picture' of reality. The priority of an element can be ranked as 'core' if it acts as a form of anchor or keystone that the rest of the ideology is 'built around' or as 'peripheral' if it sits in the marginal space of inclusion/exclusion or near the perimeter of how 'applied' elements realise the ideology's 'pure' ideas (Freeden 1996, 78–80): e.g., 'the environment' and 'sustainability' as core for ecologism, with 'labour' and 'welfare-statism' more peripheral, while for social democracy the ranking is exactly the opposite. Similarly, an ideology's density also depends on how evenly it allocates space to asserting each of the elements within its overall set. The scale of proportionality runs from highly spacious, where an element is made the principal theme of ideological thinking and action with only sparing references to other elements, to crowded, where it is tightly clustered alongside several others in a way that ensures it is only ever mentioned 'in passing': e.g., the extensive space conservatism allocates to defending 'order' (in general, and in its contingent forms), versus the rarer, usually negative mentions made of it in socialism, which almost instantly couples it with copious discussion of 'change' and 'progress'.

The size and density of an ideology together determine its *'thickness'* (or *'thinness'*), both in an absolute sense and compared to other ideologies. But the respective emphasis on ideas (and the *habitus* they stand for), and on their combination and arrangement, also informs two further criteria of characterisation, which together describe what we can call a given ideology's *robustness* (or *fragility*).

One of these additional criteria, again concerning what is included in ideologies' morphology, is ideological *strength*: how sturdy or resilient its individual ideas and derived *habitus* elements are as granular component parts of its particular combination. At the heart of this lies the question of how clearly, carefully, and extensively the elements an ideology has selected for inclusion have had their meaning specifically delimited and refined. The definition of an ideology's elements can be highly precise, with extensive stipulations of which denotations and connotations are 'ruled in' and 'ruled out' along with exacting criteria for determining the distinction between them, or somewhat vague, cashed out only superficially and leaving the full 'depths' of their meanings unplumbed and 'up for debate': e.g., the many explicit programmatic elaborations of socialism applied to 'Nordic', 'Arab' (Ba'athism, Nasserism), 'African' (*ujamaa*, 'consciencism'), 'Chinese' (Maoism, Dengism), or 'Latin American' (Guevarism, Chavism) contexts, versus the far smaller, more allusive, and more diffuse 'statements' available for conservatism or Christian democracy in the same settings. Ideological robustness is also influenced by how far the incorporation of specific elements into particular combinations and arrangements permanently fixes their intended meaning or leaves some deliberate scope for its future evolution. Such ideological firmness can veer towards rigidity, where the elements' meanings are profoundly entrenched and affirm the value of a well-constructed morphological edifice, or towards fluidity, where meanings are only more loosely attached in a way that acknowledges the psychological and behavioural desirability of contextual variation: e.g., communism's specific attachment of 'progress' and 'the future' to the revolutionary proletarian overthrow of the capitalist

What is ideology? 63

economy and dictatorial transition to a classless, stateless society, versus liberalism's more open-ended equivalents of human flourishing and improvements in our social conditions through the advance of reason and enlightened creativity. Closely related to this is the question of how far an ideology's elements are (able to be) deformed, or 'stretched', relative to their meaning in our wider societal context through their collocation with its other components (Collier and Mahon 1993; Goertz 2006, 69; Sartori 1970). Their response to such ideological strain is either highly elastic, accommodating the imposition of unusual or obscure meanings but resisting a permanent shift in favour of 'bouncing back' to their 'original shape', or more plastic, where such accommodation makes elements 'denature' and diverge to the point of incompatibility with their semantic interpretations beyond the given ideology: e.g., the idea of 'community', which in its liberal, conservative, or socialist readings retains conventional associations of 'locality', 'cooperation', and 'collection of individuals', compared with fascist efforts to tie it to a totalising corporate state and genocidal–imperialist ethno-religious homogeneity.

The last criterion of ideological characterisation, in turn again referring to how ideologies' morphology is assembled, is that of ideological *integrity* (in the sense of 'structural integrity', not ethical steadfastness): how closely its ideas and *habitus* hang together as a coherent whole in the specific way they are arranged. A core determinant of this integrity is how straightforward it is to translate an ideology from 'pure' representations of reality to 'applied' manifestations within it without incurring any 'losses' or 'remainders'. The internal consistency between its constitutive elements varies from smooth continuity, with a sound shared logic and steadfast mutual confirmation in their aims and effects, to jarring incongruity, typified by the erratic logic and seemingly capricious hypocrisy that marks what Habermas (1990) terms 'performative (self-)contradiction': e.g., the stringent anarchist institutionalisation of decentralised federal democratic coordination, industrial self-administration, and collective agriculture in Makhnovist Ukraine (1918–21) and Revolutionary Catalonia (1936–9), compared to the tension in fascism between 'left' rhetorical appeals to producerism, wealth redistribution, and cooperative central planning and 'right' policy accommodation with monopoly capitalism, private property rights, and hierarchical elitism. Equally, an ideology's integrity hinges on how well its elements are equilibrated, or balanced, with one another. The stability of its elements' morphological position ranges from predictable solidity, where the ideology imposes and seeks to maintain a crystalline immutability in its precise arrangement, to precarious volatility, where this arrangement is subject to countless tensions and recalibrations that leave it in a state of near perpetual flux: e.g., liberal efforts to carefully delineate the links between 'justice', 'freedom', 'equality', 'democracy', and other elements, contrasted with the long schisms within socialism over the morphological place of 'reform or revolution', 'the national question', and 'the mass strike'. Finally, and closely connected to this, is the ideology's vulnerability to external challenge, either in the form of conceptual scrutiny of its 'pure' representations or opposition to its 'applied' manifestations. Here, the gauge of ideological durability runs from impervious, where the ideology can effortlessly 'bat away' any threats to its 'picture' of how we should engage with our surroundings, to porous, where it is susceptible to shifts in its content and construction as a result of having to accommodate or yield to the concerns they raise: e.g., the appeals of socialism, liberalism, and conservatism to a combination of theoretical logic and empirical verifiability to shore up their claims, versus the protean forms of climate-change denialism or anti-vaxxer ideology, which continually refresh their cast list of conspiracist concerns as 'older' elements lose evidential plausibility.

Every ideology can be characterised as variously *thick/thin* and *robust/fragile* in its morphology, depending on where its constitutive elements and their combination/arrangement fall on these twelve spectrums. Some, such as liberalism, socialism, and Christian democracy, are both thick and robust, with a considerable number of elements held together in a rigorous and long-lasting constellation; others, often 'single-issue' ideologies such as nationalism or populism, lie more towards the thin, fragile end. Between them are ideologies that are thick but fragile, such as conservatism, fascism, or social democracy, which suffer 'dents' to their strength

What is ideology? 65

Table 1 The criteria of ideological characterisation

	Thickness–thinness	Robustness–fragility
Morphological *content* (ideas and derived elements)	*Size* • Complexity • Incorporation • Differentiation	*Strength* • Definition • Firmness • Response to strain
Morphological *construction* (combination and arrangement)	*Density* • Proximity • Priority • Proportionality	*Integrity* • Consistency • Stability • Durability

and/or integrity in practice or over time; and others that are thin but robust, such as libertarianism, which has consistently retained its laser focus on the centrality of individual freedom against all comers. Yet we must be careful not to see this as bestowing an illusory permanence on the depiction of ideological morphologies: ideologies are in a constant state of evolution over time and undergo regular changes that can have significant effects on their size, density, strength, and integrity (see chapter 4).

§3 What is and is not (an) ideology

If we incorporate these criteria, we can refine the definition of ideology a step further: an ideology, or an 'ism', is a combination and arrangement of (1) ideas that determines how we understand reality, and (2) a set of derived elements (a *habitus*) that determines how we engage with it, *whose (3) construction is more or less thick and robust*. But one of the lurking questions that remains as yet unanswered by this definition – a legacy of the methodological 'turn against ideology' after the Second World War (see chapter 2) – is how we can distinguish ideology, especially in the form of 'pure' abstract ideas, from the broader social category of *discourse*. In general, discourse refers to any orderly, extended exposition or exchange of information, whether through connected verbal expression or audiovisual communication, often (but not exclusively) relying on natural language. The term also connotes a degree of formality and seriousness in its content, reflected in its size and length (e.g., conversation, story), its reliance on recognised regular frameworks to connect its constitutive elements (e.g., reasoned argument, discussion) and standardised formats to present them (e.g., sermon, dissertation, lecture, treatise), and its 'roots' in specific contexts that define social boundaries on 'what can be thought' or 'said' about the topic in question. In other words, discourse shares with ideology its use of ideas to designate meanings, other specific elements to 'realise' them, and consciously formulated combinations and arrangements that build up into more complex constructs. Simply eliding the two terms and identifying *all* discourse as ideology renders the term 'ideology' essentially meaningless: it deprives it of analytical distinction and makes it nearly impossible positively to identify, measure, or critique its societal presence and effects (McLellan 1995, 61–70, 80–3; Purvis and Hunt 1993; van Dijk 2013). Instead, the task for ideological analysis is to specify *what kind* of discourse ideology represents: what kind of 'pure' ideas and 'applied' elements it contains, what kind of combinations and arrangements it builds them into, and ultimately what kind of 'sense' it 'makes' of reality.

The core of this qualitative distinction lies in how ideology presents itself as a form of discourse: what it says or implies about the kind of understanding and engagement it 'gives' us. Perhaps the central distinguishing feature of ideological discourse is its *claim to comprehensiveness*: ideologies 'think big' (i.e., 'think social') when they represent reality and manifest within it; even thinner, more fragile ideologies posit worldviews in a 'grand' sense, situating us in larger wholes and asserting macroscopic, strident in some cases even 'totalising' ambitions for the direction reality should take, although they can take microscopic forms in specific cases (Foucault 2000, 298–325, 403–17, 449–53; Gentile 2013; Larraín 1994; Schwarzmantel 2008, 3–24). In this light, every ideology claims to provide an ineluctably necessary angle – or even the best and only angle – from which to ensure that key social phenomena are readily 'visible': what it brings most prominently into view is what matters the most in reality. It puts us in the right frame of mind to engage with such major, serious phenomena, focusing our attention onto

What is ideology?

the key things in our surroundings we 'should' be aware of. An ideology prescribes standards of 'right' action intended to apply in general to the weightiest and most widespread social situations we face and ensures that we abide by the most fundamental requirements of good conduct. It makes us adhere dutifully to routines designed to ensure the 'proper' overarching functioning of society, primarily choreographing scenarios where society as a whole is 'at stake'. The social entities with which every ideology is concerned are those that 'capture' and affect us in large numbers and in a decisive, life-altering way: the largest possible edifices with which, and within which, we are expected to engage in our everyday lives. Consequently, it focuses primarily on the most complex and extensive networks and institutions with the most sweeping purposes that we encounter, preparing us with demonstrations of their scale and the far-reaching significance of their impacts on us.

This distinguishing feature is mirrored by the ideological *claim to completeness*: ideologies are designed to function 'without remainders', fully capturing the part(s) of reality they set out to explain – or even to act as self-sufficient 'closed systems', providing a watertight depiction that covers everything we may conceivably encounter in the world around us. Each ideology purports to take us to a point from which the relevant (or even total) characteristics of reality become wholly apparent and without which (conversely) they can never quite do so: what it allows us to see is 'all that there is to be seen'. It prepares us for the full gamut of possible ways reality could make us think, feel, and (re)act, and the social phenomena it makes 'stand out' in our surroundings are the only ones we will ever have to worry about in our engagement with them. Ideology makes sure we are never left 'high and dry' regarding what is expected of us in any of the social situations we may face, by telling us 'all that there is to know' about how we should engage with reality. It claims to omit none of the habits we need to master in order to engage successfully with reality: the social character it gives us is fully developed and has 'three-dimensional' mental and physical depth. The description ideology offers of how the social phenomena around us are 'organised' is supposedly a top-to-bottom account of reality, with not a single relevant detail 'left off' the way it 'renders' our surroundings. In short, ideology sells itself on how thoroughly it diagnoses the social organisms within which we operate and how fully fleshed-out an account it can provide of how we are psychologically and behaviourally integrated into them.

A third feature is the ideological *claim to correctness*: ideologies present themselves as uniquely insightful about reality and our engagement with it, to the partial or wholesale exclusion of the alternative representations offered by rival 'schools of thought', 'positions', or worldviews. Every ideology insists it (alone, or as a necessary ally, ingredient, or accompaniment to others) is capable of providing us with accurate insights into social phenomena: its perspective is the best (only, or unavoidable) place from which we can get the 'proper view' of our environment. It ensures that reality elicits the best-judged psychological and behavioural responses from us, filtering through the best available information to us from our surroundings. Every ideology maintains that (only) its account of how to engage with our surroundings is an unimpeachable guide to healthy social functioning and a truly flawless rendering of the appropriate rules of style. The patterns of psychology and behaviour it fosters in us are well grounded and reasonably justified, and the social role it expects us to play is plausible and 'written' in a way that lets us give our best societal 'performance'. Likewise, it holds that the material and relational elements in our surroundings really are aggregated in the way it describes: its social schematisation is exact and well defined and offers a recognisable illustration of how reality is 'put together'. Overall, ideology argues that every aspect of the taxonomy of social phenomena and events it outlines is well supported and reliable and that by following its suggested 'walkthrough' of our surroundings we are guaranteed not to make any missteps.

Together, these three claims separate ideology from other forms of discourse that are more fragmentary in their content and more casual and circumscribed in the guidance they give us. Ideologies stringently resist being labelled as sectional, partial, or inaccurate, and they react swiftly and vehemently to critiques (especially from rival ideologies) that seek to present them in that light. Of course, this qualitative distinction is not a hard cut-off. It is impossible to impose a pure 'ideological/non-ideological' binary on all discourse because most examples of discourse do not just operate on one register. Instead, each specific 'case' of discourse lies on a spectrum between 'more ideological' and 'less ideological', depending on how many of its registers have ideological aspects and how significant these ideological registers are to the societal role it plays. For instance, there are clear cases of discourse whose primary register is ideological (e.g., election manifestos, legal statutes, scriptural exegesis), as well as others whose ideological registers, while potentially still there, lie far more in the background (e.g., poetry collections, sports commentary, cookery recipes). Nevertheless, these claims are an important delineating tool to help us avoid creating analytically muddying elisions between discourse in general and its ideological forms in particular. They also allow us to round off our final definition of ideology: an ideology, or an 'ism', is *a combination and arrangement of (1) ideas that determines how we understand reality and (2) a set of derived elements (a habitus) that determines how we engage with it, whose (3) construction is more or less thick and robust, and which (4) claims to be comprehensive, complete, and correct.*

4
Ideology and ideologies

In our discussion of ideology in its 'pure' and 'applied' forms, there is a latent tension between how we use 'ideology' in its general and particular senses – a spectral remnant of the metonymic shift that moved the concept of ideology from '*the*' ideology (uncountable) to '*an*' ideology (countable), as well as a legacy of the methodological tension between Marxisant analyses of 'ideology' *tout court* as a barely differentiated toxicity of capitalist society and the political-scientific preoccupation with 'ideologies' read as partisan policy platforms within the framework of parliamentary-democratic electoral competition. Ideology in general has a universal social morphology, a number of consistent elements that help us 'make sense' of reality in our thought and action. But, at least hypothetically, there is an infinite number of ways in which these elements could be combined and arranged: the possibility for ideological morphologies to vary in thickness and robustness implies that even a notional single ideology can take several different forms; meanwhile, ideological claims to comprehensiveness, completeness, and correctness only exist precisely because each 'account' has to keep a wary eye out for rival efforts to make reality 'make sense *better*'. We therefore have to consider the full range of ideologies available – not just the absolute number of different separate ideological formations (ideolog*ies*, variants, strands, etc.) but also the extent of the differences between these formations

Ideology and ideologies 71

that demarcate the 'location' and permeability of their mutual boundaries.

This implies, of course, that the question of whether ideology is a singular or a plural phenomenon must – *pace* orthodox Marxism – be resolved unquestionably in favour of the latter. All of these different ideologies and ideological formations put forward rival representations of reality and guidance for how we should engage with it. But they vary significantly in how successful they are (or have been) in asserting and establishing these representations within society – judged in terms of (e.g.) their popularity, how familiar their ideas are to us, and their entrenchment through particular societal institutions. To fully analyse ideology as a social force, and ideologies as vehicles of social power, we have to go beyond describing them in a 'flat' sense by listing the characteristics and constituent features of their social morphologies and also consider them at the 'deeper' level of how they present in society – expressed in a 'three-dimensional' sense in terms of the scale ('how large') or quantity ('how often') of their appearance, as well as the reciprocal dynamics between these two levels.

Some ideological formations are *macro-ideologies* (Freeden 2003, 78ff.): they enjoy rich, long-standing mainstream social institutionalisation, rank highly in the 'tiers' of preferred individual or group self-identification, and act frequently as 'hosts' or 'modifiers' for other ideologies. Their social success is marked by the preponderant influence they exert over the overall ideological character of society, the preferential leadership and authoritative control they exercise over its power-structures, and their aggressive framing of the parameters of ideological dynamics within it – a situation classically described as their 'hegemony' or ideological 'dominance' over society, and an ascendancy they maintain by imperially suppressing ideological rivals or encroaching onto their conceptual 'turf' (Gramsci 2011; Laclau and Mouffe 1985). For instance, in various registers, liberalism and conservatism, capitalism and socialism, democratism and authoritarianism have staked out (cross-cutting) dominant positions over geoeconomic–geopolitical–geocultural conditions in long-running cycles of hostility and alignment – with some enjoying periods of intense macroregional competition, as with Latin America's long oscillation between socialist–democratic and conservative–authoritarian trends ('pink tide' versus 'blue tide', *'democradura'* versus *'dictablanda'*) or the struggle between Cold War liberal–capitalist and socialist alignments (both democratic and authoritarian) across Africa post-decolonisation (e.g., Angola, Congo, Ghana, and Mozambique, as well as Ethiopia).

Others, by contrast, are *micro-ideologies* (Freeden 2003, 94ff.): these play a newer, narrower, or more marginal social role, are a 'niche' label associated with minorities or 'fringe' groups, and may struggle to assert an independent existence 'without adjectives'. Correlatively, they exert far less influence over society, are (at least initially) excluded from social power-structures, and depend for their existence on submitting to the 'rules of the game' set by the macro-ideologies – and, as a result, they are 'subordinate' or 'subaltern', at best 'junior partners' and at worst subservient underlings to macro-ideologies' shaping of the overall ideological landscape. These include cooperativism, centred on support for voluntary collective enterprise, which is typically folded into variants of anarchism or socialism; federalism, the decentralisation of administration and legislative authority, which has liberal ('devolution'), socialist ('autonomous soviet socialist republic'), democratic ('United States', 'federal republic'), or authoritarian (*Gau, Reichskommisariat*) interpretations; and religious fundamentalisms, which are often marginalised and at most partly incorporated by 'ultra' traditionalist or nationalist conservative strands (e.g., Evangelicalism and the 'Christian right', Islamism and jihadism, *haredim* and religious Zionism, Hindutva and *Hindū rāṣṭravāda*, or Sikh Khālistānism).

Finally, there are some that sit (perhaps uneasily) between the two extreme poles of this binary: *meso-ideologies*, at the mercy of contrary 'upward' and 'downward' pulls in the circulation of social discourse. Classic examples are social democracy, now independent of its origins as a socialism–democratism rapprochement but subject to frequent encroachment by liberalism and capitalism (e.g., 'postwar consensus', the 'Third Way'); or fascism, likewise autonomous but sidelined, albeit with clear 'gateways' maintained by capitalism, conservatism, and authoritarianism (e.g., via 'national-libertarianism', 'illiberal democracy', 'authoritarian populism', or the 'alt-right').

Together, these differential status as 'macro', 'meso', or 'micro' allow us to give a sense of social hierarchy between ideological formations: large–medium–small and frequent–occasional–rare as an expression of how far each of them contributes to the overall ideological 'flavour' of society. However, the idea of *societal* 'hegemony' or 'dominance' becomes more problematic once we observe that society is not a monolith but, rather, is subject to differentiation and variation along several different dimensions. First among these are two dimensions of *synchronic* differentiation, which are based on inherent and irreducible 'multiplicities' in what we do (social action) and who we are (personal characteristics). When we engage with reality through our psychology and behaviour, we do so using a range of different types of action: we labour to create things, we give and receive them, and we use them up; we organise and compel them; we come up with rules for them; we worship them; we think and express ourselves about them; we look after them; we teach and learn about them. Each of these types of action underpins its own *domain*, or 'field', of social action, which 'collects' the materials and relations relevant to the action into domain-specific forms of conduct, processes, and institutions (Althusser 2014, 94–139, 171–208, 243; Bourdieu 1977, 97, 109, 119–20; Gellner 1988; Giddens 1985; Jameson 1981, 21; Künzler 1989; Luhmann 2012; Luhmann et al. 1982; Mann 1986–2012; Roth and Schütz 2015; Thompson 1995, 13–18) (see table 2). Ideologies are often 'dedicated' to some domains more than others, in the sense that they focus especially on them when they represent reality to us and guide our engagement with reality above all towards creating, maintaining, and transforming these domains: political ideologies (e.g., internationalism, militarism, caesarism) are concerned chiefly with how administration and coercion 'works' in society; economic ideologies (e.g., mercantilism, syndicalism, *dirigisme*) likewise with production, exchange, and consumption; legal ideologies (e.g., originalism, textualism, constructionism) and religious ideologies (e.g., literalism, restorationism, Salafism) with regulation and devotion, and so on.

Table 2 Social domains

Domain	Activities
'The economic'	Production, exchange/distribution, consumption
'The political'	Administration/coordination, coercion/repression
'The legal/juridical'	Regulation
'The religious'	Devotion
'The cultural/discursive'	Ideation, communication
'The curative'	Nurture/care-giving
'The educational/scholastic'	Instruction, study

At the same time, an irreducible aspect of our own material reality as embodied beings is that we are endowed with particular, (at least initially) innate and unchosen biological features: ageing status, sexual organs, facial markers, skin, hair, and eye colour, metabolism, congenital health conditions, motor skills, overall varying shapes and sizes, and so on. These features form the basis of *demographic* personal characteristics, which classify us as living beings according to what kind(s) of features we have: e.g., numerical age, 'generation'; sex, gender, sexual orientation, gender identity; race, ethnicity; (dis)ability, neurodiversity, 'intelligence'; 'attractiveness', body image. Again, likewise, ideologies are often chiefly preoccupied with certain demographics over others, in that they centre their importance when they define and add meaning to reality as a whole, giving them a particularly rich set of connotations and associations and stressing their contextual salience: e.g., sexism and feminism focus on how society 'treats' sex and gender; homophobia/transphobia and queer ideology likewise for sexual orientation and gender identity; racism and antiracism similarly for race and ethnicity. These domains and our demographics constantly and intimately cross-cut and overlap with each other, which creates the basis for myriad subcategories of societal differentiation and for complex 'intersectionality' between the ideologies that pertain to them (Crenshaw 1989).

But these two synchronic dimensions are also modified, enhanced, and exacerbated by long-term deep-structure trends in societal development. Advances and innovations in technology – construed broadly as any and all materials (tools, equipment) we use to carry out actions, including but not limited to turning existing materials (substances) into new ones – have fostered and facilitated deep changes in our societal arrangements (cf. Ellul 1964; Heidegger 1977 [1954]; McLuhan 1951, 1964; Smith and Marx 1994). These changes have been an ongoing feature throughout human history, but they have become more noticeable, faster, and arguably more explosive in their social effects in recent centuries (Bauman 2000). Technological development, above all in areas such as medicine, mechanisation, architecture and engineering, transport and communications infrastructure, and computing has started to push our society (or, rather, *some* of our socie*ties*) towards becoming (1) larger, with accelerating population growth and ever denser concentration in our living conditions; (2) more complex, with populations becoming increasingly specialised, mutually distinct, and hence more fragmented, sophisticated in their skills and abilities, and intricately related to one another; and (3) more fluid, with loosening ties of rootedness and permanent connection to specific spatial contexts and greater geographic mobility and interconnection. At every stage, and in every case, ideologies have been formulated with the aim of guiding us towards either supporting and bringing about these technological advances or, conversely, opposing and preventing them: futurism, posthumanism, or hypermodernism among the former; (neo)Luddism, anarcho-primitivism, and some variants of 'deep ecology' for the latter.

These technological and societal developments and their attendant ideologies add two further dimensions of *diachronic* differentiation. One is a trend towards *universalisation*: a homogenising tendency to make us and the social phenomena and events we encounter increasingly similar, blended together, and interchangeable; and a globalising scope of economic integration, political association, and cultural penetration. The ideological effect of this emerging 'global village' has been to expand the 'reach' of specific representations of reality, both in the sense of a (potentially) worldwide scale in the social circulation of their ideological symbols and messages, leading to a convergence in the degree of exposure to them and their ubiquitous recognition by people distributed across the world, and in their 'relevance' to contexts beyond those in which they were first created, fostering stronger cross-border, long-range solidarities (Inglehart and Welzel 2005; McLuhan 1962; Norris and Inglehart 2009). The second dimension is a seemingly opposite trend towards *individuation*: the atomising break-up of social phenomena and events (and of us) into many discrete, minute units without any interrelations and their (our) localising accumulation and 'squeezing' into specific and limited geographies (district, settlement, residence). Ideologically, this has eroded the grand visions, 'collective consciousnesses', and sweeping 'metanarratives' that underpinned previous solidarities – e.g., the family, religions, political parties – and instead is fuelling a pull towards increasingly subjective 'micronarratives' that in effect become synonymous with the personal 'lifestyle' worldviews we hold as the result of our embodied experience of society (Baudrillard 1994; Bauman 2001; Beck et al. 1994; Lyotard 1984). These diachronic trends coexist – albeit not always neatly and uniformly – in 'glocalised' phenomena such as 'grassroots' campaigns around 'world' issues (e.g., climate activism), internet-mediated virtual and online communities, and market-specific product variety in multinational brands (Bauman 1998).

These two diachronic trends have recursively expanded and amplified synchronic differentiation by bringing about increasing mutual autonomy between social domains, alongside a proliferation of demographic classifications (Meiksins Wood 1986; Poulantzas 1975). Ideologically, they have fostered a dramatic and ongoing vertical diffusion and 'stretching' of the arena of ideological operation: away from national wealth, state sovereignty, and ethnolinguistic monoculture and towards 'society' understood simultaneously at the most microscopic and macroscopic possible levels. In light of these four dimensions of differentiation, it is not enough to analyse ideological hegemony or dominance purely at 'a' societal level. At the very least, we need to break down our analysis of the relative standings of macro-, meso-, and micro-ideologies to a more granular level, looking at the dynamics of ideological hegemony–subalternity and dominance–subordination within (and among) synchronic categories and within (and across) diachronic periods. In other words, to approximate the 'societal' level of any given ideology's 'macro', 'meso', or 'micro' status, we have to examine the consistent homology or inconsistent variation between its status in different spatial and temporal contexts.

The range of ideologies present in society that ideology analysis has to consider – i.e., their absolute number and the extent of distinction between them – and their relative places in the societal hierarchy of ideologies varies intensely along these synchronic and diachronic axes of differentiation (Derrida 2001; Koselleck 2002). If we look at both a 'time-sliced' synchronic snapshot of the ideologies available and the *longue-durée* diachronic developments that have taken place in them, we can identify three clear sources of variation.

(1) The same ideology can articulate vastly different claims and possibilities in different geographies and at different points in time, depending on how it interacts with the stages and trajectories of development of various social domains and with the incidence and salience of particular demographic characteristics among the relevant populations. For instance, conservatism has proved notoriously adaptable, shifting its support for religious traditionalism between faiths and denominations across macroregions, moving from staunch monarchism (and absolutism) to contingent alignments with democratism and other authoritarianisms and evolving from resistance to capitalism in 1800s Europe and Latin America to enthusiastic defence of it today.

(2) An ideology's thickness and robustness (and the evolution of both over time) significantly affect its 'macro', 'meso', or 'micro' status. Its various component elements can make it easier or harder to get disparate individuals or social groups 'on board' and render it more or less likely that ideologies will split off into subcategorised variants or strands. Similarly, changes in its popularity and institutionalisation can rapidly shift it from 'insurgent' to 'established' to 'declining', especially as it can be of very different 'vintages' depending on how much time it has had to develop (Goldmann 1964). A good example is the ossification of communism in the shift from the 1910s–20s (USSR foundation) to the 1930s–60s (spread

to China, Cuba, Vietnam, etc.) and the 1970s–80s (stagnation, transformation, collapse), which saw it rapidly lose its federal, pluralist-democratic elements in favour of centralised 'party line' authoritarianism.
(3) Every ideology enjoys contingent 'points of contact' and permeation with other ideologies, which can lead to one 'hosting' or 'modifying' the other, or *vice versa*. This creates 'boundary cases': ideological 'hybrids' that do not clearly fit into any of their 'source' ideologies but which may not be stand-alone formations either, such as 'liberal conservatism', 'national-conservatism', 'national-liberalism', 'liberal socialism', 'ecosocialism', 'ecofascism', or 'anarcha-feminism'. Entire new ideologies are often born out of 'splits' within and 'encounters' between other ideologies, which have an impact not only on the unique onward trajectory of the resulting 'strands' or 'hybrids' as they become increasingly independent ideologies but also on that of their original 'source' ideologies and parallel alternative strands – since ideologies often define themselves in contradistinction to (specific) others.

Together, these effects raise questions over the granularity of 'what counts as' an ideology and when the threshold to 'count as' an ideology has been crossed, especially where a given 'thin' or micro-ideology happens to be wholly and exclusively monopolised by another 'thicker' or meso-/macro-ideology. The overall upshot of this is that we need to think of the morphology of ideologies in terms not of fixed characteristics but of 'family resemblances' or *'familles spirituelles'* ('spiritual families') and of 'traditions' (Freeden 1996; von Beyme 1985; Wittgenstein 1973 [1953]) – and acknowledge that both the 'time-sliced' and *longue-durée* societal 'distribution' of ideologies is by definition a 'work in progress' that always remains open to challenge.

§1 The preconditions of ideology

The simultaneous diversity that the co-occurrence of 'time-sliced' ideological 'families' and *longue-durée* ideological 'traditions' brings about two questions for ideology analysis. The first of these is whether it is possible to specify a clear point of origin for ideology and ideologies: a 'starting point' when they initially became a significant factor in social life. This is not an argument over labels or terminology: there is extensive consensus that the term 'ideology' was coined at the close of the Enlightenment; the use of 'ism(s)', in turn, is a slightly older invention, with recorded usage in the early Enlightenment, albeit with a clear upsurge in incidence in its closing years. Instead, the question is about whether the existence of ideology and ideologies is itself also a contingent feature of (comparatively) recent human history, or whether they are a perennial constituent part of all past and present (and conceivable future) human society – i.e., whether ideology 'has no history', as Althusser (2014) puts it. In particular, this first question turns on whether the development of human society needed to reach a certain level before it was possible even to form workable, 'useful', 'meaningful', thick, and robust representations of reality, whose claims to comprehensiveness, completeness, and correctness were at least temporarily tenable in the face of human experience, and which could be efficiently and successfully disseminated to large numbers of individuals. This is especially true of theoretical and empirical discoveries in scientific and technical insights about the world and of the achievement of sociological 'milestones' in the scale, complexity, construction, and composition of societal formations.

It is reductive to stipulate a chronological 'starting point' for ideology, as this almost always unjustifiably centres the partial perspective of a restricted geographic cluster of human social formations – in the case of the advent of 'modernity' in the early 1800s, the perspective of Euro-America. For similar reasons, it is also still too reductive to attribute it to the privileged achievement of a predefined level of complexity in any single social domain (e.g., as orthodox Marxism does for economics or democratic theory does for politics) or a defined level of salience for any single demographic characteristic. But what such 'conditional' approaches share is an emphasis on deep structural divisions in society, which motivate ideologies to emerge that claim to comprehensively, completely, and correctly represent reality *precisely because* there are one or more other ideologies there to deny and challenge these claims: class struggle, party competition, 'gender conflict', 'race war', and so on. The root of these divisions consists of the differential material and relational conditions we face in reality, based on the environments in which we are embodied (see chapter 3). Compared to other people, how materials are distributed and relations are arranged 'around' us – i.e., the social conditions we face – can be more similar or dissimilar in terms of (e.g.) our 'access' to resources or other 'stuff' and proximity to other people or the nature of our involvement, contact, or association with them. Where these interpersonal similarities–dissimilarities are repeated (consistently, starkly) across entire populations, they become structural divisions within society, creating 'like/other' distinctions between members of the population depending on which side of this material/relational similarity–dissimilarity of conditions they fall into.

Ideologies 'thematise' these interpersonal differences in conditions by using certain 'like/other' distinctions as criteria to identify clusters of individual population members as *social groups*, defined as much by who/what they *are* (people in similar social conditions) as in contradistinction to who/what they *are not* (other people in dissimilar conditions) – i.e., by their 'constitutive outside' (Derrida 1976 [1967]; Mouffe 2000). Specifically, ideology frames the structural divisions in our social conditions as more or less intense and irreconcilable oppositions between such social groups: conflicts of incentives, interests, and needs, if not necessarily or immediately in a violent form. The point of framing them in oppositional terms, rather than merely as neighbouring classifications of humans, is that what one group is or does is presented as having a direct impact on the other: one's beneficial gain is the other's costly loss, and their interactions are (at least very often) 'zero-sum'. Depending on whether, and how far, ideologies 'find' commonalities in incentives, interests, and needs between the different 'sides' of these 'like/other' distinctions, they may frame them as internecine 'friend/enemy' antagonisms (Schmitt 1996 [1932]), more civilised and 'domesticated' 'friend/*adversary*' 'agonisms' (Mouffe 2005), or even closer forms of cross-group truce, amity, compromise, or alliance. The purpose of ideologies in this context is to cement the shared material and relational position of each group's members into their self-conceptions and self-identifications: to generate and add meaning to 'group consciousness' by presenting the group *as* a group to its members in the representation of reality it gives them and thereby raise the *sociological* 'like/other' distinction to the level of *ideological* 'identity/difference' (Connolly 2002).

We can build on the insights about the ideologically generative effect of (e.g.) class struggle or party competition to identify three ways of generalising the logic of 'like/other' distinctions. The first is the existence of social *hierarchies*, which create vertical separations between social groups based on unequal distributions of materials and asymmetric relational linkages between them – collectively *and* between individual members of the respective groups. Hierarchical distinctions rest on *domination/subjection* relations in the possession and wielding of social power, which accrues to us variably as a result of our 'shares' of materials and our relational 'standings'. Within social domains, these have been by far the most prominently analysed in terms of class, defined as having material wealth and access to sources of income and/or as being situated in relations of exploitation, and often disaggregated into subsidiary occupations (e.g., entrepreneur, executive, business owner, manager, office clerk, technical worker, production worker, service worker); however, since the concept of class is heavily tied to labour and economic production, other domains also tend to express similar or equivalent stratifications in terms of 'rank', 'grade', or 'status', or (more diffusely) 'roles' in tabular 'organigrams' (Goldthorpe 2005; Oesch 2006; Wright 1998, 2008). For demographic characteristics, hierarchies are usually expressed in terms of dyadic or polyadic classifications, defined either as discrete categories or 'points' on a scalar spectrum, and the material or relational (dis)advantages or (dis)privileges these confer – which can cover the full gamut from the nuances of interpersonal perception and treatment to the construction of (e.g.) ethnoreligious 'castes' or 'sexual classes', which elide to a degree with domain hierarchies (Firestone 1970; Wolff and de-Shalit 2007). The long-term tendencies in societal development have vastly extended the 'reach' and number of hierarchies into which we are 'allocated' in our social groups, in some cases to a macroregional or even global level; but they have also brought about ever more granular fragmentation and Byzantine intricacy in the stratifications these hierarchies contain. Morphologically, the sheer ongoing proliferation of the different forms that social distinction based on domination/subjection can take creates pressures on the 'thickness' of both hegemonic and subaltern ideologies, in the sense that dominant and (especially) subjected social groups expect them to 'have something to say' about each form of distinction. We can see this tendency in both the idea of an 'imperialist white-supremacist capitalist heteropatriarchy' that must be challenged 'on all fronts' by truly intersectional emancipation movements and the convergence between some combination of securitarian–militarist, pro-private enterprise, racist, sexist, and homophobic ideas in 'anti-woke' strains within reactionary ideologies.

The second general distinction is the presence of *factionalism*, which creates horizontal separations among social groups measured by the number of members they contain. Factionalism is notionally independent of social power arrangements, although, depending on the groups' comparative sizes, it can also lead to unequal collective distributions of materials and asymmetric relational linkages between them as groups or between individual members. What makes this a horizontal rather than simply a (small-scale) vertical division is that the groups in question are in the same or very similar positions of (dis)advantage or (dis)privilege within social hierarchies, so while they are 'heterarchically' distinct they are also simultaneously part of a larger social group. Factional distinctions are based on *in-group/ out-group* relations of inclusion and exclusion, a form of limited collectivity whereby self-seeking groups and their members oppose the comparable needs and interests of others in similar societal positions. For social domains, these are typically read through the lens of parties and partisanship as expressions of organisational and strategic separation within (e.g.) a demos/electorate or a legislative chamber, and within them in terms of rival 'wings'; but the same logic can be applied to less overtly political activity, for example through 'teams' of colleagues or collaborators, 'cliques' of friends or family members, and 'fractions' of economic classes. The equivalents for demographic characteristics are fairly similar, and are often somewhat indiscriminately called 'groups' – although they are understood more through the lens of (especially ethnic) sectarianism in the case of collective divides and as majority–minority dynamics at the level of interpersonal interaction. Universalising and individuating trends in societal development have stretched the potential range and 'grounds' for inclusion in factions by raising the upper limit on social groups' potential size and numerical membership; but they have simultaneously created opportunities for embryonic intra-group schisms to reach the 'critical mass' they need to turn into fully fledged factions. The burgeoning expansion of overlapping in-group/out-group social distinctions exerts a second, countervailing pressure on hegemonic and subaltern ideologies' morphological 'thickness', as the rising number of their constituent elements sets up ever more potential disagreements – and hence splits – rooted in whether these elements deserve core or peripheral priority and more or less proportional space, or whether they should be included at all. An archetypical case of this is the late 1800s conservative–liberal struggle for supremacy within the Euro-American aristocracy and '*haute*' bourgeoisie over issues such as imperialism, free trade versus protectionism, expanding the franchise, and alleviating poverty, while at the same time Christian democracy, fascism, social democracy, and communism challenged the socialist–anarchist duopoly among the 'petty' bourgeoisie, proletariat, and peasantry by leveraging themes of nationality and chauvinism, reform versus revolution, and the salience of religion.

The last general 'like/other' distinction is that of *context*, where separations between social groups are rooted in differences of place. Like factionalism, context is *prima facie* independent of social power arrangements, but because of the 'overriding' effect of spatial and temporal contingency – i.e., 'what is there' and 'what has happened before' – it can also be associated with collective group and individual inequalities and asymmetries in material distributions and relational linkages. What distinguishes it from being merely a variant of factionalism writ large, or a specific application of it, is that contexts can both (1) 'sit above' and precede *and* (2) 'sit below' and modify domination/subjection as well as in-groups/out-groups: spatial and temporal distance may either (1) prevent the integration of hierarchies or solidarisation of factions *or* (2) act as a further ineluctable obstacle within them. Contextual distinctions are quite straightforwardly *here/there*: contrasting loci, or 'points' of situation, along with their surrounding 'areas' or 'circumstances' and the sources of social influence they contain. There is a vast terminology used to describe the intersections of here/there contexts with social domains, most of it heavily premised on a territorial understanding of space – ranging from (e.g.) global (macroregional) unions, blocs/alliances, markets, trade areas, and 'civilisations' to local (microregional) towns/cities, boroughs/counties, offices, branches, and plants, as well as national (mesoregional) states/countries, central offices, 'desks', jurisdictions, and cultures. With demographic characteristics, largely because they are intimately attached to our bodies as we engage with our surroundings, context tends to be associated less with territoriality and more with networks of common lived experience: the particular circumstantial constellation of people, objects, actions, etc., that we personally encounter by virtue of our given characteristics, and how these circumstances replicate themselves only for other people who share the same characteristics, so we are constituted as a group by the sense that 'you had to be *one of us*, and you had to be *there* to get it'. The effect of the long-term universalising trend is steadily to shift the borders of our contexts outwards so they 'scale up' into larger versions, which in extreme cases effectively *de*contextualises us by extracting and literally 'dis-placing' us from any reference to our points of origin; at the same time, however, societal individuation makes our personal set of lived experiences increasingly unique, subject to 'hybridities' (Bhabha 1994), and impossible to replicate, which *hyper*contextualises us by increasing the 'bases' of our differences with others and isolating us from spaces and networks of commonality. These perpetual shifts in here/there social distinctions at different scales acts as a third source of pressure on hegemonic and subaltern ideologies' morphological 'thickness', with the features of different territorial and experiential places motivating the inclusion of potentially very different elements within ideologies notionally belonging to the same 'family' and tradition. For instance, much of neoliberalism's success has come from its ability to adjust its core political-economic programme fairly flexibly to different contexts, endorsing specific elements and pursuing certain aims in one that would be unrecognisable in another (Harvey 2007) – whether in countries at different stages of economic development (i.e., with different proportions of manual, managerial, service, or knowledge workers) or backing women's and queer emancipation ('purplewashing', 'pinkwashing') concurrently with 'family values', sexism, and homophobia.

This trio of social hierarchies, factionalism, and context represents three general and enduring underlying sociological preconditions for ideological emergence, which we can loosely call distinctions of *class*, *party*, and *'Volk'* ('people'). They exacerbate, mitigate, and modify each other to produce a breath-taking variety of 'avenues' for ideologies to explore. Given their highly complex intersecting effects, it becomes essentially impossible to speak meaningfully of there being just one global 'dominant ideology', underpinned monologically by industrial capitalism, electoral democracy, or Euro-American culture (Abercrombie et al. 1980). Instead, we have to look more closely at the points of contact, disjuncts, and remainders between the cluster of 'dominant ideolog*ies*' that coexist in a more or less stable equilibrium in different corners of society at the same time. One case that unites all three 'like/other' distinctions is the 'world-systems' division of the globe into 'core', 'semi-periphery', and 'periphery' (Wallerstein 2004, 2011). This exhibits simultaneous tendencies towards (1) domination by post-industrial, ex-/neo-imperial, 'norm-giver' societies and the subjection of industrial–agrarian, post-colonial, 'norm-taker' societies, (2) global in-groups/out-groups created at the level of countries and meso- and macroregional bodies, and (3) a literal spatial division of the world into 'global North' (Europe and North America) and 'global South' (Africa, Asia, Latin America), which together are often summarised using broad-brush ideological characterisations such as ethnoreligious 'civilisations', 'world values' clusters, or 'liberal-democratic', 'authoritarian-populist', and 'communist' blocs (Huntington 1996; Inglehart and Welzel

86 *Ideology and ideologies*

2005). Each of the three preconditions by itself is sufficient for ideologies to arise, but, while they are mutually reinforcing, not all of them necessarily have to be present at the same time. Overall, they allow us to broaden our understanding of how both ideology and ideologies can emerge in cases and contexts that are non-industrial (e.g., heavily agrarian, post-industrial) or non-capitalist (e.g., manorial–feudalist, state socialist), non-electoral (e.g., with limited enfranchisement, 'acclamatory') or non-democratic (e.g., monarchic–aristocratic, dictatorial), and beyond the direct control of Euro-America (e.g., pre-colonial, global South). In short, ideology and ideologies can exist anywhere where there are traditions of ideas, locations and perceptions, customs and roles, organisations and procedures that lay claim to comprehensiveness, completeness, and correctness in how they 'make sense' of social reality.

§2 The morphological history of ideologies

This leads to the second question raised by simultaneous synchronic and diachronic variation in ideological range, namely whether it is possible to identify a clear trajectory for ideology and ideologies – an overarching 'trend' or underlying 'pattern' in how they have evolved up to this point (which might even enable more or less limited predictions about their future development). The demonstrable scope for ideologies to exist outside the influence of Euro-American modernity opens up a long global prehistory of ideology that significantly predates the late Enlightenment. Moreover, the extensive latitude in defining the preconditions for ideological emergence strongly implies that we need to look beyond the 'isms' associated with post-1800 political economy and cultural policy to detect the full extent of ideology's premodern existence. *Prima facie*, this suggests that the history of ideology coincides closely with the history, or even palaeology, of human thought and expression *tout court*. But we have to recall that what demarcates this history from the viewpoint of tracing advances in ideological activity are instances of division – when ideologies' claims to offer comprehensive, complete, and correct representations of reality become socially necessary *precisely because* they are not universally accepted. The clearest milestone markers to look for when tracing back the trajectory of ideological range are thus moments when there is no consensus on how to 'navigate' or 'steer' social reality. When these moments occur, they overwhelmingly centre on the question of fostering or responding to social and ideological *change*: the perpetuation or transformation of social reality and the maintenance or revision of its representations. Disagreement over this foundational question underpins many of the key binary contrasts in social thought and societal formations: 'established–innovative' (for philosophical arguments or research approaches), 'orthodox–heterodox' (religious doctrines or economic theories), 'mainstream–alternative' (subcultures or media sources), 'moderate–extreme' (partisan views or policy measures), 'conservative–progressive' (social attitudes or political aspirations), and 'reactionary–radical' (stylistic tastes or institutional intentions). These manifested in a range of premodern contexts, from uprisings by slaves, peasants, or artisans to court rivalries and intrigues and to religious dissenters and nonconformists.

Nonetheless, the turn of the 1800s saw a decided uptick in the consolidation and complexity of the divisions between (and among) individuals and groups on either side of these binary divides, in the form of four successive 'waves' of ideological development. The 'first wave' covered approximately the period 1800 to 1870, marked by rising capitalism and industrialisation, urbanisation and the rise of new classes, changing levels and aims of public expenditure and taxation, new pressures for electoral reform and the first consolidation of parties, the professionalisation and codification of law, accelerating imperial expansion and the first successful anti-absolutist and anticolonial revolutions, widespread abolition of slavery and serfdom, increased toleration of religious dissent, the emergence of regular newspapers, and the rise of modern universities. These conditions led to the emergence of the 'Big Four' ideologies in their original forms: four distinct macro-ideologies whose evolutions and interactions have consistently played a central role in influencing the subsequent contours of our societies. *Liberalism* in its 'classical'

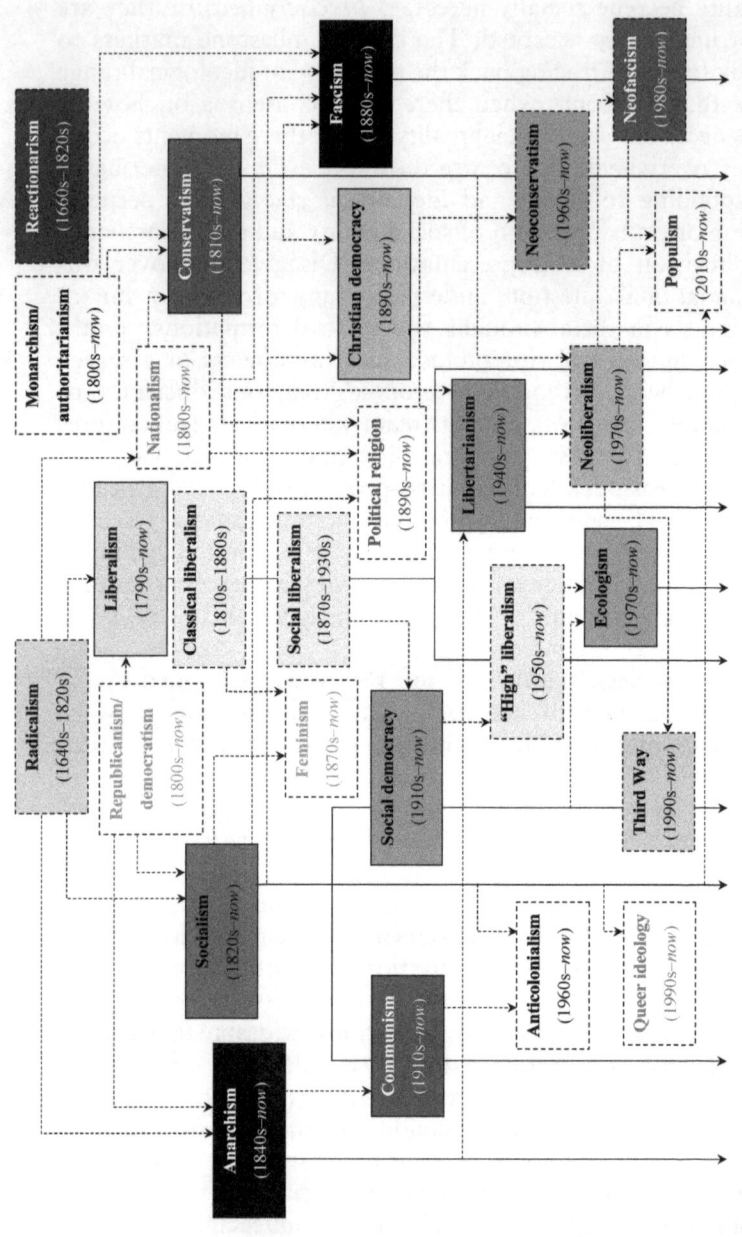

Figure 2 An overview of ideologies' historical development

form emerged around the 1810s as an ideology centred on individual liberty and rights, embracing religious tolerance and (democratic) political equality, but above all associated with economic *laissez-faire* and free trade, and promoting rationality and creativity as the foundations of social order and the superior routes to human progress. Meanwhile, *conservatism* arose largely in parallel, fixating on the tension between social order and social change, initially encapsulated in a deep hostility to capitalism and democracy, often with deep religious and traditionalist overtones, which gradually softened into an accommodationist stance as time went on. *Socialism* followed swiftly after in its reconciliation of individuality and sociality and vehemently opposed capitalism and the state in favour of a decentralised, spontaneous conception of social order. Alongside the 'Big Four', this period also saw the rise of the first micro-ideologies, which shaped and cross-cut the wider ideological landscape: *democratism* and *republicanism*, dedicated to a constitutional transfer of political rule from religiously legitimated monarchy and aristocracy to direct/representative rule by 'the people'; and *nationalism*, which sought to constitute this 'people' out of microregional solidarities based on commonalities of ethnicity, language, or territory.

The 'second wave' of 1870 to 1940 coincided with protracted volatility in the market economy and increased state intervention and industrial nationalisation, the consolidation of large monopolies/cartels and rising financial speculation, the fragmentation of the economic class structure, mass (first male then also female) enfranchisement, progressive taxation to fund welfare and public service provisions, the high point of 'new imperial' expansion, an explosion of military technology, total war and genocide, the rise of international law, anti-clerical and revivalist religious tensions, and vast advances in communications and transport (telegraphy, telephony, radio, rail, automobile, and air). These saw the arrival of a cluster of new ideological challengers to the 'Big Four', as well as the first signs of ideological fragmentation with the rise of several 'ideologies of identity'. Liberalism took on a 'social' guise and underwent first a transformation and then a nadir in this period, trying to expand its offerings of 'positive' rights, its embrace of democratic state intervention, and its accommodation to economic equality in an attempt to broaden its appeal, but ultimately becoming drowned out and overtaken by its rivals. In turn, conservatism moved to fill the space it had vacated, reversing its 'classical' position into a new enthusiasm for capitalism and growing (often democratically mediated) scepticism of the (welfarist, tax and spending) state. But its space likewise came under challenge from two new meso-ideologies: *fascism* in the 1880s, which combined a superficially paradoxical fusion of hierarchical reactionarism and violent revolutionary radicalism with a heavily racialised nationalism, religious-inflected traditionalism and the aim to subordinate capitalism to the requirements of the totalising imperial state; and *Christian democracy* in the 1890s, which sought to articulate a religiously inspired alternative to both liberalism and socialism, based on a statist–capitalist 'social economy' compromise, welfarist institutions, democratic localism and subsidiarity, and a moderate, organicist traditionalism. Socialist ideological space became abruptly contested at the start of the 1900s by the rise of two further meso-ideologies: *social democracy*, which embraced the opportunities of democratic politics and statist policymaking to achieve societal (especially economic) reforms, above all securing liberty via welfare rights and individual equality; and *communism*, which initially enjoyed extensive permeation with anarchism but soon turned decisively towards revolutionary statist anti-capitalism, premised on economic central planning, totalising mass sociality, and a quasi-federal 'soviet' (council) conception of political institutions. These meso-ideological challenges were also joined by two additional new micro-ideologies: *feminism*, which aimed to dismantle patriarchal social relationships in order to construct a society based on sexual and gender equality; and various *political religions*, including Islamism, Hindutva, and religious strands of Zionism, which fundamentally applied the logic of nationalism to social collectivities viewed through the specific prism of shared religion.

The period 1940 to 1990 represented a 'third wave' of ideological development, prompted by the legacy of total and nuclear warfare and the entrenchment of the global bipolar coexistence of parliamentary democracy and the 'social market economy' with (notionally soviet-republican) authoritarianism and central planning, along with sectoral economic diversification and the decline of mass production, decolonisation of European empires and new waves of migration, the first multilateral and supranational bodies, 'proxy' wars and anti-war activism, new women's, racial, and LGBT rights movements, growing awareness of ecological crisis, secular and fundamentalist religious trends, and more communications advances (mass media, computing, digital). These led to significant reinvention and recalibration among the 'first wave' stalwarts, a maturing (and partly stagnation) of the 'second wave', and the appearance of yet more challengers. Liberalism recovered steadily from its nadir but split into two strands: 'high liberalism', which steered its 'social' incarnation further towards justice, equality, and democratic reasonability; and 'neoliberalism', which allied with the new meso-ideology of *libertarianism* to pursue a return to its 'classical' emphasis on (especially economic) liberty and rights, albeit now with a virulently anti-statist and anti-democratic gloss. Socialism became squeezed and assimilated by social democracy and communism, which split along the fault line of the global bipolarity and consolidated their democratic–capitalist and authoritarian–anti-capitalist conceptions of equality, sociality, order, and progress. Christian democracy enjoyed a period of considerable dominance after the Second World War (especially in Western Europe and Latin America), trading on its permeability with social democracy and liberalism to position itself as a 'safe' median position on all major political-economic and cultural questions. Conservatism underwent several transformations that threatened to divide it into multiple rival meso-ideological strands, from its welfare-state accommodation during the 'postwar consensus' to the overt militarist–imperialist enthusiasm of neoconservatism and the religious traditionalism of paleoconservatism, but its overriding shift came with its close alignment to neoliberal political economy. Fascism went into steep decline after it became indelibly stained with genocide, lingering on in a chiefly Iberian and Latin American rump form and elsewhere on the countercultural fringes, while many of its substantive positions were quietly absorbed by the various new conservative strands. One other meso-ideology and two micro-ideologies also emerged in this period: *green ideology*, or ecologism, which focused on the destruction wreaked by our waste, pollution, and unchecked, unsustainable economic growth on our natural environment; *anticolonialism* and *antiracism*, which aimed to undo what they regarded as white-supremacist social structures and build a society based on ethnic and racial equality; and *queer ideology*, which articulated similar goals to feminism and anticolonialism regarding heterosexist social institutions and the achievement of equality between sexual orientations.

Finally, a 'fourth wave', beginning in 1990 and still continuing today, saw the collapse of global political-economic bipolarity with the end of the Cold War, the globalisation of economic sectors and a 'great divergence' between Euro-American and global South growth and development, new efforts at macroregional integration and nation-statist opposition, new movements for and against 'multicultural' ethnoreligious diversity, the broadening of queer activism to – at the latest count – LGBTQQIP2SAAK* (lesbian, gay, bisexual, transgender, questioning, queer, intersex, pansexual, two-spirit, androgynous, asexual, and kink) claims for recognition, new movements supporting rights of indigeneity, (dis)ability, and mental health, the accelerating urgency of ecological catastrophe, and more transport and communications advances (hybrid/electric vehicles, online and virtual technology). These have fostered both a reassertion of the 'Big Four' and a renewal of their challengers, coupled with a significant acceleration in the rise of 'ideologies of identity'. High liberalism and neoliberalism found themselves thrust back into the macro-ideological limelight through contingent alliances with social democracy and conservatism and have since tried to adjudicate between often hostile political-economic and cultural claims through a determinedly individualist lens, incurring pushback from 'postliberal' positions of various stripes. Social democracy underwent a 'Third Way' transformation that aligned it far more closely with liberal conceptions of liberty, equality, and individuality and inaugurated strategies of state–market synthesis that broke with its long-standing commitments to public ownership and close regulatory oversight. Communism went into rapid decline with the collapse of the USSR and 'liberal' turns in China and other communist states, and its 'postcommunist' residues have become reabsorbed into socialism *simpliciter*, which has experienced a pronounced resurgence in a democratic–anti-capitalist form that echoes its 'classical' origins, albeit updated with a fresh 'postsocialist' sensitivity to ecology and individual and collective identity claims. Conservatism, meanwhile, has largely continued in its alliance with neoliberalism, modified by occasional further absorptions from high liberalism, but has recently moved abruptly into reverse, pursuing an 'illiberal' turn against internationalism, multiculturalism, and on occasion even democracy, often driven by explicitly religious-traditionalist and hierarchical commitments. In this, it has been fuelled by a resurgence of fascism, which has reinvented its morphology through a hefty injection of libertarian/neoliberal political economy and a new centring of hostility to feminism, multiculturalism, ecologism, and queer identity. Christian democracy has been the major victim of these trends, with its ideological space squeezed by the social-democratic–liberal and conservative–liberal rapprochements and little to show for any substantive rejuvenation. Finally, this period has also been marked by the rise of new micro-ideologies: *populism*, centring the social importance of 'the people' and its interests, which has gained salience primarily via contingent alignments with modern fascism/conservatism and socialism; and a set of embryonic ideologies based on securing equal *transgender*, *indigenous*, and *disabled* rights.

Throughout this rich record of ideological evolution and (re)invention, every ideological family or tradition has tried to distinguish itself from its competitors by putting forward its own unique constellation of 'pure' ideas and 'applied' perspectives, dispositions, norms, practices, structures, and systems to 'make sense' of social reality. Further, each ideology has sought to assert 'its' set of these elements against those of its rivals among a greater or lesser number of people and population groups across the globe. On this basis, it is possible to give a reasonably detailed social morphology of these ideological families and traditions according to the elements they incorporate. Of course, the older ideologies especially have undergone some notable morphological transformations as a result of the societal changes and attendant ideological recalibrations that have taken place since 1800.

They have fluctuated in thickness and robustness: they have been defined more or less precisely and rigidly and in more or less complex and maximal ways; the priority or proportionality accorded their components has shifted markedly; the relationships between their components have proven of varying congruity and stability; and so on. No simple overview can satisfactorily reflect all of these subtle nuances. In the interest of parsimony, the outline offered here in table 3 points out only the core elements of ideologies where they stand out clearly from their peripheral accompaniments (in **bold**), where they are more recent acquisitions (in *italics*), or where they have become steadily lost over time (in [square brackets]) (cf. Freeden 1996; 2003, 81–93, 98–100).

As the overview in table 3 shows, some ideas and other elements crop up repeatedly in the morphologies of very different ideological families and traditions. Yet how they do so ranges from near identical alignment to diametric opposition. Elements that occupy a place of principal and seemingly unassailable importance in some ideologies play only a marginal or forgotten 'bit part' in others; those that act as lynchpins in the understandings of reality offered by some ideologies are jarringly 'out of kilter' with the readings that others put forward. These overlaps and juxtapositions are the key 'nodes' where ideologies make contact and their compositions and meanings permeate into one another, and where the dynamics of ideological division and competition play out at the morphological level.

These dynamics move along a spectrum between two extremes – essential *contestation* and essential *co-option*. Essential contestation relies on the imperfectly crystalline societal definition of the meaning of the concepts used by ideologies to describe ideas and their manifestations, which leaves ample room for indeterminacy and dispute. Ideologies carefully police the permeability of meaning between the concepts they want to 'rule in' and those they hope to 'rule out' because they belong to another ideology. They accentuate the permeability among the former to the point of eliding them into fixed compound concepts, but strenuously deny any link whatsoever between them and the latter – as with the long-standing disputes over the relative permeability of 'freedom' with 'rights', 'markets', 'the state', 'property',

Ideology and ideologies 95

Table 3 Overview of ideologies' social morphologies

Ideology	Morphology	
Liberalism	Liberty	Freedom of thought and speech, action, assembly, trade
	Rights	[Property and land], privacy, electoral franchise, *welfare, healthcare, civic, human rights*
	[Autonomy and consent]	[Contract]
	Equality	*Opportunity, resources*
	Justice	*Fiscal redistribution, public services*
	Tolerance	Moderation, *plurality*
	Democracy	Representation, parliamentarism, constitutionalism, rule of law, anti-absolutism, *deliberation, judicialism*
	Social thinking	Rationality, [utility-maximisation], education, criticality, *emotionality, abstraction, reasonability*
	Individuality	Self-interest, *particularity*
	Sociality	Organicism, harmony versus conflict, *universality, internationalism*
	Creativity	Invention, (*social, natural*) science
	Order	Market *versus* state activism/*interventionism*, security, [colonialism/imperialism], stability, *planning, institutionalism*
	General interest	Common good
	Human/social progress	Open-endedness, flourishing, *improvement, evolutionary struggle for survival*, humanitarianism, protection
Conservatism	Change	Natural growth, anti-revolution, reactionarism *versus modification* towards threats
	Order	Stability and security, *status quo*, [divinity], naturalism, historicism
	Sociality	Organicism, religious community, **nationalism**
	Individuality	Human will and wilfulness, personal flaws, *rights*
	Flexibility	Consistency versus opportunism
	[Anti-]capitalism	Private property, inequality, [anti-]consumerism
	Anti-statism	[Aristocracy], [monarchy], rule of law, localism, militarism, police, *democracy, privatisation, deregulation*, authoritarianism
	Religion and science	Biological essentialism, economism, extra-human authority
	Tradition	Cumulation, familiarity
	Utopia	Nostalgia, romanticism, anti-experimentalism
Socialism	Equality	Class, anti-hierarchy
	Liberty	Emancipation, *rights*
	Economic priority	Historical structural explanation, determinism, exploitation
	Anti-capitalism	Cooperation [versus competition], planning versus market
	[Anti-]statism	[Abolition], instrumentality, entryism, revolution, *democracy*
	Sociality	Collectivity, [commune], syndicate/trade union, internationalism, group versus individual identity
	Creativity	**Labour/work**, *intellectuality*
	Order	**Production**, *party*
	Welfare	Anti-poverty/immiseration, expropriation, redistribution
	Social progress	Future orientation, critique of past/present, [predictable laws], inevitable process *versus human agency*, positive

96 Ideology and ideologies

Ideology	Morphology	
Anarchism	Liberty and equality	Anti-hierarchy, anti-authority, person, [class]
	Economic priority	Production, exchange
	Anti-capitalism	Cooperation, mutuality, **possession versus property**
	Anti-statism	Spontaneous order, democratic self-government, federalism, peaceful transition versus violent revolution
	Sociality	Producer/consumer cooperative, workers' association, syndicate
	Individuality	Voluntarism, creativity, anti-prevailing norms
	Welfare	Anti-poverty, self-management
	Human/social progress	Present orientation, critique of past/present, anti-inevitability
Fascism	Change	**Decline versus regeneration**, revolution, violence
	Order	Organicism, biological naturalism, anti-privacy, anti-individuality
	Nationalism	Irredentism, **militarism**, imperialism, [anti-]internationalism
	Racism	Ethnic purity/health, antisemitism, antiziganism
	Reactionarism	Anti-liberalism, anti-communism
	[Anti-]capitalism	Corporatism versus central planning, protectionism, welfarism and state intervention
	Statism	**Totalism and totalitarianism**, bureaucratism, state terror, party, **leadership cult**
	Religion and science	**Eugenicism**, biological/theological sexism, heterosexism, anti-disability
	Tradition	Familiarity, rejuvenation versus radical overhaul
	Utopia	Nostalgia, myth, futurism
Christian democracy	Change	Natural growth, anti-revolution
	Order	Stability, *status quo*, divinity, naturalism
	Sociality	**Organicism**, religious community
	Individuality	Human will and wilfulness, rights
	Reactionarism	**Centrism**, moderation, anti-extremism
	Flexibility	Consistency versus opportunism
	[Anti-]capitalism	Private property, trade unionism, **social market economy**
	Statism	**Subsidiarity**, anti-communism, democracy, cross-party collaboration
	Religion and science	Biological essentialism, economism
	Tradition	Cumulation, familiarity
	Utopia	Nostalgia, romanticism, anti-experimentalism
Social democracy	Liberty and equality	Citizenship, class, anti-hierarchy, *full employment*
	Political priority	Party, constitutionalism, rights
	Democracy	[Anti-]capitalism, managed competition, *social market economy*, cross-party collaboration
	Statism	**Parliamentarism**, reformism, anti-revolution
	Sociality	**Trade union**, [producer/consumer cooperative], internationalism, *nationality*
	Individuality	Personal identity expression
	Creativity	Labour/productivity, *good life*
	Welfare	Anti-poverty, **taxation, redistribution, public services**
	Human/social progress	Critique of past/present, gradualism, present-orientation, anti-inevitability

Ideology and ideologies 97

Ideology	Morphology	
Communism	Equality	Class, [anti-hierarchy], [anti-elitism]
	Economic priority	Historical structural explanation, determinism, industrialism, rapid development
	Anti-capitalism	State planning, [cooperation], [collectivisation]
	Statism	Revolution, [vanguardism], *bureaucratism, anti*-democracy, [de]centralism, violence, *state terror*
	Sociality	[Anti-private property], [*soviet*/council], internationalism, mass identity, *nationality, totalitarianism*
	Creativity	Labour/productivity
	Order	Party, *leadership cult*
	Social progress	Future orientation, historical process, spontaneity *versus management*
Libertarianism	Liberty	**Freedom of choice**, thought and speech
	Rights	[Natural origin], **property**, accumulation
	Economic priority	Anti-politics
	Anti-statism	Discretion [versus rule-making], **deregulation**, decentralisation, **privatisation**, anti-welfarism, anti-fiscal policy, international institutions
	Anti-democracy	Anti-majoritarianism, elitism, *authoritarianism*
	Market society	Competition versus central planning, globalisation, *nationalism*
	Rationality	Criticality, scepticism, [idealism]
	Individuality	**Self-ownership, anti-collectivism**, self-interest, egoism
Green ideology	Environment	Conservation and control, anti-ecological degradation and marginalisation, natural rootedness, biological/organic sociality and solidarity, agrarianism, [historical nostalgia]
	Sustainability	Renewable resource exploitation, anti-waste and pollution, *vegetarianism/veganism, degrowth, rewilding*
	Social justice	Civil rights/liberties, **welfarism**, fiscal redistribution, state intervention and incentivisation, [anti-]capitalism
	Democracy	Grassroots mobilisation, federalism and **localism**, mass movement, extra-state movements
	Non-violence	**Pacifism** and anti-militarism, reformism, passive resistance
Democratism/ republicanism	Political priority	Statism, **partisanship**, citizenship versus subjecthood, mass mobilisation, popular legislation, [nationality], *public opinion, internationalism*
	Democracy	[Anti-monarchism], [anti-aristocracy], electoralism, mass franchise, parliamentarism, *plebiscitarism, deliberation*
	Constitutionalism	Sovereignty, separation of powers, (de)centralism, rule of law, *judicial scrutiny, anti-technocracy*
	[Anti-]capitalism	[Workplace democracy], [producer/consumer cooperatives], regulation, fiscal policy, *anti-communism*
	Demos	Anti-elitism, [property qualification], [gender requirement], [racial requirement], minimum age requirement

98 Ideology and ideologies

Ideology	Morphology	
Nationalism	Exceptional worth of nation	Shared traits, common good via protection/domination, unity, anti-individuality, emotionality, biological loyalty/solidarity
	Superiority of own nation	Sovereignty, anti-internationalism, chauvinism
	(Anti-)imperialism	Colonial expansion versus resistance to foreign rule
	Purity	Ethnic/cultural monism, anti-tolerance, anti-minority rights
	Centralism	Anti-localism, elision of private/public spheres, concentration versus separation of power
	Political-economic unity	Intervention, protectionism, fiscal activism
Feminism	Gender	Social construction, roles, **anti-inferiority**/pathologisation, essentialism versus fluidity/spectrum, intersectionality
	Sex	Naturalism versus moral (in)significance, sexual pleasure
	Anti-patriarchy	Anti-asymmetric power relationships, anti-subordination, **equality**, human rights versus men's rights, universality versus particularity, electoral franchise
	Labour	Gendering of occupation/class, exploitation
	Embodiment	Ownership, objectification, sexual trauma/violence
	Social thinking	Rationality versus **emotionality**, affect, empathy
	Caregiving	Social justice and altruism, marriage versus celibacy/divorce, family and childbearing
Political religion	Exceptional worth of religion	Shared rituals, common good via privileged access to truth, unity, (anti-)individuality, emotionality, psychological loyalty/solidarity
	Superiority of own religion	Devotional supremacy, divine legitimation, providential future, anti-secularism, (anti-)chauvinism
	(Anti-)persecution	**Proselytising expansion** versus **resistance to discrimination**
	Purity	Cultural monism, (anti-)tolerance, (anti-)minority rights
	(Anti-)centralism	Hierarchy versus diffuseness, elision of private/public spheres, doctrinal integrity versus local variation
	(Anti-)political–cultural–economic unity	Withdrawal versus intervention, *laïcité* versus theocracy, fiscal activism, welfarism
Anticolonialism/ Antiracism	Race	Social construction, roles, **anti-inferiority**/pathologisation, essentialism, intersectionality
	Ethnicity	Naturalism versus moral (in)significance, beauty and aesthetics
	Anti-white supremacy	Anti-asymmetric power relationships, anti-subordination, **equality**, anti-slavery and discrimination, anti-illegalisation and incarceration, **religious/cultural tolerance**, universality versus Eurocentrism, electoral franchise
	Labour	Racialising of occupation/class, exploitation, globalisation
	Embodiment	Ownership, (in)equality of life value, state and group violence
	Social thinking	Rationality versus emotionality
	Decolonialism	Anti-white settlement, immigration, social justice, foreign aid and reparations

Ideology and ideologies 99

Ideology	Morphology	
Queer ideology	Gender identity	Social construction, roles, **anti-inferiority/pathologisation**, essentialism versus fluidity/spectrum, intersectionality
	Sexual orientation	Naturalism versus moral (in)significance, beauty and aesthetics, sexual pleasure, questioning, (self-)exploration
	Anti-cisheteropatriarchy	Anti-asymmetric power relationships, anti-subordination, **equality**, anti-homophobia, anti-transphobia, anti-illegalisation and incarceration, anti-medicalisation, **religious/cultural tolerance**, universality versus particularity
	Labour	Occupational exclusion versus inclusion
	Embodiment	Ownership, **(in)equality of life value**, state and group/individual objectification and trauma/violence
	Social thinking	Rationality versus **emotionality**, affect, empathy
	Queering	Identity (re)assignment, **(non)conformity**, stereotypes and subversion, revisionism and anti-normalisation, marriage and **sexual partnership dynamics**, family and childbearing

'equality', and 'democracy'. Likewise, they stress that the relative adjacency and distance they ascribe to these concepts is logically well founded and appropriate to their overarching social context and, conversely, are keen to highlight areas of poor logical or contextual 'fit' in other ideologies' equivalent determinations – such as contrary accusations of the association of 'democracy' with either elitist 'parliamentarism' or ochlocratic 'tyranny of the majority'. Essential contestation also leads ideologies to engage in something of an 'arms race' in the level of care (i.e., dedicated attention and effort) with which they define their concepts, as they circumscribe, colonise, or discredit new potential connotations in a bid to ensure that 'their' definition remains the most societally relevant, and hence dominant – as with decontestatory tracts by rival ideologies on individual concepts of 'equality' (Tawney 1931), 'justice' (Rawls 1971), or 'the political' (Schmitt 1996 [1932]).

Along similar lines, ideologies are keen to ensure an overarching perception of the essential fixity of the 'core' of their concepts' meanings. Generally, they either insist on the 'original and best' nature of their 'decontestation' versus those of other ideologies or claim that any newly accommodated connotations were always 'natural' extensions of the core meaning – e.g., the Chiangist (Kuomintang), Maoist (communist), and Wangist (collaborationist) appeals to Sun Yat-Sen's 'three principles of the people' to underscore their competing visions for China. Ideologies also enter a persistent struggle over the potential 'gaps' between their decontestation of their concepts' meanings and the contingent vernacular consensus, either in order to 'drag' societal understandings closer to their position or by denying that this consensus 'is really talking about' these concepts at all – e.g., the social liberal and later neoliberal effort to first expand and then contract prevailing connotations of 'the state' and its (welfarist, interventionist) social role. In all of these cases, ideologies challenge the meanings that other ideologies have ascribed to the concepts in question and 'decontest' them to assert the comprehensiveness, completeness, and correctness of the (alternative) meaning that they want these concepts to 'have'. This can take the form of an 'ownership dispute' over which ideology claims the 'right' to incorporate a particular element, or a 'battle of wills' where each ideology tries to assert 'its' semantic restriction of the element's meaning within society at large – e.g., successive (Trotskyist, Titoist, Maoist, Hoxhaist) communist efforts to claim sole representation of the Leninist or Stalinist legacy, denouncing other rivals as 'revisionists'.

Essential co-option, meanwhile, takes an inverse approach and relies on the societal need for some kernel of consensus on delimiting the meaning of these concepts, however narrow or ephemeral, in order for them to play a viable part in social discourse in the first place. Ideologies rely on permeabilities of meaning between their concepts and those of other ideologies to act as 'chinks' in the other ideologies' morphological armour: openings that allow them to 'swoop in', challenge their semantic 'stranglehold' over these concepts, and steal them as new additions to their own morphological 'offerings' – as with fascist attempts to lay claim to 'progress' and 'reform' through their own reactionary–radical fusion or conservative uses of 'worker' to refer to business owners at the expense of the unemployed/'precariat'. On the same principle, ideologies carefully note where other ideologies' logical construction and contextualisation of their conceptual arrangements is 'uncontestable' and, instead, make a play to absorb these parts of their morphologies by emphasising their continuity with their own adjacency–distance arrangements

Ideology and ideologies 101

– as happened extensively with the concept 'social', originally a core socialist concept, which was steadily appropriated by liberal, conservative, Christian-democratic, and fascist ideologies with various 'charitable', 'national', or 'ethnic' connotations. Essential co-option also works by ideologies deliberately ignoring 'grey areas' and maintaining strategic incompletenesses in their conceptual decontestations, in order to 'hold open the door' to rapidly (and credibly) adjusting them to new connotations when the opportunities for semantic expansion present themselves – e.g., 'justice', which usually occupies the same semantic space as 'welfare' or 'fairness', but can be turned towards far more retributive, disciplinary connotations of 'law and order', 'desert', 'authority', or even 'state terror'.

By the same logic, ideologies are also often tacitly willing to let the 'core' of their concepts' meanings 'drift' quietly and (im)perceptibly over time, either by letting them 'expand' in response to new contextual conditions or by 'dropping' enough superseded connotations to let their meanings appear perpetually 'current' rather than 'antiquated' – e.g., social democracy's core focus on 'labour' and 'the worker' migrating semantically away from 'class struggle' or 'anti-capitalism' and towards 'welfare-statism', 'codetermination', and 'collective bargaining'. Ultimately, essential co-option is a key part of ideologies' strategy to ensure that their concepts' meanings always remain within safe 'touching distance' of the vernacular consensus, so that they can 'pick their battles' semantically in cases where society as a whole remains unwilling to adopt their particular decontestation – e.g., the tactic of 'strategic essentialism', mobilising ideological resistance around 'broad-brush' gendered, racialised, queered, ableist 'othernesses' jointly imposed by dominant ideologies in vernacular language (Spivak 1988, 1996). With all the various forms of essential co-option, ideologies remain tacitly open to the limitations of their own claims to comprehensiveness, completeness, and correctness, specifically on the assumption that other ideologies' rival decontestations may hold the key to 'shoring up' their own semantic 'positions'. Perhaps the best way to visualise this is as a form of conceptual 'headhunting' where one ideology 'poaches' a particular element from another with a view to 'shaking up' its morphology, or as a 'merger and acquisition' where it 'asset-strips' the other ideology's morphology, either wholly incorporating it as a new 'subsidiary' variant or 'spinning it out' into a new ideological hybrid – as with conservatism's chameleonic self-reinvention by appropriating elements of democratism (e.g., *Volkspartei* campaigns, plebiscitarism), nationalism (chauvinism, protectionism), or populism ('red scares', anti-technocracy), or its wholesale absorption of first 'social market economy' and then neoliberal political-economic programmes.

§3 Ideological categorisation

The changes that two centuries of societal development have wrought in the preconditions of ideological emergence, coupled with the increasingly complex dynamics of ideological competition between a growing list of 'players', have driven the proliferation of ideologies – 'families' and traditions, subsumed strands and variants, 'hosts', 'modifiers', and hybrids – to an unprecedented height. As a result, ideology analysis has given significant consideration to the question of whether all of these ideological formations can be categorised and compared using as sparing as possible a list of overarching universal criteria. While ideologies' self-identification has evidently moved on considerably from the mere binary endorsement or rejection of social and ideological change, there is still something attractive about being able to categorise ideologies qualitatively or quantitatively by the degree and nature of their support for, or opposition to, the societal *status quo* – and, at the next level up, in terms of the 'aspects' or 'directions' in which they would like to see social reality perpetuated or transformed. Fundamentally, this is the logic that underpins the best-known of these overarching ideological categorisations: the left–centre–right 'ideological *spectrum*', which fuses together several of the binary contrasts regarding social and ideological change (Freire 2015; White 2011). The label 'left', 'left-wing', or 'leftism', which consolidated in the 1840s to 1880s, typically connotes progressivism, often radicalism, and the reform or revolutionary overthrow of the established order, as well as varying degrees of social, political, and economic change in the name of greater freedom, power, welfare, and comfort for ordinary people – with undertones of favouring political and economic equality, democracy, fraternity, solidarity, and internationalism. The terminology of 'right', 'right-wing', or (more rarely) 'rightism' followed suit in the 1850s to 1930s and is, conversely, associated with reactionarism, professing support for the established order, opposing social equality and extensive political reform, and favouring traditional attitudes, practices, policies, and ideas – with connotations of aristocracy, monarchism, theocracy, capitalism, authority and hierarchy, duty, and nationalism. The label 'centre' or 'centrism', which dates from the 1870s, is in essence a positional comparison meaning 'neither left nor right', but it also connotes moderation, aversion to extremes, and the search for median points of compromise. Used as an informal metric of comparison since the French Revolution and the early years of the 'first wave', at least since the mid- to late 1800s, the left–centre–right spectrum has become the confirmed *de facto* description of ideologies' relative 'positions'.

The position of some ideologies on the spectrum is easy to deduce from their morphology and familiar from their vernacular associations. Socialism and communism lie firmly on the left and conservatism equally solidly on the right, to the point that these 'isms' and their spectrum positions are often treated as semantically and functionally synonymous. Liberalism is more variable: it is typically located in the centre (Europe) but also contingently associated with the left (North America) or right (Latin America), reflecting the local development of the liberal tradition and the underlying ideological skew of the respective societies. But, beyond these positions, the ideological spectrum faces two key problems. First, these ideologies are 'easy' to categorise only against a background global context that is overwhelmingly capitalist (in various forms), split more or less evenly between democracy and authoritarianism (also in different forms), and with extensive macroregional variations in (especially religious) cultural norms. By contrast, in the early 1800s, liberalism was a radical advocate of (in Europe) capitalism and (in Latin America) decolonisation against conservative defences of feudalism, latifundism, and imperialism; meanwhile, in the late Cold War, secular 'state socialist' regimes favoured maintaining order and *nomenklatura* hierarchy, while liberal and (often devoutly religious) conservative dissidents were anti-system reformists and radicals. Second, it is not always obvious where other ideologies fit, even those that have a long-established societal presence. Anarchism is a particular 'hard case', usually categorised as left but with some sharply rightist strains; while social democracy and Christian democracy are paradigmatic inventions of respective 'centre-left' and 'centre-right' compromise. Fascism and libertarianism are both typically categorised as (extreme) right, due to their associations with genocidal totalitarianism and untrammelled capitalism respectively; but this underplays strands of both that exhibit proximities with the left, largely on account of the former's extensive historical co-option of social-democratic 'mixed economy' policies and the latter's co-option of anarchist suspicion towards state institutions.

One way to rectify this is to disaggregate the left–centre–right spectrum into multiple dimensions, which allows for a more precise and nuanced 'positioning' of ideologies. These dimensions form spectrums in their own right, and ideologies can be distinguished from one another according to the overarching 'distribution' of their locations on each of these separate spectrums – i.e., using multiple points of reference. The simplest form of this is a two-dimensional model, of which the best-known since its initial postulation in the 1950s to 1960s is the categorisation of ideologies along 'political-economic' and 'cultural' dimensions. The first of these dimensions is strongly tied to the representation of different class interests and views on societal inequalities of wealth and income and concerns especially the evaluation of state involvement in the market economy via taxation, welfare policies, regulation, and investment – running from *interventionism* to *laissez-faire*. The second dimension is defined more diffusely, covering issues such as views on the demographic and moral integrity of society, tolerance and celebration of individual difference and preference, religiosity and secularism, hierarchical order and protean voluntarism, support for the nation-state or global institutions, and the overall degree of 'permitted' (internal) ideological diversity and contestation – running (broadly) from *monism* to *pluralism*. Again, the definition of these dimensions is tellingly a product of the mid-1900s global *status quo*: a tense bifurcation between, on the one hand, societies operating under capitalist and 'state socialist' modes of production and exchange and, on the other, those who valued hierarchy and strong collective unity and those who favoured protections for personal freedom and diversity. Nonetheless, this disaggregation already allows for more granular ideological comparisons. In political-economic terms, communism and socialism lean towards interventionism, conservatism and libertarianism favour *laissez-faire*, with anarchism, social democracy, fascism, Christian democracy, and liberalism clustered into more middle positions. In cultural terms, communism and fascism are strongly monist, libertarianism and anarchism highly pluralist, with conservatism, Christian democracy, socialism, social democracy, and liberalism arrayed along the spectrum between them.

These political-economic and cultural 'ratings' can be combined to create an ideological 'compass', with the political-economic and cultural dimensions as its axes (see table 3). This compass accommodates at least some of the most 'broad-brush' differences between the 'Big Four' macro-ideologies and their meso-ideological challengers and thus offers a convenient 'snapshot' of the extent and points of synchronic variation between ideological *familles spirituelles* in a given spatial–temporal context. It can accommodate the micro-ideologies that 'orbit' macro- and meso-ideologies, and it can model the loci and outcomes of dynamics of hosting, modification, and hybridisation that play out between them, locating these minor and dependent ideological formations 'between' their 'source' ideologies in both political-economic and cultural space. The ideological compass can also represent diachronic variation reasonably clearly, usually using arrows to trace ideologies' political-economic and cultural evolution over time. The left–centre–right spectrum does not align neatly with either of these dimensions, and it is also too simplistic to see it as merely a 50:50 'average' between the two. At least since the consolidation of 'ideologies of identity' during the 'third wave', the proportionality of cultural concerns within ideologies has been growing at the expense of political-economic foci, although this development has not taken place at the same pace across all of them (Inglehart 1977, 1990, 2018). On the ideological compass, the left–centre–right spectrum is thus best approximated as a curve that shifts or rotates in 'compass space', which is currently being pulled ever further away from the 'horizontal' (political-economic) towards the 'vertical' (cultural) axis. Coupled with decadal trends towards ideological polarisation, the result in Europe especially is an embryonic coalescing of two opposing clusters: a 'Brahmin left' that supports political-economic interventionism and cultural pluralism and a 'Merchant right' favouring political-economic *laissez-faire* and cultural monism (Kitschelt 2010; Kriesi et al. 2008; Piketty 2020, 807–965).

Although the ideological compass certainly improves on the nuance of the ideological spectrum, it still has two significant limitations. First, it still requires major compromises in characterising ideologies by 'clusters' of their constituent elements, which relies on looking at the 'average result' of where each individual element (e.g., 'progress', 'privacy',

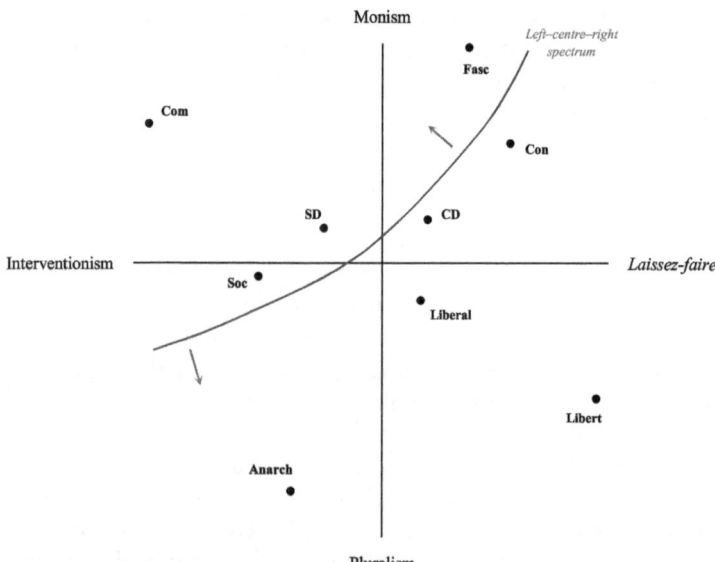

Figure 3 The ideological compass

'order', 'localism', 'due process', 'expertise') falls on either political-economic or cultural dimensions to determine where the ideologies 'fall' on these dimensions 'overall'. In particular, the contestability of meaning associated with individual ideas, dispositions, practices, structures, and so on, means that they can sometimes connote completely opposite ends of the two dimensions, which makes it difficult to determine the ideologies' exact place on the relevant spectrum, and hence their location in 'compass space' – e.g., 'faith' denoting theocracy or freedom of worship, 'rights' as private property or welfarist claims. Second, the disaggregation of left–centre–right into two dimensions is still of limited benefit in categorising thinner ideologies, especially 'single-issue' formations. Their core element(s) may not by themselves clearly connote any of the grand concerns of political economy or cultural policy, and they may lack the adjacent and peripheral elements required to contextualise their ideological claims adequately, making them 'unplaceable' on either if not both of the compass's axes – e.g., 'the people', 'the constitution', 'the environment', 'growth', 'reason'. There have been several attempts to modify the ideological compass by adding other dimensions of categorisation: religiosity, humanitarianism, and nationalism (Ferguson 1939, 1940, 1941, 1942); freedom–equality (Rokeach 1973); and secularism–traditionalism and survival–self-expression (Inglehart and Welzel 2005). However, there is as yet no consensus at all on which of these make for the most promising and insightful replacements or complements for the political-economic and cultural dimensions; above all, it is not clear that any of them has acquired sufficient proportionality or priority across all the ideologies currently available to 'add value' as a consistently meaningful criterion of analysis.

The addition of further criteria to disaggregate and complement the political-economic and cultural dimensions brings the efforts to categorise ideologies ever closer to reflecting the full scope of their morphological diversity. But, in doing so, it risks losing the main benefit of the ideological spectrum or ideological compass approaches and ultimately defeating the central point of categorisation – namely, to provide a useful 'at-a-glance' overview of the range of ideologies available. Ultimately, attempts to find universal criteria for ideological categorisation face a trade-off between (1) their heuristic value as a simple, manageable set of scalar or continuum 'dimensions', easily visualisable in diagrammatic form, and (2) the impossibility of capturing the full extent of ideologies' complex and constantly evolving morphology, due to the imperfect correlation between the elements that any categorisation is forced to compress into as low a number of dimensions as possible. One possible solution is to abandon the strategy of trying to mark ideologies' location on the compass using only single points and instead to reflect them as 'freeform shapes' – to capture the concept of 'family resemblance' and the suggestion that there is a certain non-infinite ideological space within which the *longue-durée* tradition moves. Another solution is to develop alternative ways to visualise ideologies entirely, such as an ideological 'star plot' or 'spider-web chart', or using 'sliders' to represent the various dimensions of comparison. But this depends on establishing a more meaningful consensus on what the extra dimensions should be; until this is achieved, the ideological compass and the left–centre–right spectrum remain the stubbornly durable analytical tools of choice for ideology studies to categorise the wealth of ideologies available in contemporary society.

5
The experience of ideology

So far, we have looked at how ideology is defined and how it works, the different ideological families and traditions into which it can be divided, the social preconditions for their emergence, and how they can be categorised and compared. But, from our position as members of society, these descriptions of how we 'use' ideology in our psychology and behaviour, and how we can observe and diagnose it, offer only a partial picture of our encounters with it. What has not been covered up to now is how we 'receive' ideology, how it 'works on' us, how it is 'used on' us – in short, what it is like for us to experience ideology. Here, we can make two starting observations. The first of these is that ideology is something we fundamentally experience *individually* (Boudon 1989, 5–8). The individual is the 'smallest unit' of ideology, in the sense that individual psychology and behaviour is the 'lowest level' at which ideology operates. Of course, this can be (and is often) mediated through collectivity, in that we experience ideology because of our membership in a given social group that is distinguished by particular similarities in its (our) social activity or personal characteristics. But the 'group' aspect of our ideological 'treatment' is ultimately the expression of our 'similarity' with these separate individuals' social conditions – i.e., our equivalent positions in social hierarchies, on the same 'side' in social factions, or within the same cultural contexts (see chapter 4). The steady rise in societal complexity has created an ever greater variety of available social tasks, roles, and developmental paths for us to pursue, while at the same time attributing social salience to a growing list of our personal mental and physical characteristics. This has led to a vast cumulative proliferation and mass expansion of the groupings of similarity into which we can be 'slotted'. The overlaps and intersections between these groups become increasingly unique to our personal 'roster' of salient factors, which translate into our own particular 'constellation' of hierarchical, factional, or contextual positions across all categories of social valence. At the same time, *even though* we are members of domain-based or demographic groups, we move in concentric 'circles' of social 'connections' – family and friends, neighbours, local community, colleagues, team-mates, club co-members, etc. – that are not populated exclusively by members of any of these groups but, instead, reflect our own personal 'cross-section' of other people from different groups whom we encounter as part of our day-to-day social interactions (Kadushin 2012, 108–34). As ever more areas of social life are subjected to ideological representation, then, our experience of ideology becomes ever more individuated because it is more distinctly calibrated to us – even as the sweep of ideological currents attached to these ideological meanings becomes ever more global (Bauman 1998, 2001).

The second observation is that, in the first instance, we are *oblivious* of our individual experience of ideology. Even as fully developed adults with full control over our mental and physical faculties, we are only aware to a limited degree of the precise ideological nature of our surroundings and our engagement with them. But when we first gain consciousness as neonatals, and later infants and pre-pubescents, we are wholly unaware that we have been allocated a certain perspective within social reality, that we are exposed 'defencelessly' to specific others who are oriented by certain dispositions, abide by certain norms, and follow certain practices, and that we are integrated along with them into certain structures and systems that have been 'set up' around us (Lyotard 1992) – let alone that where and how we 'start out' in life is the product of many previous iterations of ideological 'steering'. Instead, our individual experience

The experience of ideology 111

of these social phenomena and the effects of ideological processes is primarily as the outcome of contingent chance, as if we have been 'thrown' haphazardly into a particular 'corner' of reality (Heidegger 1962, 174–6, 184–5, 219–25, 233–6, 321–5, 329–33). In the first instance, it seems purely providential to us that 'this' is the part of reality in which we 'happen' to have appeared, and that we 'happen' to have 'manifested' in it in a particular biological form (i.e., in bodies with certain mental and physical characteristics). At the same time, our surroundings are not *per se* instantly (made) clear but are 'disclosed' to us only gradually through processes of cumulative experience (ibid., 105–6, 256–73, 344–8, 384–400). It seems entirely random to us that 'this' is the part of reality that 'happens' to be appearing to us and that we 'happen' to be encountering it in a certain way (i.e., via specific constellations of materials and relations). In short, when we are born, we enter a reality that is 'always-already' ideological, without any sense of what this means (for reality or for us). Instead, we are left to play catch-up; we have to 'hit the ground running' in order to 'get up to speed' with how this ideological world works.

This early developmental stage is the closest we come to occupying a position 'outside' ideology, in the sense that our early-years psychology and behaviour – prior to our gradual 'self-alienating' development of a social-comparative subjectivity, prompted by the onset of the 'mirror stage' (Lacan 2006, 75–81, 671–702) – is the nearest to being 'purely' determined by the biological constraints of our mental and physical faculties, untrammelled by the 'additional' modifiers ideology imposes. At this developmental stage, our vantage-point onto the world, the lens through which we see it, the primer and script we stick to, and the design plan and simulation we follow are 'authentically' our 'own' and instinctual in one particular sense, namely that (at least initially) they are not affected by any symbolic 'inputs' that lie outside our direct, immediate control (Kristeva 1980). This is reflected in the rudimentary psychology and behaviour we exhibit at this stage: (1) 'childish' imagination and fantasy (Glynos 2008; Lacan 1994, 60, 89, 185, 273; Žižek 1996), both positive (e.g., make-believe) and negative (e.g., fear of monsters), and (2) 'unguided' creative play

(Huizinga 2016; Lyotard 1993 [1986], 112), which together bridge and explore the divide between pleasure, pain, and transgressive *'jouissance'* (libidinal enjoyment/'pain-beyond-pleasure') (Kristeva 1980; Lacan 1994, 184, 234, 281; Lacan 2006). Both are unsettled, unstructured, and undifferentiated, pre-existing our 'abjection' ('casting-off') into the 'mature' period of independent self-formation in a world with pre-settled, pre-structured, and pre-differentiated meaning (Kristeva 1980, 1982). In both cases, what characterises our neonatal or 'infantile' experience of social reality is a profound incomprehension, especially of any notion of *finitude*, or limitation by the existence of other people or objects (Heidegger 1962, 126, 378–80, 399, 436–8, 466, 476; Levinas 1969 [1961], 33–52, 109–21, 287ff.). Social reality appears to us as a realm of towering, limitless possibility, with no reason to restrict the ways its constituent materials and relations or their representations can be combined and arranged. Our memory of this early-years incomprehension is the closest we have to an 'unfiltered' experience of reality on which we can draw in (intensively ideologised) social life. But from all of our later positions of having-been-ideologised, it is fundamentally imperfectly reaccessible and replicable – at best a recollection and object of 'fascination' lurking in the shadowy recesses of our psychology and behaviour (Kristeva 1982).

However, crucially, this is not to say that, when we enter the world, we are as yet 'pristine' or 'untouched' by ideology. On the contrary, based on the spatial and temporal contexts in which we are born, the distribution of social materials and arrangement of social relations around us, our own personal mental and physical characteristics, and the equivalent situations of the people in our social circles, we are immediately made the objects of intense and intensive ideological representation. We are given an ideological meaning and attributed a social significance and value, which determines the 'place' we occupy in *others'* ideological maps, lenses, primers, scripts, and so on – i.e., how others view and treat us. Ideology *objectifies*, or 'reifies', us all as a material part of social reality that, like any other 'stuff', can be combined and arranged as part of ideological structures and systems (Honneth 2008; Langton 2009, 223–66; Lukács 1923; Nussbaum 1985;

Silva 2013). Moreover, thanks to the proliferating range of different ideologies available, *we* are increasingly subjected to attempts at essential contestation and co-option. We can be treated as synonymous or antonymous with ('standing for' or 'against') other specific concepts and meanings: we are harbingers of chaos or civilisational collapse or personifications of duty and chastity. We may be 'put' adjacent to (associated with) or distant from (disassociated from) other logical or cultural connotations: 'strong and stable' and 'too big to fail', 'Axis of Evil' or 'leader of the free world'. We can be obsessively pored over and micro-managed to the point of fetishistic essentialism or dismissively ignored and sweepingly defined to the point of parodic stereotype: we are hailed as geniuses or slavered over as voluptuous, derided as shallow or mocked for our 'funny accents'. Ideologies may flexibly embrace or stubbornly defend against 'changing their mind' on our meaning and significance: we may be 'chavs' deserving of ASBOs one moment and subjected to patrician 'hug a hoodie' overtures the next, 'expats' or 'guest workers' in one context and 'illegals' or 'cockroaches' in another. Ideologies can also either dispute to the point of denialism or accommodate to the point of uncriticality the accepted vernacular consensus on our meaning versus the one they have specified for us: e.g., conservatives denying green ideologists' liberal-approximating 'rightwards' tack by insisting on viewing them as 'hippies' or 'tree-huggers', and socialists exaggerating it by terming them 'neoliberals on bikes'. Ultimately, ideological objectification ends up placing us on a spectrum between the extremes of lionisation and demonisation; in both cases, ideology 'allocates' us a 'bloc' ideological identity that others use to understand and engage with us *as social phenomena in their environments.*

There is a stark tension between our ideological obliviousness and our ideological objectification, which we must overcome if we are to start 'making sense' of social reality. As ideological *objects*, we are the equivalent of 'intermediate goods' or semi-finished products; we have been extracted from the mass of 'raw material' provided by humanity at large and 'allocated' as individuals to specific societal processes in accordance with our ideological representations. In order for us to become 'final goods', we need to have our mental and physical faculties refined in such a way that we can play an active part in 'steering' social reality in the way the ideological representations in question 'want' – i.e., to become ideological *subjects*. For this, we have to acquire an understanding of how we 'fit into' reality according to the prevailing (hegemonic as well as subaltern) ideological conception(s) by which we are objectified. We need to internalise the ideological 'role' in which we have been 'cast' – what is (and is not) available to us, expected or required of us, how we are encouraged or incentivised to think, feel, and act – in order to gain an understanding of how to 'work' the ideological tools that our surroundings offer us to 'make sense' of social reality (Therborn 1980, 15–30). There are two aspects to this: in general, an awareness of what the 'uses' of ideological perspectives, dispositions, norms, practices, structures, and systems are to 'making sense' of social reality; and, in particular, 'getting used to' the 'inner logics' (i.e., the basis of the comprehensiveness, completeness, and correctness) presented by the ideologies circulating in our surroundings.

The force of the shift from ideological objects to subjects is that we need to *subjectivise* what is otherwise still just an *objective* manifestation of ideology. We have to make the *ideological* vantage-point, lens, primer, script, design plan, and simulation – i.e., the ones that a given ideology offers us – *our own* vantage-point, lens, and so on. By doing so, we make them 'authentically' ours in a *different* sense, namely that we individually, personally adopt and 'take ownership' of them, modifying or overwriting whatever rudimentary or vestigial 'pre-ideological' psychology and behaviours we might have had previously. Through ideology, our imagination and fantasy become 'bound' and our play becomes 'guided' by the parameters of existing reality and its available representations. Crucially, we need to adopt an *a priori* position of ideological 'immanence' (Antonio 1981; Buchwalter 1991; Finlayson 2014; Stahl 2017) – i.e., taking on the ideological map and *habitus* with which we are presented – whether or not we ultimately accept or reject our ideological 'allocation', since social action from a 'transcendent' position of rootless oblivion is equally unconducive to either perpetuating or transforming our ideologically determined social 'place' (of meaning, significance, value, purpose, etc.). The first stage is always 'adjusting to' the ideological characterisation we are 'dealt' in order to get our bearings. Only then can we answer the follow-on question of whether or not we choose subjectively to 'claim' (or 'reclaim') the identity and the shared objective representation that we have been 'dealt' – and from there on to establish 'chains of equivalence' with others who have been similarly ideologised, which can act as a common basis for subsequent parallel or joint subjective ideological activity (e.g., expressions of solidarity, strategic exchange, joint mobilisation, power-sharing) (Laclau and Mouffe 1985, 130–44, 164–82).

§1 The formation of ideological subjects

At least to start with, subjectivisation is not predominantly an internal process. There is no meaningful point at which we consciously 'choose', 'opt into', or autodidactically 'acquire for ourselves' our initial ideological subjecthood from a position of complete non-subjectivisation. Instead, the process is *prima facie* external, taking the form of deliberate and sophisticated *subjectification* (*assujettissement*) (Butler 1997; Foucault 1977, 1982b). Formally speaking, *anybody* or *anything* can subjectify us – any other individual, social group or network, or social institution – by impressing on us a specific ideological map and *habitus* that we adopt at the expense of our previous psychology and behaviours. This is the process of *interpellation*, or 'hailing' (Althusser 2014, 189–97, 261–70; Therborn 1980, 15–20, 77–85), which we experience as a 'call' ('*Ruf*') or 'appeal' (Heidegger 1962, 314–15), whereby we are 'summoned' to our social role as subjects of (within, under, according to) a given ideology. But the core responsibility for processes of subjectification – above all, the authorship of the ideological perspective, dispositions, norms, and so on, that we are supposed to adopt – lies with particular systems (and their constituent structures and practices) that are distinguished by having this as their identifiable ideological function, along with whatever other purpose(s) they might have within society. These are ideological *apparatuses* (Althusser 2014, 74–93, 103–47,

198–206, 218–31; Therborn 1980, 84–9): complex organised assortments of people and the means (e.g., tools, instruments, equipment, vehicles, machinery) and methods (e.g., techniques, operations, strategies) they use to accomplish the specific task of 'getting' us to adopt and internalise ideological maps and *habitus*. They have a 'psychosocial' function, in that they define the meanings and connotations of the 'pure' ideas and 'applied' manifestations that an ideology contains and assert their 'hold' over our psychology and behaviour by disseminating them to us via judicious interventions in our social lives. Ideological apparatuses and their interpellative function form a central component of ideological 'hardware' in society's overarching ideological *dispositifs* ('schemes', 'devices', 'deployments'): the sum total of the various interconnected ethical and scientific dispositions, normative rules and laws, practical techniques, structural tools, and institutional systems that 'go into' shaping societal conditions to resemble how a given ideology represents them, unified into an overarching integrated, complex *Gesamtkunstwerk* ('total artwork') (Agamben 2009, 14; Althusser 2006 [1993–4], 47, 105, 141; Caborn 2007; Foucault 1980, 194–228; Jäger 2009).

The term 'apparatus' conjures up the image of a highly stylised, quasi-official institution, not unlike a state propaganda ministry. This impression is not helped by Althusser, who ties ideological apparatuses (IAs) to a monolithic conception of the 'State' as an all-encompassing political–legal–cultural entity (ISAs). But we should not necessarily think of apparatuses in such rigid, architectural terms – or, in fact, in terms of discrete social entities at all. Instead, it is better to think of them more as a broad but distinct category of networks, bodies, or communities, whose perceived 'apparatus-ness' and social 'permanence' is a result of their perennial presence in society (*in some form*) and their consistent, immediately recognisable ideological function. Our encounters with them are far more commonly (inter)personal than institutional – through other people we know and spend time with, work or learn alongside, campaign or worship with. Similarly, ideological apparatuses are not always necessarily visible. As ideological subjects, we are not always (or even usually) in a position to 'trace' the full line of connections between the representations of social reality we 'hold' and a definite 'author' (i.e., another identifiable subject or group of subjects) who provably 'came up' with them. In fact, one of the core 'naturalising' features of ideology is precisely to hide that these representations have been 'come up with' at all (Bourdieu 1977, 164; 1990, 71, 139; Norval 2000, 326). That this is a fundamentally unsatisfying solution to the question of ideological 'responsibility' is shown by the lasting mark it leaves on our psychology: in place of the all-consuming 'unsettlement' at the chaotic, self-contradictory nature of reality, we are left with a residual concern about the final inexplicability of our objective 'place' and subjective role in society.

Ideological apparatuses are far from homogeneous, and we experience their operations and effects in a large variety of different ways (Althusser 2014, 94–139, 164–70, 218–72). First, they take very different forms across the various *domains of social action*, where they 'prepare' us to engage in the specific types of action with which each domain is concerned by 'socialising' our psychology and behaviour to fit that of 'the kind of subjects who' engage in each type of action (see table 4). They are specialised in qualitatively different ways of ensuring that we adopt our particular guiding ideological maps and *habitus* – what we can call the *dimensions* of ideological subjectification (Bourdieu 1977, 87–9; Foucault 1977; Therborn 1980, 17, 25, 34, 53, 116). Each of these different types of ideological apparatus 'tackles' the 'project' of subjectifying us from a different angle. (1) They cultivate different 'facets' of our 'overall' ideological subjectivity: they make us ideologically and hence socially 'well-rounded' (as 'children', 'students', 'workers', etc.), in order for us to be able to function in a way that is consistent with the 'expectations' of our ideological maps across all the different societal situations with which we are confronted, spread across all the different domains through which we engage with reality. (2) They are mutually complementary, with the more or less subtle/gentle or blatant/violent approaches they take to subjectifying us acting as 'carrot-and-stick' combinations that give us different 'reasons' to adopt the particular ideological representation(s) they are 'selling' us. By the same token,

118 *The experience of ideology*

Table 4 Ideological apparatuses across social domains

Domain	Examples of apparatuses	Subjectification
Economic	Business association, trade union, performance review board, 'human resources' team	Remuneration, fining
Political	Parliament, party, government information service, bureaucracy, intelligence agency, police, military	Supervision, disciplining
Legal/juridical	Court, judiciary, prison, detention centre, law firm, bar council/association	Sanctioning, rewarding
Religious	Church, place of worship, faith group, seminary, 'mission', international network/foundation	Ritualisation, reification
Cultural/discursive	Newspaper/magazine, radio station, TV channel, online and social media forum/website	Formulation, dissemination
Curative	Nuclear and wider family, friendship group, social club, social care, hospital, counselling service	Conditioning, raising
Educational/scholastic	School, university, vocational programme, skills learning and enhancement course	Qualification, training

these different apparatuses also give ideology 'full coverage', in that there is no domain (i.e., part of reality) in which we are 'safe' from, or able to 'avoid', processes of ideological subjectification.

Second, these ideological apparatuses from different social domains 'enter in' to subjectify us at very different stages of our life cycles. It is clear that some apparatuses are restricted in their usefulness only to certain ages, periods of life, or stages of personal development – above all our 'immediate' and 'wider' families, primary and secondary schools, and (if relevant) universities or trade schools – which means that we are 'passed' from one apparatus to the next as they grow or diminish in relevance to the (ideological) social role we are expected to 'play'. The precise course and sequence of our life-cycle encounters with different apparatuses is determined by their controlling ideologies' conceptions of what the trajectory of evolution of an individual's social action should look like over the course of their life: e.g., nurture and

The experience of ideology 119

education, consumption, voting, working, parenting, and retirement (cf. Therborn 1980, 87) (see figure 4).

However, even once we are 'out' of a particular apparatus, its subjectifying effects do not immediately stop; we (and they) rely on our memory, our cognitive 'schemata', our 'muscle memory', 'force of habit', and so on, to keep us 'keeping up' the perspectives, dispositions, norms, and practices with which we have been inculcated. This is especially strong with early-years socialisation, which plays a dominant and durable role in shaping our adult psychology and behaviour, barring the 'shock' effects of significant crises in later life (Bouchard and McGue 2003; Specht et al. 2011). Instead, apparatuses' effects are cumulative over time: we experience the subjectification from different life-cycle apparatus encounters as multiple superimpositions of domain-specific 'variants' of the ideology in question. As every 'new' apparatus arrives, the proportional importance of 'older' apparatuses and the maps and *habitus* they have 'given' us becomes gradually downgraded: 'key' parts of our 'older' subjectifications are shifted to our longer-term memory, and the 'less relevant' parts are quietly forgotten. This means that our subjectification is never a *fait accompli*: the psychological and behavioural 'expectations' it imposes on us are 'ideal-type' aspirations or 'asymptotes' towards which we are always 'in the process' of developing, and as such our ideological subjectivities are constantly 'on trial' (Althusser 2014, 187–201, 261–6; Kristeva 1980; Parsons 1967 [1937], 601–9; Weber 1978 [1922], 20–1).

Third, insofar as it is possible to 'trace' at least partly the 'authorship' of the ideological representations that we hold, this can be attributed to multiple ideological sources within different social domains and their apparatuses. Here, there is a range of possibilities: from identifiable individual 'influential personalities' who are so personally significant in defining and disseminating ideology that they act as 'opinion leaders', through to 'reference groups', whose role in both is far more evenly spread, mutually dependent, and collective, and who thus constitute ideological 'opinion climates' (Bernays 2005 [1928], 73–6; 2011, 88; Gramsci 2011; Kadushin 2012, 135–61; Lane and Sears 1964, 34, 40–1, 70; Merton 1968, 279–334; Noelle-Neumann 1993, 28,

120 *The experience of ideology*

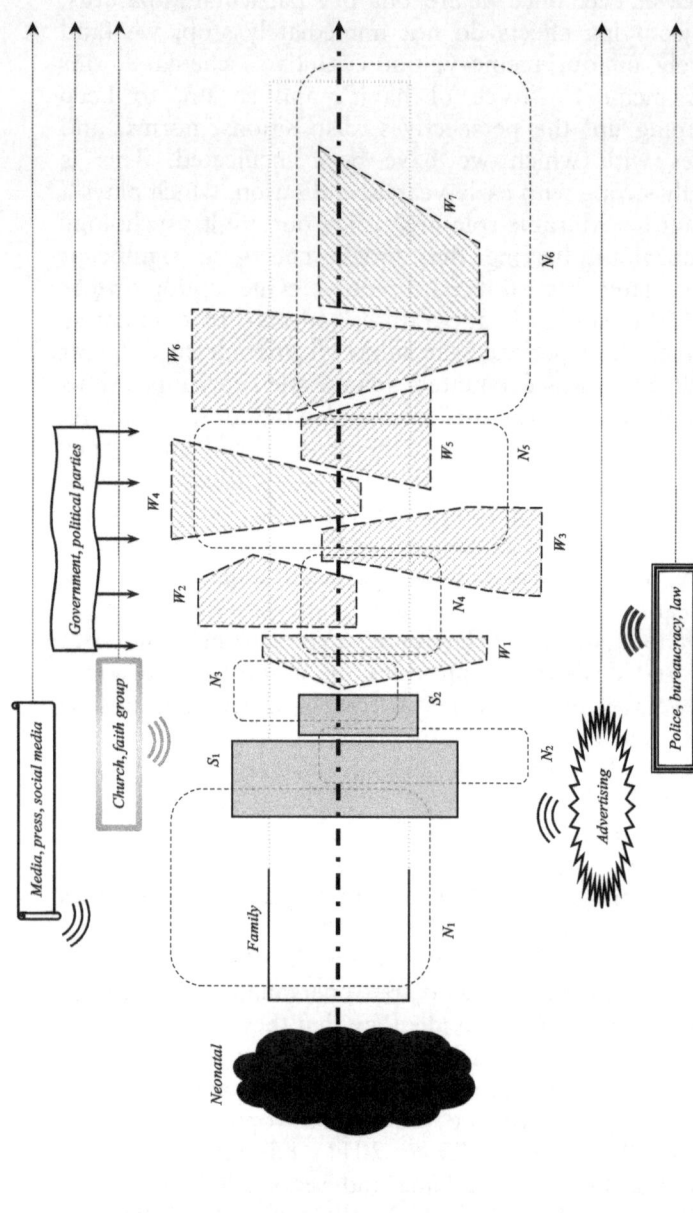

Figure 4 Ideological apparatuses' operations over the life cycle
N = neighbourhood, S = schooling, W = work
Source: Adapted from Therborn 1980, 87.

124, 169; Ostrowski 2021, 163; Zaller 1992, 41, 45–6) (see figure 5). Of course, these individuals and group members will have been ideologically subjectified in turn – and will, like us, also be continuing to have their subjectivities constantly reaffirmed to them – so their 'authorship' is to a large extent a matter of their perpetuating and 'building on' the '*status quo*' that their ideological representations had attained at the point when they first 'received' them. But the purpose of allocating 'authorship' to these subjects is not to attribute complete ideological originality to them but, rather, to identify a degree of agential responsibility for who 'runs' ideological apparatuses – which otherwise appear (somewhat fictitiously) as blank, faceless structures without anyone to 'staff' them.

'Running' here can have three possible meanings.

(1) Some of these individuals and groups 'determine' ideological apparatuses in that they explicitly formulate the ideological representations (etc.) they use to subjectify us. These are typically referred to as the *intelligentsia*: academic theorists and scientists, researchers, publishers, publicity agents, or journalists (Bernays 2011, 94, 124; Bourdieu 1977, 96–7, 116–17; Mannheim 1936, 136–46; Weber 1978, 500–18).

(2) Others 'direct' apparatuses thanks to the favourable (privileged, advantaged) position they occupy within the domination/subjection relations in the relevant social domains, which gives a pre-eminent role in constructing apparatuses and deciding what ideological representations they use. Though it has been frequently challenged for presenting an excessively binary 'have/have not' understanding of social power-relations, the most enduring collective term for these groups and individuals is the concept of the *elite*, modified to incorporate the polycephalous nature of the people it includes: high-level politicians and government officials, major business figures and trade union general secretaries, senior judges, church and faith-group leaders, school governors and university executives, or directors of arts and cultural bodies (Mills 2000; Poulantzas 1975; Therborn 2008).

(3) Insofar as 'ordinary' people perpetuate ideological representations (etc.) – which ranges from, at minimum, passively parroting the ideological content they are 'given' to a more proactive approach of 'riffing on' this content, extending its logic, or applying its implications to their 'local' circumstances – they act as 'marginal', low-level 'apparatchiks', 'operating' ideological apparatuses by providing a background *doxa* (Bourdieu 1977, 159–70; 1990, 36, 66, 68, 110–11), which offers 'bottom-up' support and reinforcement for (other) people's subjectification (as well as their own). While there are evidently significant hierarchical individual and group distinctions among members of this category, they resemble one another in their greater remove from the creation of apparatuses and the ideologies they disseminate, which in this case justifies their description as a *mass*. But the mass's 'contribution' to ideological apparatuses is far less ideologically thorough and explicit than that of the elite or the intelligentsia, acting more as a general 'tendency' that reinforces core elements of the ideology's morphology: in essence, it provides the 'mass collusion' necessary for ideologies to act as legitimating devices within society (Žižek 1994, 7).

A final additional element that 'localises' ideological apparatuses' influence for us is the effect of our social circles, which act as immediate *peer groups* that bring ideological maps and *habitus* 'close to home' (Lane and Sears 1964, 40–1; Price 1992, 58, 67). Ultimately, this complex of overlapping, mutually supporting practices by different 'contributors' to ideological apparatuses plays a major part in the *dispositifs* through which ideologies' 'hold' on society is maintained (Ostrowski 2021, 165).

Finally, while ideological apparatuses certainly reflect the prevailing ideological conceptions available in society at any given point, they are not straightforwardly monological exponents of the *same single* ideology. Here, again, the need to depart from a conception of ideology as a singular phenomenon becomes acutely apparent: it is just too much of a methodological stretch to flatten all the demonstrable contemporaneous and intertemporal differences between the apparatuses to which we are subjected into the claim that they still only 'put out' different shades of the same underlying morphological complex. Apparatuses from different social domains and at various periods of our life cycles expose us not just to separate social dimensions and sources of ideology but to multiple ideolog*ies tout court*, whose societal influence ranges from macro-ideological hegemony to micro-ideological subalternity.

Which ones they represent is heavily determined by the contingent presence and salience of 'like/other' distinctions of (1) hierarchy, (2) factionalism, and/or (3) context, which put in place particular preconditions for the emergence of a specific range (spectrum, compass) of ideologies.

(1) Contrary to Althusser's conception of ISAs as uniformly legitimating existing societal conditions, and thereby asserting the prevailing relations of domination/subjection, ideological apparatuses that fulfil this role are also met by others – '*counter-apparatuses*' – that critique and seek to discredit these conditions and challenge domination by taking the side of the subjected (Therborn 1980, 86). The rival ideologies these apparatuses formulate and disseminate take wholly opposite stances on how to 'steer' reality, encouraging us to act (respectively) to preserve and redistribute/rearrange the prevailing constellations of materials and relations: e.g., to foster 'order' and 'authority' by defending the status quo or 'progress', 'freedom', and 'equality' by reforming it.

(2) Likewise, in part through the proliferation of individual ideological apparatuses that fall into the same category (operating in the same domain, on the side of the same hierarchical group), they may easily come to foster or reflect sectional fractions within it, asserting the needs and interests of 'their' in-group at the expense of those of 'other' out-groups. Their ideologies may lie closer or further apart on major questions of how to 'steer' material and relational reality, but their key point of opposition is their meta-level pursuit of strategies to expand the comparative size of 'their' in-group's

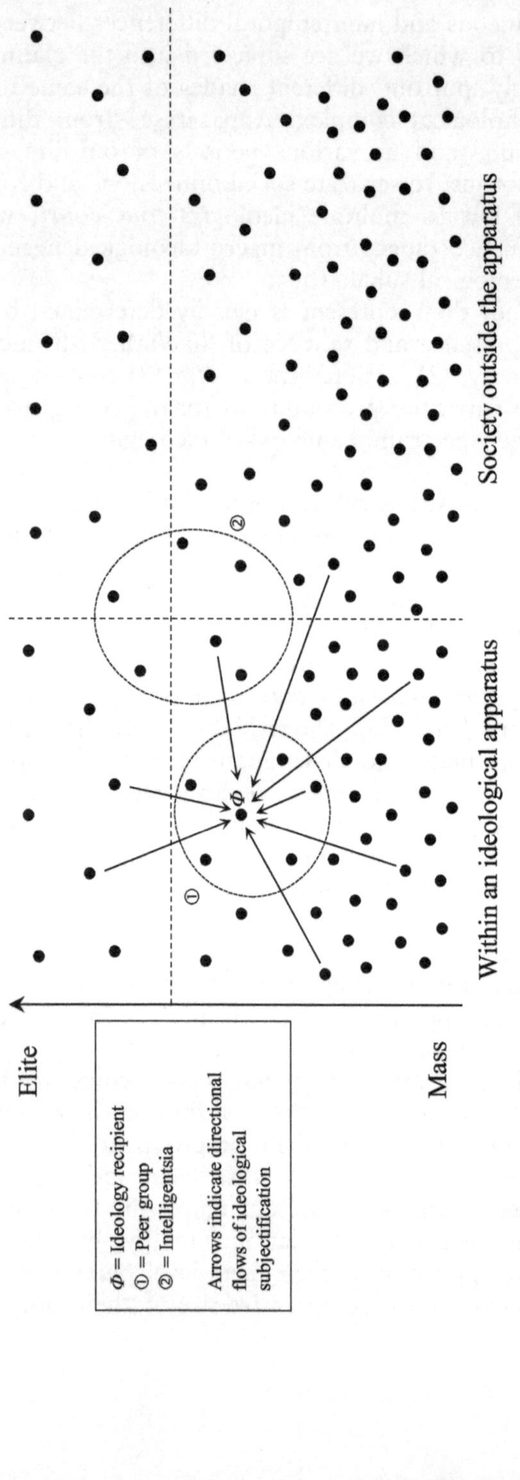

Figure 5 Sources of ideological influence
Source: Ostrowski 2021, 165.

membership as a share of the larger social category and simultaneously to shrink or eliminate that of its out-group competitors: e.g., anarchist, communist, or socialist factions battling for control of a trade union; or liberal, libertarian, and nationalist factions vying for dominance inside a conservative party.
(3) Ideological apparatuses are also highly differentiated by where they are situated and what scale of 'area' they are intended to 'cover', which at the very least leads them to reflect significant contrasts from one locus to another but also often results in their affirming the absolute priority of their 'here' over everyone else's 'there'. Whatever else their ideologies may contain, this leads them to include in their morphologies an insistence on the uniqueness and superiority of their own 'place' (and its attached social circumstances) in a way designed to outshine or denigrate any others: 'local interest' stories in regional papers versus pro-government propaganda in national tabloids; or designated 'women's', 'BAME', or 'LGBT+' networks and caucuses in companies, parties, or movements.

In each case, there may also be additional apparatuses that seek to bridge these 'like/other' distinctions by offering ideological content that stresses ways of finding commonalities between them. This can take place through 'compromise' alterations in the material/relational basis of hierarchies, 'reconciliatory' *modus vivendi* settlements that balance factions' needs and interests, or 'exchanges' that acknowledge the compatibility of intercontextual contrasts – e.g., works councils and board 'co-determination' practices, arbitration and conciliation bodies, interparty cabinets, (socialist, liberal, etc.) 'internationals', interfaith centres, or national embassies. Again, a cross-cutting immediate determinant of our ideological influences is which ideological apparatuses the members of our social circles mainly 'get' their maps and *habitus* from – e.g., family members, friends, and neighbours who 'always vote for X party', who 'know someone involved in Y', or who 'have been reading a lot about Z recently'.

§2 How ideological subjectification works

Framed in these terms, this complex of ideological apparatuses, pervasive throughout society and exercising a ubiquitous influence over our social lives, can appear to exert an oppressive, invasive force over our psyches and behaviour. Our postnatal experience is seemingly one of becoming both increasingly and irrevocably entangled in the lattices of structures expressly designed to bring about our social compliance and ever more deeply buried under an avalanche of ideological content – an image of how ideology 'works on us' that is ultimately Marxist in origin, but which also unites several later ideology theory traditions. But this form of *subjection* is not primarily what *subjectification* is meant to achieve. It is not meant to 'trap' or 'prevent' us from exercising our agency but, rather, 'mould' the faculties that underpin it in such a way that our conformity to ideology – our 'use' of it – becomes 'second nature' to us. We consciously accept and 'join in with' our subjectification, 'helping it along' by 'practising' and 'copying' our ideological examples through *'mimesis'* ('imitation') (Bourdieu 1977, 26, 96, 116, 125, 138, 167; 1990, 73). When we 'overwrite' our 'pre-ideological' psychology and behaviours and adopt the new ones that ideology is telling us we 'should have', the point of subjectification is for our 'new ways' to become reflexive, instinctive, and unconscious as rapidly as possible. In our everyday lived experience, we are not meant to (and typically do not) 'come up against' the restrictions ideology imposes on our psychological and behavioural engagement with reality. Because we have internalised our ideological 'role', we already automatically 'stay within' our ideological 'parameters': we are quite happily ensconced in our acquired vantage-points, our eyes have become accustomed to our lenses, our primers are well thumbed, we know the lines in our scripts 'backwards', we are familiar with our design plans, and we can dextrously 'power through' our simulations. In light of this, past the early-years stage of ideological subjectification (education, raising, etc.), and beyond an initial 'orientation period' once we start to be subjectified by a new apparatus, apparatuses do not need to be omnipresent and can recede into a far more background presence. Typically, they step in only 'at the margins', *in extremis*, in cases where our ideological subjectivity needs 'shoring up' – specifically, when we threaten to 'go wrong'. For the most part, we can be left to *self-subjectify* ideologically by merely ensuring that we faithfully 'stick to', build on, and act 'in the spirit of' the perceptions, habits, etc., with which we have been inculcated. The memory of our previous subjectification, bolstered by our awareness of the existence of ideological apparatuses that will 'step in' if they have to, is enough to keep us doing so most of the time. In other words, apparatuses operate on a 'carceral' (prison-like) model only in marginal situations; most of the time, their effects on individual psychology and behaviour are far more 'panopticist' (Foucault 1977).

Our experience of ideological subjectification is rarely that we are directly, blatantly 'belaboured' by self-declared ideological apparatuses in a formal, institutional sense. Instead, most of it is heavily skewed towards indirect, subtle 'nudges' that reach us more or less circuitously, often in forms that do not necessarily present as ideological (Hausman and Welch 2010; Kosters and van der Heijden 2015; Lepenies and Małecka 2015; Mols et al. 2015). In both cases, we encounter moments of subjectification in the form of ideological *cues* (McLuhan 1964; Zaller 1992, 45, 47): 'nuggets' of information in the form of messages that encode specific ideological content drawn from aspects of a given ideology's map and/or *habitus*. These cues can be compared on a number of dimensions. First, in the amount of ideological content they embed, or what proportion of 'its' ideology's morphology each cue tries to deliver: isolated elements by themselves or in relation to others, focusing only on core elements or also including more adjacent/peripheral content, and so on. At one polar extreme, cues can be *macroscopic*: fully elaborated, 'all-purpose' statements containing all (or as many as possible) of an ideology's constitutive morphological elements, such as philosophical 'grand theories', party programmes or manifestos, scriptural exegeses (e.g., Christian biblical, Jewish *Mishnah*, or Islamic *Tafsīr* commentaries, Hindu *Smṛti* texts, and Buddhist *vinayas*), or constitutional preambles. These are the closest that ideological cues come to exhibiting the full degree of comprehensiveness, completeness, and correctness to which ideologies lay claim; macroscopic cues are intended to 'spell out' the full contours of the ideology's map and *habitus*, leaving nothing to our imaginations. At the other extreme, they can be *microscopic*: selected 'extracts' tailored to specific aspects of our psychology or behaviour, containing only the 'bare minimum' of an ideology's morphological elements that are relevant in a given situation, as with 'government guidelines', 'health tips', 'honours systems', media awards, 'good marks', or 'tellings-off'. With these, the aim is not to demonstrate the ideology's claims through the sheer 'weight' of their substantive content but to pinpoint precisely the 'right' part(s) of its ideological map and *habitus* to 'prove' to us that the ideology has all situations (and specifically *this* situation) 'covered'. As with all such binaries, most cues lie at a *mesoscopic* level somewhere in between these two extremes, which do not display the ideology in its fullest extent but are more fully elaborated than just situation-specific 'pointers' – offering a 'mid-range magnification' that gives us the sense of a 'bigger picture' or 'there being more to it' than just the situation at hand, as a kind of justification-by-insinuation (Freeden 2003, 65).

Second, cues vary in how frequently they are designed to be deployed, which also has an effect on the level of morphological detail they go into: a general overview or more precise stipulation, designed to trigger immediate understanding or only build it up incrementally over time. Some cues are conceived as *one-shot* occurrences, which deliver as much information as possible in one 'go' (in one place, one format, at one time) about what elements the ideology contains, what meaning it gives them, and how they are combined and arranged: textbooks, national 'declarations', sacred texts, keynote lectures and speeches, *'magnum opus'* monographs. In this form, cues go out of their way to pre-empt any problems that the psychological and behavioural instructions they give us might incur – e.g., when we 'transfer' them from one domain to another or over the course of our life cycles – because the underlying ideology is not thick or robust enough in certain areas, and to foreclose as many possible avenues of ideological contestation as they can predict. Others, by contrast, work on the principle of *frequent repetition* and try to deliver their information over as large and diverse a number of 'goes' (places, formats, times) as possible, reinforcing one another and altogether 'adding up to' a 'picture' of the ideology that lies 'behind' them: rote-learning for tests and exercises, 'thoughts for the day', advertising posters and commercials, daily 'op-eds' and news headlines, or campaign slogans. This form of ideological dissemination is meant to be flexible and cumulative, designed to ensure that we are never too far 'out of reach' of reminders to keep us 'in line' and allowing us to 'get used to' the ideology's psychological and behavioural demands quasi-impressionistically as its definition emerges across contexts and over time. Again, many cues fall in between 'one-off' and 'constant' provision and are delivered *periodically* – not quite as encyclopaedic or exhaustive 'grand statements' but more intermittently, uniquely, and thoroughly than as a 'production-line' of rote-learning increments.

Finally, cues differ in how far they present themselves as statements of (an) ideology at all, in the sense of whether they make any reference to its morphological content: 'talking about' particular dispositions, norms, etc., or more presenting a 'just so story' of reality *tout court*. At one end, some are *overtly* ideological and do not try to hide that they are particular ways of representing the world, bracketed under specific families and traditions labelled as more or less well-established 'isms': texts on ideologies ('X-ism', 'theory of Y', 'doctrine of Z', etc.), statements by politicians and activists, commentary by 'paid contributors', religious symbols (Hindu *auṃ* and *sri chakra yantra*, Christian crucifix, Jewish 'star of David' and *menorah*, Islamic crescent, etc.), flags and rosettes or other coloured items (e.g., socialist/communist red, conservative blue, anarchist black, fascist brown, liberal yellow, Christian-democratic or libertarian orange, feminist or queer pink/purple, ecological or Islamic green). These explicitly tie their content – no matter how macroscopic/microscopic or one-shot/repeated – linguistically and semiotically by connotation to their 'wider' ideological *hinterland*. They do not leave any doubt about what sociological bases of hierarchy, factionalism, or contextual specificity underpin their emergence and social aspirations, and they often self-categorise in contradistinction to other ways of representing the world in ideological 'spectrum' or 'compass' space. At the other end, cues can be *covertly* ideological, framed in a way that denies or downplays (1) their particularity, often by presenting as 'the only' way to represent the world to which 'there is no alternative', and (2) their connection to specific families and traditions, usually by claiming to be 'non-ideological': 'common-sense' criticism, statistical presentations, 'fact-finding', 'impartial' expert opinion, 'fashion statements', purchasing options. Here, there is no link to any ideological *hinterland* but instead explicit attempts to 'naturalise' the cues' content – however macroscopic/microscopic or one-shot/repeated – by tying it to either discourse 'in general' or discursive forms that are presented as notionally ideologically 'neutral' (e.g., 'basic maths', 'statistics', 'science', 'philosophy', 'literature'). They are silent about the causal relevance of different sociological 'like/other' distinctions, in favour of claiming universality in their social aspirations (e.g., *Allerweltspartei*, cosmopolitanism), and they refuse to self-categorise in 'spectrum' or 'compass' terms, claiming to be 'realistic', 'pragmatic', or 'cross/non-partisan'. As before, many ideological cues lie in a liminal *semi-overt* space between these overt and covert extremes: they do not boast about their affiliations to any particular ideological family or tradition in 'ism' terms, but nor do they try to claim not to have any, leaving their *hinterland* to remain as a tacit connotation lurking behind their substantive content.

§3 The limitations of ideology

In principle, the upshot of the many intersecting layers of ideological subjectification is that we are 'set for life', in ideological terms, in our psychological and behavioural engagement with reality. To summarise: we are given a map full of ideas to represent chaotic, self-contradictory reality; we are given a *habitus* derived from these ideas, whose elements shape and guide every facet of our experience of reality, how we think and feel about it, how we act towards and within it. The combination and arrangement of these ideas and elements can be more or less thick and more or less robust, which makes the 'picture' of our engagement with our surroundings more or less simple and consistent – and distinguished by the claim that it gives a 'full picture' that is all we need to come to terms with reality. The last 200 years have seen several waves of significant expansion in the synchronic and diachronic range of the 'full pictures' we have available to us, to keep pace with the proliferation of social hierarchies, factions, and contexts brought about by tendencies towards increasing global complexity and differentiation. We have a prodigious wealth of ideologies to choose from, and precise ways to categorise ourselves in relation to one another. The same increase in complexity and differentiation has created a growing range of sophisticated apparatuses with the task of cultivating the ideological subjectivity we need to escape our infantile stance towards reality and instinctively 'use' our ideological maps and *habitus* in our psychology and our behaviour – a subjectivity they 'remind' us of periodically over the course of our lives. From the side of ideology, there is nothing else that it can offer us – and nothing more that we need – in order to join in with the processes of 'navigating' and 'steering' reality as fully 'fleshed-out' participants.

The one remaining question we still have to consider is what determines whether ideology and ideological subjectification succeeds or fails to achieve this outcome – where we remain only partly 'fleshed-out' and are not perfectly subjectified into the 'role' ('our' particular) ideology defines for us. There are six factors that can play such a determinant role, the first three of which represent serious breakdown risks in the subjectification process. The most fundamental is how amenable or resistant we are to adopting the psychology and behaviour that ideology 'expects' of us. This can manifest as, respectively, enthusiastic willingness versus outraged refusal to 'use' the map and *habitus* with which ideology provides us: whether we dutifully take on the mindsets, habits, and worldviews it is trying to 'pitch' to us, or whether we try to 'negotiate' or 'oppose' them with alternatives of our own devising (Hall 1973, 1980). Refusal can have several causes. Due to a mixture of genetic attributes and prior attempts at socialisation, we may lack the openness to accept ideological cues or the conscientiousness to absorb them or the competence and dexterity to apply their content in our actions. This can start in the very earliest years of our lives, caused by insufficient prosocial early-years education, cold, erratic, or inattentive parenting, experience of criminality, or physical abuse and expresses itself as 'disruptive behaviour', 'oppositional defiance', or other 'conduct disorders' (Gelhorn et al. 2005; Latimer et al. 2012; Murray and Farrington 2010; White and Renk 2012). It may be additionally exacerbated by dysfunction within our ideological apparatuses, such as instability (e.g., parental stress and conflict, family poverty, adoption or separation, school delinquency), which can leave gaps in their efforts to subjectify us, or a skew towards heavy-handed negative dimensions of subjectification rather than more light-touch or positive alternatives. Such dysfunction is often associated with ideological 'overload', which happens when we receive cues that are explicitly ideological but not tailored to our needs or drilled into us well enough to actually help guide our 'normal' psychology and behaviour – e.g., loud, generic propaganda or mass advertising that vapidly 'talks over our heads' – which simply makes us find them off-putting. If this means that we fail to adopt the ideologies that these cues are trying to 'sell' us, this can foster a contrarian mindset in us, where we define our subjectivity precisely in opposition to the ideological tendencies with which we are routinely confronted and become susceptible to ideologies that define themselves in similarly rejectionist terms (e.g., countercultures, extremism) (Nucci 2014).

A closely related factor is whether or not there is any (residual) tension between our subjective and objective ideological positions. The question here is whether the ideological map and *habitus* we 'use' fit neatly, or sit drastically at odds, with those 'used' by others around us: whether how we see the world and carry out our everyday tasks within it tallies with the way expected of us (and others like us), or whether we find ourselves having to 'carve our own path' in order to 'stay true' to who we 'really' are and how we see ourselves. Again, there are several potential reasons why such 'at odds'-ness might come about. We may have several ineliminable, irreducible mental or physical attributes that a prevailing ideology does not consider or even tries to erase in its conception of subjecthood, or we may lack other attributes that the same ideology emphasises or prizes highly: we can never quite get ourselves to think and feel the same way other people do about (e.g.) family drama or celebrity gossip; our skin and hair may be the 'wrong colour' or 'wrong texture' for the available range of beauty products; or we cannot find anyone else around us who is as good as we are at climbing trees and having a kickabout or as interested as we are in playing an instrument or reading poetry. This is made worse by the 'averaging' tendencies of ideological apparatuses, which try to 'force' all of us into a 'one size fits all' subjectivity that is always going to be far more 'suited' to – and, in fact, is potentially based on – some people's psychology and behaviour than others'. Such omissions become especially problematic when subjectification processes rely on highly elaborated cues that try to hide their ideological nature, which claim to express the 'full extent' of 'the only possible' account of the attributes we can have and how we can engage with social phenomena, and which imply that anyone who is not fully 'captured' by this account is to that extent 'unnatural' and 'out of place' in society. Where this ideological tension is not reconciled, the effect for us as individuals is social dislocation or disjunction, where our subjectivity sets us on a collision course with the ideological formations in our surroundings. This leaves us misrecognised and marginalised by them, partly 'trapped outside' and ostracised, and vulnerable to the mental and physical trauma of intense (violent, targeted, incessant) subjectification attempts.

The third core factor is how far reality matches or deviates from how it is ideologically represented to us. We can measure this by whether our ideological map and *habitus* are actually 'useful' in helping us 'make sense' of our surroundings: whether we can go through life in our environments insouciantly and unscathed based purely on the 'nudges' and instructions ideology gives us about it, or whether anything remains 'uncharted', 'out of focus', or 'hidden from view', and we are forced to improvise to avoid bumping into objects in our 'blind spots'. Perhaps the most enduring risk to ideological subjectification is that, thanks to our many ongoing and iterative interactions with a host of social phenomena and events, and constant stochastic development in the composition and constellation of the materials and relations that constitute reality, we may at any point encounter something 'weird' that ideology insists 'should not be there': an experience we find strangely titillating or nauseating; a person or object that seems jarringly 'out of place'; or a catastrophic, cataclysmic, or miraculous event that is so unforeseen (and unforeseeable) as to defy explanation (Badiou 2005; Fisher 2017). This is not helped by the 'ploughing-ahead' tendency of ideological apparatuses, which continue trying to 'prepare' us for the familiar, well-established 'reading' of reality (and our engagement with it) even if it jars with our actual experience and exhibit considerable 'lag' before an 'authorial' change to the representations they are disseminating fully filters through them. As with the last factor, this tendency becomes particularly toxic if it relies on a mixture of fully developed and purportedly 'non-ideological' cues, which combine to frame anything that their (notionally complete and 'neutral') content 'leaves out' as an 'impossible anomaly'. If it proves infeasible to overcome such ideological discrepancies, we experience a critical rupture, in which our subjectivity is either forcibly detached from the ideological formations we have swirling unhelpfully around us, or we continue to cleave to one or other of them at the cost of condemning ourselves to social ineffectuality.

The next two determinant factors are contingent risks that depend on the diversity and mutual distinctness of the ideologies available in our given societal context. One is how broad or narrow a variety of alternative sources of ideology we are exposed to. This affects whether the multitude of competing individuals and groups who claim the 'authority' to influence our ideological maps and *habitus* are more convergent or in conflict with one another: whether we take the lead impressionably in how we think, feel, and act from an overbearing parent, a particularly inspiring teacher, a powerful media magnate, or a charismatic local preacher, or whether we find ourselves 'collating' a host of suggestions and pieces of guidance that do not overlap with one another at all. We may enjoy the company of a large and ideologically highly disparate set of social circles thanks to the various domains of social activity in which we are engaged – further refined by the hierarchies and contexts in which we are situated. This may 'pull' our subjectivity in contrary directions rather than reinforcing it through a narrower set of cues with consistent content: friends and colleagues from many 'walks of life', active in a wide range of careers (teaching, nursing, civil service, estate agency, law), representing a diverse array of ethnic backgrounds, genders, sexual preferences, etc., with very different social identities, interests, needs, and incentives as a result. In turn, this is exacerbated by cases of persistent conflict and lack of a clear epistemic hierarchy among the various 'personnel' in particular ideological apparatuses, especially where their strategy of ideological authorship and dissemination rests on overturning rather than building on the activities of other (previous or parallel) apparatuses and sources: i.e., whether we are expected to respond to a 'new-fangled' consensus among the intelligentsia, the passing whims of the elite, or the latest 'moral panic' amplified by the 'echo-chamber' of the mass. Where such conflict takes the form of competing barrages of repeated cues that offer us only glimpses of fragmentary idea-extracts or how to apply them, we are confronted with a series of 'mixed messages'; these prevent us from seeing the 'bigger picture' that could help us properly contextualise and navigate the more situation-specific ideological injunctions. If the set of ideological sources is too amorphous, this paralyses us in our thinking, feelings, and action, and our subjectivity becomes torn between many different 'authorial' interpretations of the available ideological formations. We become liable to have a less precise grasp on the psychological and behavioural engagement expected of us, become more hesitant in carrying it out, and *in extremis* we may evade and withdraw from our social 'obligations'.

The other determinant is the range of cross-cutting alternative ideologies that are trying to influence our psychology and behaviour at any given time. This is one of the strongest factors in our subjectification, as the incidence of several rival ideologies – and, given the trends of societal development, an ever growing number of ideological 'options' – presents us with multiple alternative maps and *habitus*, each of which is ostensibly 'the (only) one' we are supposed to 'use': we may encounter a lot of mutually reinforcing signals pushing us towards (e.g.) casual bigotry, instinctive patriotism, studying a 'mathsy' subject at university, or 'going to work in the City', or we can face a plethora of attacks on these 'foregone conclusions' from the side of humanist romanticism, hard-line Marxism, theological traditionalism, or cosmopolitan liberalism. Thanks to our particular demographic characteristics, coupled with our places in specific contexts and positions within hierarchies across multiple social domains, we are confronted with a number of ideologies that may be factionally divided, but which can all more or less comparably 'speak to' our situation within social reality – which provides us with multiple unrelated (and potentially incommensurable) subjectivities we can adopt. This is amplified by ideological discontinuity between and even within ideological apparatuses, either successively (over our life cycles) or in parallel (across different domains), where the processes of subjectification for any of these ideologies fail to overcome definitively the 'hold' of the other ideological subjectivities, leaving unresolved clashes between the psychology and behaviour each of them expects from us: e.g., having one parent who is devoutly religious while the other is a resolute atheist; moving from an 'old-fashioned' private school to a progressive 'red brick' university; migrating between countries and across continents. Here, we may also be drawn into an 'arms race' of incessant cues that are heavily saturated with the terminology of social distinctions, and which seek to delegitimise other rival subjectivities by accentuating their immanent inconsistencies and deficiencies and downplaying any areas of mutual compatibility. Where these ideologies are too orthogonal, we are forced to internalise ideological social polarisation, where our subjectivity itself becomes the object of essential contestation between the various rival ideological formations vying for our support. This can leave us diffident, torn, and unable to commit definitively to any of the psychological and behavioural requirements 'on offer', while also still exposed to the 'essentialising' ideological predations from different sides (Butler 1988; Phillips 2010).

Finally, how strongly these previous factors affect us depends on how much of an opportunity we have to 'process' consciously our (successful or failed) subjectification. The step from acquiring an ideological map and *habitus* from cues to becoming proficient at 'using' them takes a variable amount of time and effort. This may allow complications arising from contrarianism, dislocation, ruptures, paralysis, and polarisation to 'creep in' and disrupt our subjectification process: we may face immediate pressure to 'deliver' on our ideologically expected tasks and outlooks, leaving us 'playing catch-up' and fighting just to 'stay afloat' in the subjectivities with which we have been inculcated, or we may end up 'ahead of the (learning) curve' and thus able to 'detach' somewhat from apparatuses' efforts to subjectify us. Here, a great deal depends on how much 'spare capacity' we have 'left over' in our mental faculties to indulge in ideological reflection and experimentation – i.e., self-oriented argumentation and persuasion, criticism and justification (Billig 1991) – 'for its own sake', after we have already 'used up' the effort required to carry out our 'everyday' thinking, feeling, and action as mandated by our subjectivities. In part, this benefits from apparatuses being 'set up' in a more 'subdued', even 'patchy' way that allows us 'breathing space' and temporary 'respite' from ideological subjectification processes, rather than delivering relentless, omnipresent 'blanket coverage' for every aspect of their social activity. Rather than a stream of relentless microscopic details, this ideological 'set-up' relies on more intermittent fuller accounts that give us a worldview statement we can linger over and get 'stuck into', allowing us to think back over our experiences, ask (and where possible answer) 'deep and meaningful' questions of ourselves and of others at a level closer to that of intelligentsia-type ideological production than mass ideological consumption. The more scope we have to 'work through' the map (and other elements) with which we have been inculcated, the more we become able to 'take ownership' of our ideological position. We adjudicate between different psychological and behavioural expectations, 'take control' of decisive moments of ideological (de)contestation and co-option, and thus consciously accept, reject, or (often) hybridise different subjectification processes to 'build' our 'own' subjectivity.

Each of these factors inhibits the success or provokes the outright failure of ideological subjectification. Yet while they are certainly mutually reinforcing, and often take place in tandem, not all of them necessarily have to be present at the same time for this to happen. The effect of any one of them by itself is enough to create a category of subjects who do not (entirely, or at all) conform to (some, or any) ideologies' representations of social reality, and who are minded to question the meanings encoded in the ideological cues circulating in society. This, of course, makes these representations by definition imperfect, endangering above all their claims to completeness and correctness. In this way, these instances of ideological failure or even incomplete ideological success 'unmask' the particular representation of reality that a particular ideology is trying to inculcate in us. But they do not do so immediately. First and foremost, they 'cast doubt' on the ideology, prompting us either (1) to block out and explain away any challenges to the overall ideological 'picture' as 'blips', 'glitches in the Matrix', or even 'exceptions that prove the rule', which do not undermine its fundamental rightness and usefulness, or (2) individually or collectively to 'adjust' our ideological positions to accommodate the challenging factors as merely new developments within the ideology's tradition. But in particularly extreme cases of failure, such as when several of these factors are 'in play', neither of these responses is enough, because it is simply no longer tenable for us to use the given ideology to inform how we 'navigate' and 'steer' reality – i.e., the ideology simply no longer 'does what it is meant to do'. We experience this as anything ranging from gradual disenchantment with our prior ideological position to a sudden shock of revelation. 'Unmasking' exposes the limitations and the existential falsity of the given ideology's claims to comprehensiveness, completeness, and correctness, as well as its morphological inadequacy – both in its content as well as in its construction. But it also 'pulls back the curtain' on the mechanics of ideology. It reveals that ideology is 'merely' a vantage-point, lens, primer, script, etc., rather than a 'true' statement of where we are located among social phenomena, what we can see, how we can act, and so on. It also 'exposes' the existence of ideological apparatuses as well as the lines connecting their 'authors' to us as 'recipients' of the ideological maps they have formulated.

There are several possible outcomes of ideological subjectification failing by being 'unmasked' in this way. In the first

The experience of ideology 139

instance, as our prior ideological position is eroded, this increasingly forces us to confront the aspects of 'pure' reality that defy the representations, distinctions, simplifications, points of reference, explanations, etc., that this position offered us – in other words, to confront the 'real' reason for our ideological disenchantment. But by definition, having 'lost' our ideology, we now no longer have the means we need to make chaotic and contradictory reality appear to us in a way that 'makes sense'. Insofar as we can even confront the discomforting 'non-sense' of 'pure' reality, it appears to us as an unsymbolised, unrepresented 'spectral supplement' that alludes to the real 'kernel' that caused the breakdown in our past subjectification; this in turn 'haunts' us with persistent, lingering attempts to capture this kernel via (ineffectual) ideological representations, which we can never quite fully shake off (Derrida 1994; Žižek 1994). Depending on the speed with which the unmasking has taken place, we are led to engage in a more or less frantic 'grasping for straws' as we look for an alternative, 'better' set of representations that can replace the ones we relied on previously – specifically, or so we hope, a set of representations that does not suffer from the 'gaps' of our last ideology, so that we can continue (*some*how, *any*how) to be able to 'navigate' and 'steer' reality *at all*.

Here, there are two possible options. Either we cast out on our own and try to come up with a new ideological map of reality entirely by ourselves, which essentially returns us to (a parodic imitation of) our infantile 'fantasmatic' psychology, 'unguided' play behaviour, and transgressive '*jouissance*'. Or, far more commonly, we 'seek harbour' (even if only temporarily) in one of the other ready-made alternative ideologies (strands, variants, families) available in our contexts. This, in essence, is what ideological change amounts to: replacing one 'mask' with another (Howarth et al. 2000, 4, 9; Laclau 1997, 299; Norval 2000, 333; Žižek 1994, 3, 6–7, 11, 21, 25) in a process resembling something in between Ebenezer Scrooge's (self-)reinvention after his three ghostly Christmas visitations and a straightforward 'Damascene conversion'. The alternative to this – i.e., delaying or avoiding replacing the old ideological 'mask' over reality with a new one – carries the risk of sliding into a situation where we start to find reality more and more confusing, overwhelming, disorienting, incomprehensible, and meaningless. If this persists, we become increasingly unsure of how to feel, think, or act, which induces a form of directionlessness or *anomie* (Durkheim 1893, 482, 491): a mismatch, or 'derangement', between the 'authentic' dispositions, norms, practices, etc., we use at our discretion to engage with reality and (any or all of) those circulating in society as ideological cues. We experience *anomie* psychologically as panic, despair, and horror; we experience it behaviourally as paralysis and ineffectuality. If left in place, it imposes profound individual and collective costs on us: dislocation, dysfunction, breakdown, *in extremis* (social or literal) death. We cannot survive in a world without meaning, and we rely on ideology to provide this meaning *even if* this means taking into account the possibility that *no specific individual* ideology has the ability to deliver meaningfulness in perpetuity. Or, to put it another way: ideolog*ies* may change, but ideology endures.

6
The dimensions of ideology studies

The cumulative insights of analytical engagements with the concept of 'ideology' from across the spectrum of social research methods and approaches have led to a number of 'leaps forward' in our understanding of how we 'recount' or 'tell' ideas. We have learned to see them as more or less thick and robust map-like representations of reality, manifesting in a series of elements that guide our psychology and behaviour, which claim to be the only full and right way to address the 'big questions' of our experience. These ideological maps come in a growing range of parallel families, each with its own tradition of morphological development, which are prompted by the incidence of hierarchical differences and factionalism within a given cultural context and which can be categorised according to various dimensions of comparison. Lastly, we 'hold' these maps thanks to becoming constituted as ideological subjects by a series of apparatuses spread across society which disseminate ideological cues to us over the course of our lives – although this process also has its limitations, which creates space for us to change or entirely lose our ideological 'positions'. But, despite these significant advances in the study of ideology, 'ideology studies' as a discrete area of social research is still only just on the cusp of becoming a subfield in its own right. It has lagged behind other subdisciplines and subfields that began as passing minor thematic considerations in social theory or social science and have since 'declared autonomy' and enjoyed rich intellectual evolutions in their own right – class theory, democratic theory, media studies and mediology, or opinion polling research. Moreover, in the absence of a single, firmly established subdiscipline of ideology studies, a number of competing 'study of ideologies' subfields have emerged in the space where it ought to be, examining more or less similar and overlapping aspects of different social groups, social movements, or schools of social thought: e.g., feminism, sex, and gender studies and populism studies (1960s–); critical race theory, anti-, de-, and postcolonial studies (1970s–); and nationalism studies and queer studies (1980s–).

It is not hard to pin the blame for this on the inherent duality between pejorative and non-pejorative views of ideology – led by their Marxisant and political-scientific champions – neither of which seems remotely inclined to cede its claim to analytical primacy. Instead, the civil war of terminological (de)contestation has waged on, with the spoils of victory swinging from one side to the other (as outlined in chapter 1). The upshot for the contemporary 'state of play' in ideology studies is a kind of stalemate: a considerable degree of pluralism, with no school obviously hegemonic, and all of them largely content to let others analyse ideology in their own preferred way. Both orthodox and revised variants of 'older' approaches coexist freely and somewhat interchangeably with more modern ones: across monographs, journal articles, and other contributions, Marxists and post-Marxists, neo-Gramscians and Althusserians, Foucauldians and Frankfurt Schoolers nestle alongside a wealth of scholarship influenced by Arendt and Bourdieu, Laclau and Mouffe, Žižek, Butler, and Freeden. The 'state of the subdiscipline' is thus a parcelised patchwork of methodological fiefdoms: academic researchers who self-identify as 'ideology theorists' tend to occupy lone positions within most social-scientific or sociological departments and faculties, and their particular orientations are heavily influenced by or subsumed within the prevailing institutional trends and priorities for the methods and foci of social research. The main organs of ideology studies so far have also refused to impose any definitional constraints or centralised 'steer' on ideology research but have largely been willing to follow the trends in the 'study of ideologies' and other cognate social research subfields to see where they lead. Indeed, the prevailing consensus within ideology studies so far has been that this pluralism has largely suited and been beneficial to fostering the nuance and diversity of individual ideology theorists' research outputs.

But as the 'rediscovery' of ideology as an analytical concept since the 1980s has become embedded as a burgeoning *renaissance* in dedicated ideological research, ideology studies is on the threshold of entering a new phase. Its consolidation and growth is being fostered by the institutionalisation and development of new ideology research initiatives and networks, leading to an ever clearer emergence of ideology studies as an entity. This raises inevitable questions about the definition of 'ideology and its study today'. Even if it is not quite there yet, by force of its own analysis, 'ideologology' can expect to face growing pressure to self-decontest through an interminable succession of 'forks in the road' of 'ruling in' versus 'ruling out', forced choices between preserving its current pluralism or succumbing to a conceptual equivalent of the 'iron law of oligarchy'. In either case, establishment of an 'ideology studies' subdiscipline changes the nature of how to conceptualise the coexistence between different approaches: 'coming at' the concept of ideology 'from different angles' shifts subtly from a coinciding shared focus of analysis (ideology) in different 'corners' of social research to the presence of rival neighbouring 'spiritual families' and (variously) *longue-durée* traditions of 'ideologology'.

The logical extension of this is that the availability of multiple 'options' within the overall construct of ideology studies creates ample opportunities for 'ideologological' hybridisation as researchers encounter and learn from points of useful synergy between different approaches. The long-standing 'Cold War' between Marxisant and political-scientific approaches is starting to become at the same time marginalised and extensively superseded, as ideology theorists increasingly draw inspiration from disciplinary sources (e.g., anthropology, history, or media analysis) untouched by this debate. Such hybridisation is a direct equivalent of the emergence of ideological hybrids from substantive contact and permeation between different 'source' ideologies, which has (at least for the time being) taken on a wholly different geopolitical, geoeconomic, and geocultural significance since the end of the US–USSR bipolarity. It is also, tellingly, already the case within the existing roster of ideology theory approaches: for instance, Marx and Freud were both influential in different ways (and in combination with other sources) for the Frankfurt School and Althusser, whose approach in turn was taken in different directions by Foucault and Deleuze and Guattari; meanwhile, Althusser's gloss on Gramsci and Lacan has equally influenced Žižek, Butler, and Laclau and Mouffe, although Žižek shifts in a more Hegelian direction while the others are closer to Foucault, Derrida, and in Butler's case the Frankfurt School and the feminist tradition. We are just starting to see the first signs of a 'new wave' of hybridisations, albeit currently still largely contained within analyses of specific ideologies.

In this light, it is important to get a sense of the methodological contours of ideology studies – what we might call the morphology of 'ideologology'. The sources of the various approaches to ideological analysis are a range of disciplines and subdisciplines within the social sciences and humanities, which have cultivated approaches that are relevant and adjacent to the study of ideology for a greater or lesser period of time within their own internal trajectories. At their epicentre are a group of perhaps the most self-consciously ideology-theoretic approaches, all of which are associated with *social and political theory*, and which focus on the relationship of ideas and meanings to contextual distributions and arrangements of political and economic power. As ideology studies matures into a subdiscipline, it is to be expected that social-theoretic and political-theoretic analysis will continue to lie at its core. But, at the same time, this analysis also draws extensively on inputs from other subdisciplines and subfields where these overlap with social and political theory's assumptions, priorities, and frameworks of analysis. The next most significant are approaches drawn from *intellectual history* and *linguistics*, which play a leading role in studying ideological traditions at different timescales and in relating ideas and texts to the way language itself acts as an instrument of social power. Closely related to these are approaches borrowed from a subdiscipline that previously proved more successful in carving out an autonomous space in social research, that of *communication studies*, which broadens the focus onto non-textual and non-linguistic expression of ideas. Lastly, ideology studies also relies on the insights generated by the contemporary approaches to two major subdisciplines whose foci used to be intimately connected to ideology theory before the early to mid-1900s. One is *social psychology*, which ties ideology to the various cognitive traits and felt experiences that shape how we formulate ideas and arguments; the other is *comparative political science*, which connects the concept to the specific ways in which we can express our social views in contemporary (democratic) political institutions.

§1 The social- and political-theoretical epicentre

To the limited degree that it is possible to speak of 'dominant' approaches to ideology studies, three of the ones that fit this description best are housed within social and political theory. The first of these is *conceptual morphology*, which sees ideology as a framework of distinctive patterned conceptual configurations that allow us to understand the social (specifically, political) world (Freeden 1996, 2013). As one of the approaches at the forefront of the turn towards vernacular thinking and expression, it looks for ideology in explicit political statements – i.e., statements geared towards 'providing and controlling plans for public policy' and 'justifying, contesting, or changing the social and political arrangements and processes of a political community' – by people in a variety of political roles, from professional politicians and journalists to grassroots activists and voters, of course alongside the theoretical output of intellectuals. It sees ideologies as mutually distinct and distinctive patterned configurations of concepts (e.g., liberty, equality, order, security, democracy, rights), which are created out of indeterminate, unlimited possible combinations by processes of 'essential decontestation' that impose specific meanings on these concepts and build them into contingent vocabularies governed by quasi-grammatical rules. These ideologies compete for control of the public language we use to represent, establish, maintain, and transform our societal (especially political) arrangements by thematising certain concepts as central to 'making sense' of society and contesting how their rivals have decontested these concepts' social meaning and significance. When examining ideological sources, the conceptual morphologist focuses on the structural arrangement (i.e., position, configuration) of the ideology's concepts, in particular how this affects their explicit meaning and implicit connotations through their mutual logical and cultural 'adjacency' – i.e., their necessary semantic connection as part of concretising each concept's meaning and their cultural contextualisation within temporally and spatially circumscribed prevailing practices, social institutions, systemic ethical theories, or societal technologies. This casts them in the role of an interpretative (antipositivist) sociologist of ideas, who aims to generate a '*Verstehen*' ('understanding' from the other's perspective) of the constellations of meaning(s) that undergird our political views and worldviews by distilling out the essential political ideas that frame how we think and express ourselves. Overall, conceptual morphology aims to produce a concise map of the combinations and arrangements of ideas that make up an ideology and their changing character over time, in order to discover which of its features are 'ineliminable' constants and which are more 'optional' and variable.

The second of these 'core' approaches is the modern form of *ideology critique*, which keeps alive the direct lineage via the Frankfurt School and Lukács back to Marx and Engels, and which maintains the view of ideology as an illusion that legitimates social arrangements by 'masking' relations of domination/subjection (Geuss 1981; Fisher 2009; Jaeggi 2008). In general, the ideological sources it examines share conceptual morphology's linguistic priorities, but it also reserves space for a trenchant critique of how ideological content becomes embedded in mass-cultural artefacts (especially art and music) and their aesthetic symbolism, in all cases with a view to highlighting the tensions between their 'illusory' qualities and the 'reality' of our social existence and action. It maintains the original Marxist reading of ideology as a set of ideas that legitimate (and are reciprocally sustained by) societal conditions of domination by distorting the true nature of these conditions and disguising the real interests that those subjected to them have in overturning them. But it shifts the task of 'unmasking' ideology away from historicising and negating its content as reducible to dominant (class) interests and towards using its inherently unstable ideas as an 'anchor' to situate transformative social struggles within existing social reality. Consequently, the ideology critic engages with ideological sources primarily via 'immanent critique', which entails identifying the logic and meanings of the (explicit or implicit) ideals, presuppositions, or 'truths' they endorse and juxtaposing them to how they are realised in society's rules and institutions. Their aim is to find areas where the two are inadequately congruent or even outright contradict each other, creating opportunities for emancipatory societal change – albeit without providing a direct alternative, to avoid constructing a similarly contradictory ideological replacement. They thus play the part of an investigative sleuth motivated by an activist commitment to tear down the ideological edifice as a whole, issuing a grand *j'accuse* against its tangled web of deceit and dissembling to lay bare the (awful) truth about our material and relational conditions, and pointing the finger at the 'rotten system' (rather than the 'bad apples') responsible for creating and perpetuating ideas and symbols to distract us from them. Ideology critique sees ideology analysis as explicitly tied to projects of political-economic emancipation for subjected groups and individuals. It hopes to achieve this through large-scale transformation of capitalist society, especially in its patriarchal, racist, homophobic, and colonialist forms – not necessarily with a specific view to realising socialism or communism in its Marxian conception, but certainly an intersectional post-capitalism (albeit not normally framed in ideological terms).

The third set of prominent approaches are the contemporary expositions of *poststructuralism*, successors to the debates of the 1960s and 1970s, which treat ideology as socially shared systems of ideas that reflect social relations of domination and which manifest in social expression (Laclau and Mouffe 1985; Malešević and MacKenzie 2002; Howarth et al. 2000; Žižek 1989, 2006). Located within cultural studies, these approaches are often highly interdisciplinary, synthesising their insights about ideology from observing and interpreting a deliberately expansive list of social phenomena that can embed structured meaning. Nevertheless, they exhibit a clear preference for popular media (films, television, computer games, comics, fiction) and widespread social practices, especially those that are unquestioned, either because they are so everyday or because they are taboo. Like ideology critique, poststructuralist approaches argue that social conflict and domination lie at the heart of societal order but part company with it abruptly on the question of their relation to ideology. For poststructuralism, discourse constitutes all possible social meaning and experience, so that, although ideology certainly lets us 'misrecognise' contingent social formations as 'natural', there is no alternative pre-social reality that we can escape to by way of uncovering an objective truth outside ideological 'illusion'. This means we can never definitively 'unmask' ideology, and our critiques can only provide alternative interpretations to make our societal experience meaningful. In turn, this makes 'dislocation' and 'antagonism' between competing interpretations inevitable, but it also suggests that any consensual ideological legitimation of society's arrangements relies on the collusion of its members. Accordingly, when the poststructuralist examines ideological sources, they focus on the 'myths' we use to give ourselves a sense of necessary (but ultimately impossible) 'closure' in our 'dislocated' social orders and the 'imaginaries' (or hegemonic myths) that define the foundations and horizons of possible discourse. Similarly, they evaluate the processes of (de)contestation, concretisation–resistance, and 'constitutive exteriority' by which we try to pin down the meaning of concepts and identities – even while their substantive content can be diluted ('empty signifiers') or contextually altered ('floating signifiers') and remains immune to final determination. In this way, the poststructuralist takes on the guise of an effortlessly wide-ranging cultural critic delivering a monumental *exposé* of how we hold – and why we should not hold – onto certain agreed meanings by which we 'create' the world we experience, by bringing to our conscious awareness the preconscious influences on how we perceive it, think and feel about it, and act within it. For poststructuralism, harking back to the legacy of 'deconstruction', the ultimate aim is to provide a cogent critique of the processes and content of ideology's attempt to use particular ideas to naturalise, reify, and legitimate our social experiences. If successful, such a critique allows us to rid ourselves of pathologies that twist our understanding of these experiences and to open up avenues to pursue alternative schemes of interpretation.

The other two social and political theory approaches may not be as explicitly focused on ideology *per se*, but their insights have been bound closely into ideology analysis. Originating in the philosophical subdisciplines of ontology and phenomenology, the methodology of *hermeneutics* regards ideologies as sets of ideas that delimit the indeterminacy of messages as they circulate between authors and audiences in society by selecting, privileging, and prioritising certain meanings. This is one of the most overtly textual approaches, focusing on the meanings that are embedded in words, by themselves and in a reciprocal 'hermeneutic circle' through their collocation with others – although its analytic tools also lend themselves to examining a broader cross-section of media messages diffused and received in society (Thompson 1990). It focuses on texts as conventionalised ways for authors to communicate their contexts with their audiences, both in the sense of how they individually understand their own experiences and the intellectual traditions into which they are conditioned (Gadamer 2013). In particular, it focuses on their 'polysemy', their ability to support many (even unlimited) co-possible meanings within the constraints of spatial and temporal context, especially where they are 'authorless', lacking a definitive 'figure' who can clarify their intended meaning (Ricœur 1974, 1976, 1985). When a hermeneuticist examines a source, they look at the unintended 'surplus of meaning' it conveys via the excess meanings/connotations of the words it uses and systematically outline different pathways we can take to interpret its meaning. These pathways can focus on literal (historical, textual), moral (psychological), allegorical (typological), or anagogical (collective) meaning (Jameson 1981, 16ff.); 'esoteric', secret, generally inaccessible meaning in need of revelation or 'exoteric', external meaning that veils the hidden meaning (Strauss 1952, 1964); and meaning in line with socially 'dominant' interpretations or with 'negotiated' and 'opposed' alternatives (Hall 1973, 1980). Their role is therefore akin to that of a secularised exegetical theologian who methodically contemplates our experientially and traditionally coloured reflections to generate an interpretative *'Verstehen'* of them. They explore (and where necessary critique) the unequal partnership between authors and audiences and identify the ideological frameworks of understanding with which we have been imbued to 'cut down' on any variability and unpredictability in our reception of meanings. For hermeneutics, the key task is to outline the range of meanings that the ideas that an ideology comprises can have within the various social contexts in which it operates. They seek to uncover the gains and losses in denotation and connotation these ideas have undergone in the process of constituting them as an ideology, as well as the choices made (when, how, by whom, etc.) to impose semantic limitations on them.

Alongside hermeneutics, a series of approaches have gained ground that examine ideology from the angle of *rhetoric*, which sees ideology as clusters of argumentative stances on pervasive social (usually political) themes to be deployed in contexts of 'ordinary' thinking and discursive exchange (Billig 1991; Finlayson 2007, 2012, 2013). In its choice of sources, rhetorical analysis focuses above all on personal opinions, but it is determined to turn ideology analysis away from merely examining 'attitudes' and information-processing cognitive rules ('real' mental states) and towards their linguistic expressions ('real' action) – and consequently examines above all (trivial and non-trivial) conversational situations to uncover their underlying intricate social regularities. It assesses the complex and contradictory patterns of talk, 'interpretative repertoires' (explanation, accounting), and 'registers of voice' we use to accomplish different expressive tasks, as well as how ideology provides the sources to support 'for/against' argumentative dynamics between opinions and counter-opinions. This approach turns conversations into an interpersonal game, with strategies and tactics, where the criterion of 'winning' is often based on constructing a mythical (rational) 'universal audience' to act as putative arbiter. The rhetorician evaluates their ideological sources by exploring

The dimensions of ideology studies 151

juxtapositions within discursive situations of 'ordinariness/ extraordinariness' between its personnel, their contexts, and their opinions. They are especially sensitive to political recruitment and mobilisation and to the evolving historical patternings that contextually alter the meanings of appeals to the conflicting commonplaces and prejudices that make up 'common sense'. Their role is consequently not unlike that of a sports commentator analysing a debating competition, stressing the 'play-by-play' of pervasive ideological strategies of (un)reasonable argumentation and persuasion, criticism and justification, concealment and exposure – with the aim of showing how the ideological history of 'common sense' is being (re)written through our everyday rhetoric. Rhetorical analysis thus assesses ideology through a quasi-critical lens, arguing that our conversational interactions occur within a wider social patterning that informs how we interact discursively, and that evolutionary patterns especially of historical social inequality are present as distorted echoes in the language we use to do so.

§2 The social-scientific and humanistic penumbra

These five approaches from social and political theory align to varying degrees with seven others from across the humanities and social sciences. In the conceptual and semantic analysis of ideology and ideologies, the closest allies to social and political theory have been approaches from the (modern) history of ideas. The British 'Cambridge School' of *contextualism* (Dunn 1985, 1996; Pocock 1972, 2009; Skinner 1969, 1978, 2002) and European *conceptual history* (*Begriffsgeschichte*) tradition (Koselleck 2002, 2004, 2018) see ideologies as collections of paradigmatic ideas – shared conventional representations of past, present, or future social facts – which define their intellectual environments and whose meanings evolve contingently over time. For them, the primary sources of interest are historical works, either by specific individual authors or by carefully delineated groups of interlocutors engaged in explicit exchange, and either pinpointed to specific periods of particularly febrile activity or spread out over a *longue durée* of societal transformation. Often, but (as of more recently) by no means exclusively, the focus of their interest is targeted at major (canonical or canon-adjacent) social and intellectual figures. Both approaches share a common focus on the centrality of accurately characterising the (economic, political, cultural) societal context in which these works and authors are situated as a way to 'get to the heart' of what their ideas 'really' (i.e., 'originally') meant. Conceptual history attaches the 'horizon' of this meaning to the key events and predominant practices 'of the time', while contextualism narrows its focus specifically onto moments of rapid or radical changes in social power-configurations. When analysing ideological sources, the historian of ideas maps their ideas and any discrepancies or shifts between them onto this background, examining how their connotations and surrounding concepts fuse 'diachronic' legacies of past meanings with 'synchronic' present formulations and identifying key agents who drove forward processes of ideational development, as well as how far these processes reflected their semantic intentions. Thus they play the part of ideological chronicler, operating at the intersection between archaeological recovery and archival preservation of the changing (prevailing and marginal, established and neglected) ways in which we have used and combined ideas to meaningfully represent our societies as they were previously, as they were at the time, and as we hoped they would be. In particular, they trace how we invoke ideas to legitimate the maintenance or transformation of societal arrangements at times of social struggle. In the end, intellectual and conceptual history alike are concerned with how ideologies take shape and develop as traditions, focusing on the cumulations and (dis)continuities in the ideas they contain and the meanings they give them, the key authors and other social causes that drive their development, and their recursive effects on the moral character of our societies.

By contrast, for social and political theory approaches that lay greater weight on discursive analysis, the main points of overlap have been with methods that focus on the processes and outputs of linguistic expression. The techniques of *critical discourse analysis* (CDA) (Fairclough

1989, 1992, 1995a, 2003; van Dijk 2008, 2009, 2011; Weiss and Wodak 2003; Wodak 2013; Wodak and Meyer 2009), lately bolstered by the addition of methods from *corpus linguistics* (Nartey and Mwinlaaru 2019; Vessey 2013, 2017), share with poststructuralism the view that ideology as expressed in social discourse is both conditioned by, and a medium for, social conflict and power-relations. But unlike poststructuralism, and more in line with rhetorical analysis, its focus is principally on the interpersonal communicative uses and manifestations of language, primarily but also not exclusively by major (i.e., powerful) social (above all political) figures. This can include rendering them in textual forms (e.g., via transcripts) but chiefly concerns mediated and unmediated speech. Another difference from poststructuralism is CDA's insistence that there is a pre-social reality that exists 'outside' the language that seeks to represent it, which is populated by identifiable social structures and agents that are responsible for domination and who cause social conflict. Under this view, the linguistic rules and discursive strategies that govern how we collocate ideas and define communicative contexts are deliberate instruments of this domination and conflict. When they examine a linguistic source, the critical discourse analyst conducts a granular structural analysis, breaking down its lexical content into syntactical parts-of-speech, parsing grammatical elements such as modality and tense, phonetic attributes such as stress and intonation, and interactive features such as turn-taking, to assess how speakers deploy them to assert their asymmetric social power-positions in relation to others within the given discursive situation. This casts them as a kind of forensic philologist ally to the ideology critic, evaluating the 'truth behind' how we articulate what we think by 'unmasking' what this can tell us about the strategies of dissimulation and manipulation to which we are subjected and identifying the specific power centres that consciously and purposefully implement them. Like the contextualist historian, they examine how these strategies foster or resist the legitimation (through normalisation) of the dominating social structures. Ultimately, the aim of CDA is to show how the ideas we hold are shaped and conditioned by power and how the language through which we express ourselves is itself a medium for us to exercise power in turn, producing meanings that steer our social practices, which constitute (perpetuate and transform) our societies.

At a kind of mid-point between conceptual/semantic and discursive extremes lies *content analysis,* which focuses on the meaningful lexical content of language and consequently understands ideology as the sets of ideas to which reference is made in socially significant expressions (Berelson 1952; Hosti 1969; Kracauer 1952; Krippendorff 2004; Krippendorff and Bock 2008). Its sources are primarily documentary texts (e.g., newspapers, books, magazines, correspondence, government publications), but it also analyses oral texts (speech), iconic texts (pictures, symbols), audiovisual texts (TV, radio, film), and hypertexts (online). From all of these, it non-invasively collects data by measuring (e.g.) word frequencies, text length, and audiovisual durations to track the presence of certain concepts and, from there, discern meaning about the text's ideological symbolism or revealed underlying attitudes. It examines 'who says what through which channel to whom with what effect' (Lasswell 1948), focusing especially on ideological 'agenda-setting', which determines how social issues are chosen to be covered as 'news stories', how their 'framing' organises observable patterns and trends in the ideas, words, images, and themes deployed to represent them, and how 'gatekeeping' via media conventions and editorial priorities restricts who is given 'standing' (i.e., high-status voice) to comment on them. Overall, the aim of this approach is to establish how cultural, historical, and institutional contexts affect how ideas are generated and diffused to mobilise mass opinion. The content analyst conducts systematic (usually computer-aided) readings of texts and artefacts, assigning them labels ('codes') with the help of an *a priori* coding scheme ('codebook') to indicate the presence of relevant content, and maps its patterns and meanings either via statistical overviews of word distributions or semantic analysis of intentionality and 'latency' in interpretation. They use 'Key Word in Context' routines to capture the meanings provided by words' textual surroundings and semantic grammatical models for statements of ethical norms, folklore narratives, utopian schemes, strategic plans, and social role attributions. As a (more) positivist equivalent to the conceptual morphologist, they essentially take on the role of a lexicographer, who treats us as actively engaged in constructing meaning about social ideas, and who outlines replicable and systematic methods to analyse our patterns of communication in order to understand the meanings we ascribe to social issues within our contexts and precisely characterise the social pervasiveness of ideological language. Content analysis overlaps with conceptual morphology and intellectual history in that it focuses on the ideas that make up ideologies, but it supplements their insights with a statistical approach to evaluating their evolving meaningfulness. It relies on precise, granular measurement of ideological density as a function of the relative incidence of ideas within their immediate lexical and situational contexts – and ultimately how this determines who has social legitimacy and power.

Ideology studies has become increasingly aware since the mid-1900s that the main traditions of ideology theory have a tendency to over-centre textual sources. Accordingly, the contemporary subfield also includes some approaches that are cognate to linguistics but broaden their lens of focus to include the ideological meaning of a far greater range of forms of expression. The modern forms of *semiotics*, such as psychoanalytic *semiology* (Kristeva 1980) or *dispositive analysis* (Bührmann and Schneider 2007, 2012; Caborn 2007; Jäger 2009; Paulus 2015; Villadsen 2021), expand the view of ideology to include ways in which social phenomena of all kinds can act as sign processes and symbolic systems that manifest ideas. They consciously seek to decentre texts as the primary objects of analysis, treating them instead as 'paratextual' supporting frameworks for ideology's manifestations in non-discursive social actions, the psychological states that underpin them, and the social objects to which they attach. These, they argue, must be analysed *in toto* in terms of their various places and functions within the overarching ideological *dispositif* and its sets of shared meanings. Semiotics thus examines how social sign-systems map onto, and reflect, ideological combinations and arrangements of ideas, tracing their effects in any social activity or process that uses signs to communicate meaning to any of our senses. This includes how they shape linguistic prosody, music, poetry, and rhythm, as well as how regularly patterned aspects of objects' forms or construction (e.g., architectural style, component parts) concretise ideological meanings. As the semiotician examines these highly diverse ideological sources, they systematise the various ways in which they can signify meaning (e.g., designation, likeness, analogy, allegory, metonymy, metaphor) as well as the 'syntactics' of the formal relations between them, the 'codes' representing ideological values and connotations that govern how we communicate agreed meanings by different 'modalities' of transmission (auditory, visual, tactile, olfactory, gustatory, kinaesthetic), and the echoes of pre-social and early-years indeterminacy that threatens our stable acceptance of shared ideological 'semiosis'. They mirror the poststructuralist cultural critic by becoming, in effect, an art critic, unpicking how meaning is attributed to social signs and objects of all kinds – especially where it spurs (un)conscious and (un)intentional emotions or aesthetic instincts – and elaborating how discursive and non-discursive practices sustain the ideological 'status' of social objects and our psychology, and consequently also underlying social power-relations. Overall, semiotics broadens the view of ideology analysis to cover the full gamut of purposive social strategies that attribute ideological meaning not just to our discursive expressions but to every facet of our psychological and behavioural engagement with our environments. Crucially, it treats these not just as a 'supporting cast' of analytical foci to the 'main event' of textual analysis but as important evidence of how ideology is 'materialised' in society.

The need for ideology studies to understand how ideology works at the level of cognition, which precedes the ideological manifestations on which the approaches outlined so far focus, brings it into contact with experimental insights that sit at the intersection of psychoanalysis and neuroscience. The first of these, *social psychology*, treats ideology as a conscious manifestation of largely pre- or unconscious psychological traits, which are partly genetic and partly social in origin, and which have demonstrable effects on what and how we think (Brader and Cikanek 2019; Carney et al. 2008; Gerber et al. 2010; Jost et al. 2009, 2013; Marcus et al. 2000, 2005; Mondak 2010; Mondak and Hibbing 2012). As a heavily empirical approach, the sources it examines lie

The dimensions of ideology studies 157

primarily at the 'output' end of our processes of thinking and expression: observable survey data and derived statistical models that correlate responses coding for certain personal traits with others coding for discrete ideological positions. Unlike many of the more interpretative approaches, it reverses the direction of causality between ideology's social presence and the ideas we hold, focusing on the cognitive components and 'schemata' that underlie our conscious assertions as predictors of ideological 'elective affinities', and which mediate our real and perceived social group identifications. These include above all personality traits (e.g., honesty–humility, emotionality, extraversion, agreeableness, conscientiousness, and openness to experience), emotions (e.g., joy, sadness, anger, fear, disgust, eagerness), and reasoning (rationality, reasonability, heuristics). To generate sources of ideological information, the social psychologist presents a group of experimental test subjects with specific questionnaires or cognitive tasks that are framed in such a way that subjects' responses map onto pre-coded criteria to catalogue (e.g.) the speed or method with which they process information, their enthusiasm or aversion towards specific prompts, or their implied values and moral frameworks. In this, they are perhaps closest of all the contemporary ideology studies approaches to the scientific philosophy of mind that the *idéologues* first set out to formulate in the early 1800s. Yet, of course, they operate with a far more systematic model of the various components of our thinking processes and a far more interpersonal–interactive and less anthropological–geographical understanding of contextual social influences – as well as a conception of ideology implicitly geared towards the political domain. In essence, social-psychological ideology analysis aims to establish robust hypotheses and gather replicable, statistically significant evidence regarding the correlation and causality between how ordinary people 'process' their social experiences and the moral stances they hold on salient issues, which combine together into their relative ideological 'placements' in society.

The second of these approaches, *emotion and affect theory*, moves its area of focus to an even deeper level of our social experience, arguing that ideology should be seen first and foremost not as an arrangement of ideas but as a febrile array of 'affects' – protean states of mind or body resulting from our embodied encounters with our environments (especially other bodies) (Ahmed 2004; Gregg and Seigworth 2010; Leys 2011; Thagard 2006; Tomkins 1962-3, 1991-2). Affect theory has extensive synergies with rhetorical and semiotic analysis in its aim to move ideological analysis away from the narrow focus on cognition and language. But it aligns more closely with social psychology in its 'turn' towards bodily forces that are not under our 'conscious' control, of which we are not even necessarily aware, but which lie at a crucial intersection of our innate, genetically 'hardwired' biology and the ideologies circulating in society. It accuses social theory of taking our bodies for granted and of neglecting the many subtle, visceral ways we react to our imbrication with our environment (e.g., emotions, feelings, moods, sensations, 'vibes', atmospheres). Affect theory sees these as the primary motives for our 'later' psychology and behaviour, in particular our understanding of the material and conceptual possibilities of (past, present, and future) social phenomena. It emphasises the felt intensities that characterise how we first experience a social event or process, as well as the 'affective resonance' that allows us to communicate these experiences non-verbally (as 'authors') to others (our 'audiences'). In turn, it expands this to a view of politics as a 'performance' that amplifies our affects, where ideology leverages affective author–audience dynamics to raise the dramatic 'experiential value' of political displays (e.g., speeches, rallies). The affect theorist looks at sources of ideology in how we use our bodies and their movements to reflect our affective states (e.g., face, voice, gaze, posture, gesture, gait) and how our non-verbal repertoire captures affective nuances (e.g., timing, staging, oration, gesticulation, sound, silence). They link these to our substantive ideological beliefs by constructing 'cognitive-affective maps' that attach interconnected, recognisably patterned ideological concepts to emotions with positive and negative valences. Similar to the poststructuralist and the semiotician, they act as a kind of drama critic, examining how affect connects our bodies and integrates us by felt compulsion into social groups conceived as bustling *mises-en-scène*, in which we articulate what our affective experiences mean to us via highly variable 'affective-discursive practices', which position us differently towards hegemonic ideological discourses and thus 'cast' us in different 'roles' in the 'theatre' of social power-relations. Overall, affect theory insists that ideology analysis needs to take far more seriously the pre-cognitive 'sensuous' aspects of power understood as an 'affective economy', to avoid the fallacy that power is manifested primarily in our thoughts and language and better capture the large- and small-scale ways in which emotional thematisation interacts with our social lives.

The final 'corner' of contemporary ideology studies reflects the close alignment – which already existed in the classical period of ideology theory and has only strengthened since then – between ideologies and the pursuit of concrete policy aims through state institutions, which have become steadily more accountable to the views that circulate among populations today. The long-dominant loci of ideology analysis in political science, *comparative politics* and *opinion research*, regard ideology in a conscious sense as the creation of political elites, a tool to unite and distinguish clusters of substantive public policy positions, which are reflected in the attitudes and opinions of the mass public (Bartolini and Mair 1990; Dalton 2002; Lane and Sears 1964; Lipset and Rokkan 1969; Price 1992; Sartori 1969, 1976; Zaller 1992). Like social psychology, this is a predominantly empirical approach and, likewise, relies on survey data and statistical sampling to map the proportional shares and distributions of discrete ideological stances among the population. However, it supplements this for elites with roll-call data on legislative votes and affiliations and institutional data such as electoral results or policy documents. It is also oriented towards a highly specific set of ideological 'markers', including political party support and voting turnout, political attentiveness, issue salience and prioritisation, and how 'surface' attitudes and opinions can be categorised in ideological space ('conservative–liberal' linearity, 'political compass', etc.) – all with the overarching aim of testing how cohesive or fractured elite and mass ideology is, both internally and in relation to each other. Like the social psychologist, the political scientist relies on a sample of test subjects (usually survey respondents) to answer explicit (binary or multi-option) questions on specific issues. These questions are deliberately framed in order to test (e.g.)

how respondents 'receive–reject/accept–sample' (RAS) information to form their opinions, how they rank the direction, intensity, degree, certainty, firmness, salience, or importance of their opinions, and how responses can be disaggregated along a range of demographic criteria (e.g., gender, age, social grade, region, voting history). This converges closely with the role of the opinion pollster, who tries to provide representative statistical indications of how successfully personal political commitments and social (economic, cultural) attitudes are reflected and mobilised by political movements and organisations and what generalisable observations or predictions this lets us make about the ideological character of society as a whole. Finally, for comparative political science, the purpose of ideology analysis is to collect granular findings within and across different political jurisdictions regarding the status and development of correlations between demographic group self-identification, substantive political understandings and attitudes towards specific policies and other salient social questions, and a narrow set of ideological behaviours such as stated (dis)approval of political leaders or voting in elections and referendums.

§3 The 'ideology studies compass'

Altogether, these twelve approaches cover the analytical domain of ideology studies as it stands in the early to mid-2000s. Each of them offers its own distinctive and indispensable perspective on the nature and workings of ideology, which combine to reveal the many overlapping effects it has on who we are, and how we think, feel, and act in our social encounters. As ideology studies gradually coalesces into its own autonomous subdiscipline, the final question to consider is whether, and how, its approaches can be categorised and compared by means of a parsimonious set of universal criteria – in exactly the same way as several qualitative and quantitative ideology studies approaches have themselves done for ideological families and traditions. The first such criterion is the *level of analytical focus* with which a given approach is predominantly concerned. Ideology studies approaches take very different views on the various aspects of what ideology can tell us about 'how the world works', which makes the actual combinations and arrangements of ideas and their derivations that ideologies comprise more or less intrinsic or instrumental objects of research interest for them. Some focus on ideology's observable *surface-level* manifestations within our direct day-to-day experience of social life: words or symbols, substantive opinions or voting choices, published texts or media broadcasts. Other approaches, meanwhile, are interested mainly in the *deep-level* personal and societal factors and processes that underpin these more visible manifestations, which do not ordinarily appear in an observable fashion and are only indirectly implied by our social experiences: structural division and conflict embedded in the fabric of society, deep-seated traumas or irreducible genetic traits, and representational maps or cognitive schemata. Ideology studies ultimately needs both types of approaches: the risk of relying too heavily on surface-level analysis is that it takes ideological phenomena too much at face value without providing an adequate account of their societal causes; meanwhile, the problem of prioritising deep-level analysis is that it reduces ideological phenomena to the status of 'second-class' epiphenomena and undervalues a large swathe of our social experiences.

The second criterion is the *type of analytical methodology* that an ideology studies approach primarily deploys. Approaches may use very different frameworks, techniques, and procedures to understand ideology and ideologies, which to a great extent are directly inherited from the prevailing research principles that govern their overarching disciplines of origin. On one side, ideology studies rests extensively on the formulation of *theoretical* accounts that are intended to capture the general characteristics of ideology and ideologies, as well as the rules governing how they operate: concepts such as 'polysemy' or 'imaginaries', models such as 'morphology' and 'RAS', or methods of 'immanent critique' and 'deconstruction'. On the other side, it also relies on *empirical* processes of gathering and documenting many different kinds of ideological evidence to inform and validate its analysis: survey samples and official records, constructed databases and archival collections, hypothesis tests and coding frameworks.

162 The dimensions of ideology studies

Again, ideology studies benefits from approaches that fall on each side of this distinction: the danger of maintaining a mostly theoretical analysis of ideology and ideologies is that it can prove impossible to substantiate its claims or test its predictions via actual ideological phenomena; at the same time, pursuing primarily empirical analysis of specific 'cases' of ideological relevance may lose sight of how to situate its findings within a more 'global' conceptualisation of what ideology is and how it works.

Together, these two dimensions of analytical focus and analytical methodology can be used to create an 'ideologological' compass (see figure 6). Much like the political-economic/cultural ideological compass developed to compare substantive ideologies, this one gives us an at-a-glance 'snapshot' of the extent and points of synchronic similarity and difference between ideology studies approaches – including the relative location of 'hybrid' approaches and, when relevant, the trajectory of approaches' diachronic change.

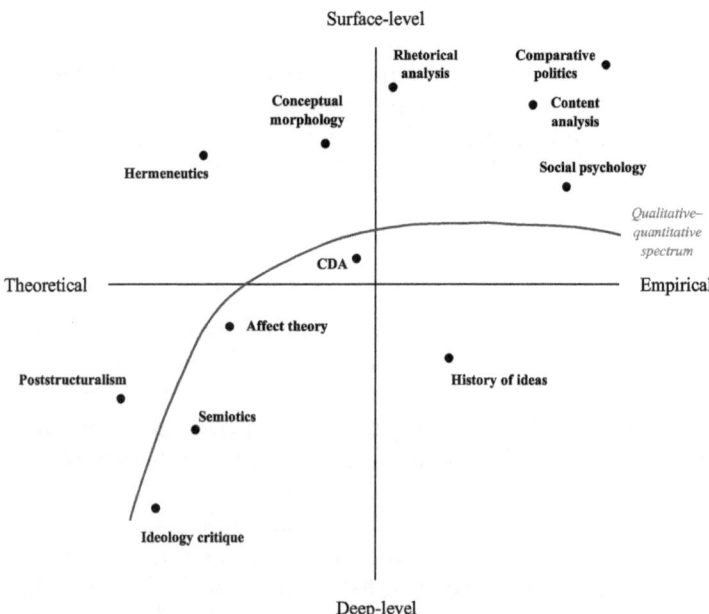

Figure 6 The ideology studies compass

The dimensions of ideology studies 163

A question remains whether it is possible to reduce this snapshot even further to a single criterion of comparison, namely whether ideology studies approaches lean more towards *qualitative* (interpretative) or *quantitative* (positivist) analysis – i.e., whether they prefer to examine ideology from the angle of evaluating the meaning of experiences, documents, artefacts, and non-numerical information or to concentrate on collecting numerical and statistical data about ideology and drawing deductive inferences from it (cf. Leader Maynard 2013). Insofar as it is possible to frame this as a linear spectrum, it tracks from the deep-structure/theoretical to the surface-level/empirical quadrants on the compass, with poststructuralism and ideology critique and comparative politics and content analysis respectively representing 'polar opposites' among 'ideologological' approaches. However, a more accurate reflection of the openness within ideology studies is to characterise the group in terms of clusters. Some approaches are *predominantly* qualitative: ideology critique, poststructuralism, hermeneutics, semiotics, and affect theory. Others are predominantly quantitative: content analysis, social psychology, and comparative politics. But there is also a healthy group of syncretics that sit fairly squarely in between the 'outer' clusters, which are perhaps the most able and inclined to draw profitably from approaches on either side of them: conceptual morphology, rhetorical analysis, CDA, and the history of ideas. This is not to say that the more definitively qualitative or quantitative approaches are less able to collaborate meaningfully with one another – merely that doing so requires a more careful negotiation of the differences of focus and methodology between them.

7
Conclusion

The death, the resurrection, and the life of ideology and its study have been proclaimed – with variable justification – on numerous occasions in the history of modern social thought. At the point of writing, the latest and arguably most successful period of reanimation now stretches back over nearly half a century. This book unabashedly sides with those who see ideology not only as very much alive but on the brink of entering a promising new era in its existence. It is meant to serve, above all, as a companion for those who want to better understand ideology in theory and practice: what it is, what causes it, what it does to/for us, what forms it takes in society, how it has changed in response to deep historical developments, and where it fits alongside the other familiar concerns of social life and social research. It is a work of what I have called 'ideologology': a substantive account of ideology following in the footsteps of Destutt de Tracy, Schopenhauer, Feuerbach, Marx and Engels, and their many successors in ideology theory.

At the same time – like many other theories of ideology, explicitly or implicitly – it is also a meta-level commentary on this field of ideology theory and latterly the burgeoning subdiscipline of ideology studies. Who counts as an ideology theorist, what constitutes the intellectual business of ideology theory, what expectations it raises for ideology theorists' social engagement, what society's effect is on the shape and contours of ideology theory, and – most acutely – who is in, who is out, and who is leading the charge as the boundaries of ideology studies crystallise: these questions of 'ideologolog-ology' (!) are equally vital for students and theorists of ideology to consider, and I have tried to sketch an answer to them too throughout this book.

Another way of saying this is that any theory of ideology and ideology studies is itself also a certain way of representing a particular part of our (intellectual) engagement with reality: it is, in a sense, an ideology too, and as such it shares the characteristics it ascribes to its subject-matter. One perfectly plausible approach to this book, then, is to view it in the same morphological terms it applies to the concept of ideology: as a map that 'charts the features' of ideology and ideology studies; a lens that 'colours and clarifies' how to view them; a primer that 'outlines the rudiments of good usage and style' for conducting ideological analysis; a script with 'carefully specified instructions' for doing so; a design plan of the 'edifice' of ideology theory; a simulation 'guided tour of the motions to go through' when analysing ideology; and a vantage-point 'onto (or, rather, within)' ideology and ideology studies. As a book of ideology *theory* rather than ideology *practice*, some aspects of its 'ideologological morphology' are inevitably more thoroughly elaborated than others – but what this self-application of its analytical concepts suggests is that, as a work of theory, it is inevitably 'committed' in some way.

Of course, the idea that ideology theory may be ideologically committed is nothing new. The historical overviews of the evolution of ideology theory (chapter 2) and the range of ideological families and traditions (chapter 4) evince some obvious overlaps, especially in their responses to major historical events and changing societal conditions – although not so closely that their developments have moved entirely in tandem. Moreover, ideology theorists over the last 200 years have often held clear normative commitments to certain ideologies, with some of those with the strongest ideological commitments (rather deliciously) being the most adamant about the post- or non-ideological nature of their substantive views. These have included leading communists such as Marx and Engels, Gramsci, and Althusser; more nuanced anti-capitalist progressives such as Arendt, Foucault, Bourdieu, and Butler; avowed liberals such as Lippmann, Aron, Boudon, and Freeden; conservatives such as Bell and Minogue; and even the solitary Christian democrat Noelle-Neumann.

I am happy to concede that this book may betray my normative commitments in a similar way. But the commitments to which I am referring pertain to the methodological assumptions that underpin how I have formulated the account of ideology outlined here. Some are easily stated: a clear endorsement of *morphological* analysis as the way to understand ideology's components; a kind of *'neo-Destuttism'* in treating ideologies as both psychological and behavioural, uniting abstract mental phenomena with their concrete physical manifestations; a sympathetic orientation towards *historicising* both ideologies and ideology theories; the need to negotiate a 'middle path' between the insights of *structuralism* and *poststructuralism*; and a strong penchant for *syncretism* and *compatibilism* in combining ideology theorists of many different backgrounds, including several who might react with considerable surprise (and even resistance) to the interlocutors with whom I have juxtaposed them and the theoretical synergies and homologies with which I credit them.

To illustrate the effect of these commitments, we can return to the central questions in the study of ideology I identified at the start of the book and outline my position within each binary. On ideology's truth or falsity, I side more with the former – not to minimise its distortionary potential but to recognise that it is impossible to 'access' reality except on *some* ideological terms, so ideological representation is indeed 'true as far as we are concerned'. By the same token, I endorse the view of ideology's necessity, since even achieving a critical stance towards an ideology presupposes substantive and methodological assumptions that in themselves 'add up to' an alternative ideology. My reading of ideology's temporariness or permanence leans towards the latter, although I find it unconscionably ahistorical and reductionist not to acknowledge how ideologies and their social priorities have evolved and proliferated over time, especially since the early 1800s. This leads smoothly into a pluralistic conception of

Conclusion 167

ideology as a rich tapestry of different families and traditions, as much out of sensitivity to their members' clearly distinct and mutually distinguishing self-conceptions in relation to those on 'other sides' as because ideology studies itself loses significant breadth and diversity if 'ideology' alone is its focus. On ideology's individuality or collectiveness, I negotiate a median position, albeit recognising that the smallest unit of society 'in the last analysis' is always the individual, not as an atom but as a node enmeshed in many intersecting social ties. I also tread a middle path on ideology's explicitness or implicitness, since, although symbolic and 'non-ideological' expressions can embed extensive ideological content, analysing these ideological forms (re)converts them into textual–linguistic formats that trade in the conscious definition and articulation of ideas.

In other words, to put it glibly: 'It's no use, Dr Marx – it's ideology (pretty much) all the way down.' But just because we cannot 'escape' ideology in the sense to which Marxist theory and its social-critical successors aspire, that is no reason to damn our social lives as inherently doomed to inauthenticity, give ourselves over to helpless despair, or abandon our dedication to social meaning and reasoning, order and justice, stability and change. Those are fallacies that ideology studies must abandon, just as it is enthusiastically hurtling away from the 'end of history/end of ideology'. I have tried to show that ideology's deep entanglement with reality and our experience of it is not necessarily as frightening as some strands of ideology theory traditionally suggest. Instead, I hope this account has started to illuminate a relatively stable equilibrium of ideological self-awareness: acknowledging the inevitability and necessity of ideology *in general*, but also the inexorable potential for reality at any point to 'show up' the inadequacies and limitations of the *particular* ideology to which we happen to have subscribed up until then. With this self-awareness in our arsenal, we can still embark on projects of ideology critique, and still spur on programmes of positive transformation, while remaining frank with ourselves about the further degree of social and intellectual emancipation to which this process leads.

References

Abercrombie, Nicholas, Stephen Hill, and Bryan S. Turner (1980) *The Dominant Ideology Thesis* (London: Allen & Unwin).
Agamben, Giorgio (2009) *What is an Apparatus? And Other Essays* (Stanford, CA: Stanford University Press).
Ahmed, Sara (2004) *The Cultural Politics of Emotion* (Edinburgh: Edinburgh University Press).
Allport, Floyd H. (1937) 'Toward a science of public opinion', *Public Opinion Quarterly* 1/1, 7–23.
Althusser, Louis (2006 [1993–4]) *Philosophy of the Encounter: Later Writings, 1978–87* (London: Verso).
Althusser, Louis (2014 [1970]) *On the Reproduction of Capitalism: Ideology and Ideological State Apparatuses* (London: Verso).
Antonio, Robert J. (1981) 'Immanent critique as the core of critical theory: its origins and developments in Hegel, Marx and contemporary thought', *British Journal of Sociology* 32/3, 330–45.
Arendt, Hannah (1976 [1951]) *The Origins of Totalitarianism* (New York: Houghton Mifflin Harcourt).
Aron, Raymond (1955) *L'Opium des intellectuels* (Paris: Calmann-Lévy).
Badiou, Alain (2005 [1988]) *Being and Event* (New York: Continuum).
Barbalet, Jack (1998) *Emotion, Social Theory, and Social Structure: A Macrosociological Approach* (Cambridge: Cambridge University Press).

Barrett, Michèle (1992) *The Politics of Truth: From Marx to Foucault* (Cambridge: Polity).
Barth, Hans (1977) *Truth and Ideology* (Berkeley: University of California Press).
Barthes, Roland (1957) *Mythologies* (Paris: Seuil).
Barthes, Roland (1964) *Éléments de sémiologie* (Paris: Seuil).
Bartolini, Stefano, and Peter Mair (1990) *Identity, Competition, and Electoral Availability: The Stabilisation of European Electorates, 1885–1985* (Cambridge: Cambridge University Press).
Bateson, Gregory (1991) *A Sacred Unity: Further Steps to an Ecology of Mind* (London: HarperCollins).
Baudrillard, Jean (1983) *Simulacra and Simulation* (New York: Semiotext(e)).
Baudrillard, Jean (1994) *The Illusion of the End* (Cambridge: Polity).
Bauer, Otto (1907) *Die Nationalitätenfrage und die Sozialdemokratie* (Vienna: Wiener Volksbuchhandlung Ignaz Brand).
Bauman, Zygmunt (1998) *Globalization: The Human Consequences* (New York: Columbia University Press).
Bauman, Zygmunt (2000) *Liquid Modernity* (Cambridge: Polity).
Bauman, Zygmunt (2001) *The Individualized Society* (Cambridge: Polity).
Beck, Ulrich, Anthony Giddens, and Scott Lash (1994) *Reflexive Modernization: Politics, Tradition and Aesthetics in the Modern Social Order* (Stanford, CA: Stanford University Press).
Bell, Daniel (1960) *The End of Ideology: On the Exhaustion of Political Ideas in the Fifties* (New York: Free Press).
Bennett, Maxwell R., and Peter M. S. Hacker (2003) *Philosophical Foundations of Neuroscience* (Oxford: Blackwell).
Berelson, Bernard (1952) *Content Analysis in Communication Research* (Glencoe, IL: Free Press).
Bernays, Edward (2005 [1928]) *Propaganda* (Brooklyn, NY: Ig).
Bernays, Edward (2011 [1923]) *Crystallizing Public Opinion* (Brooklyn, NY: Ig).
Bernstein, Eduard (1901) *Wie ist wissenschaftlicher Sozialismus möglich?* (Berlin: Verlag der Sozialistischen Monatshefte).
Bernstein, Eduard (1911) 'Die Intellektuellen in der Reichstagswahl', *Sozialistische Monatshefte* 17/25, 1580–5.

Bhabha, Homi K. (1994) *The Location of Culture* (London: Routledge).
Billig, Michael (1991) *Ideology and Opinions: Studies in Rhetorical Psychology* (London: Sage).
Bouchard, Thomas J., and Matthew McGue (2003) 'Genetic and environmental influences on human psychological differences', *Journal of Neurobiology* 54/1, 4–45.
Boudon, Raymond (1989 [1986]) *The Analysis of Ideology* (Cambridge: Polity).
Bourdieu, Pierre (1977 [1972]) *Outline of a Theory of Practice*, trans. Richard Nice (Cambridge: Cambridge University Press).
Bourdieu, Pierre (1990) *The Logic of Practice*, trans. Richard Nice (Cambridge: Cambridge University Press).
Bourdieu, Pierre (2010 [1979]) *Distinction* (Abingdon: Routledge).
Brader, Ted, and Erin Cikanek (2019) 'The emotional foundations of democratic citizenship', in Adam J. Berinsky (ed.), *New Directions in Public Opinion* (Abingdon: Routledge), 202–35.
Brant, William A. (2013) *Mental Imagery and Creativity: Cognition, Observation and Realization* (Saarbrücken: Akademikerverlag).
Brown, Wendy (1995) *States of Injury: Power and Freedom in Late Modernity* (Princeton, NJ: Princeton University Press).
Buchwalter, Andrew (1991) 'Hegel, Marx, and the concept of immanent critique', *Journal of the History of Philosophy* 29/2, 253–79.
Bührmann, Andrea D., and Werner Schneider (2007) 'More than just a discursive practice? Conceptual principles and methodological aspects of dispositif analysis', *Forum: Qualitative Social Research* 8/2.
Bührmann, Andrea D., and Werner Schneider (2012) *Vom Diskurs zum Dispositiv: Eine Einführung in die Dispositivanalyse* (Bielefeld: transcript).
Butler, Judith (1988) 'Performative acts and gender constitution: an essay in phenomenology and feminist theory', *Theatre Journal* 40/4, 519–31.
Butler, Judith (1990) *Gender Trouble: Feminism and the Subversion of Identity* (New York: Routledge).
Butler, Judith (1993) *Bodies That Matter: On the Discursive Limits of 'Sex'* (New York: Routledge).

Butler, Judith (1997) *The Psychic Life of Power: Theories in Subjection* (Stanford, CA: Stanford University Press).
Butler, Judith (2004) *Undoing Gender* (New York: Routledge).
Caborn, Joannah (2007) 'On the methodology of dispositive analysis', *Critical Approaches to Discourse Analysis across Disciplines* 1/1, 115–23.
Carney, Dana R., John T. Jost, Samuel D. Gosling, and Jeff Potter (2008) 'The secret lives of liberals and conservatives: personality profiles, interaction styles, and the things they leave behind', *Political Psychology* 29/6, 807–40.
Collier, David, and James E. Mahon (1993) 'Conceptual "stretching" revisited: adapting categories in comparative analysis', *American Political Science Review* 87/4, 845–55.
Collins, Patricia Hill (1990) *Black Feminist Thought: Knowledge, Consciousness and the Politics of Empowerment* (Abingdon: Routledge).
Connolly, William E. (2002) *Identity/Difference: Democratic Negotiations of Political Paradox* (Minneapolis: University of Minnesota Press).
Crenshaw, Kimberlé Williams (1989) 'Demarginalizing the intersection of race and sex: a black feminist critique of antidiscrimination doctrine, feminist theory and antiracist politics', *University of Chicago Legal Forum* 1989/1.
Crenshaw, Kimberlé Williams (2017) *On Intersectionality: Essential Writings* (New York: New Press).
Dalton, Russell J. (2002) *Citizen Politics: Public Opinion and Political Parties in Advanced Industrial Democracies* (New York: Seven Bridges Press).
de Man, Paul (1982 [1979]) *Allegories of Reading: Figural Language in Rousseau, Nietzsche, Rilke, and Proust* (New Haven, CT: Yale University Press).
Debray, Régis (1996 [1994]) *Media Manifestos: On the Technological Transmission of Cultural Forms* (London: Verso).
Deleuze, Gilles (1988 [1986]) *Foucault*, trans. Sean Hand (London: Athlone Press).
Deleuze, Gilles (1991 [1966]) *Bergsonism*, trans. Hugh Tomlinson and Barbara Habberjam (New York: Zone Books).
Deleuze, Gilles, and Félix Guattari (2004 [1972, 1980]) *Capitalism and Schizophrenia*, 2 vols (New York: Continuum).
Derrida, Jacques (1973 [1967]) *Speech and Phenomena and*

Other Essays on Husserl's Theory of Signs (Evanston, IL: Northwestern University Press).

Derrida, Jacques (1976 [1967]) *Of Grammatology* (Baltimore: Johns Hopkins University Press).

Derrida, Jacques (1994 [1993]) *Spectres of Marx* (London: Routledge).

Derrida, Jacques (2001 [1967]) *Writing and Difference* (London: Routledge).

Destutt de Tracy, Antoine (1804–15) *Élémens d'idéologie*, 5 vols (Paris: Courcier).

Dunn, John (1985) *Rethinking Modern Political Theory* (Cambridge: Cambridge University Press).

Dunn, John (1996) *The History of Political Theory and Other Essays* (Cambridge: Cambridge University Press).

Durkheim, Émile (1893) *De la division du travail social: étude sur l'organisation des sociétés supérieures* (Paris: Félix Alcan).

Durkheim, Émile (1895) *Les Règles de la méthode sociologique* (Paris: Félix Alcan).

Eagleton, Terry (1991) *Ideology: An Introduction* (London: Verso).

Elias, Norbert (1939) *Über den Prozeß der Zivilisation* (Basel: Haus zum Falken).

Ellul, Jacques (1964) *The Technological Society* (New York: Alfred A. Knopf).

Engels, Friedrich (1987 [1878]) *Anti-Dühring*, in Marx and Engels, *Collected Works*, vol. 25: *Engels 1873–83* (London: Lawrence & Wishart).

Fairclough, Norman (1989) *Language and Power* (London: Longman).

Fairclough, Norman (1992) *Discourse and Social Change* (Cambridge: Polity).

Fairclough, Norman (1995a) *Critical Discourse Analysis* (Boston: Addison-Wesley).

Fairclough, Norman (1995b) *Media Discourse* (London: Edward Arnold).

Fairclough, Norman (2003) *Analysing Discourse: Textual Analysis for Social Research* (Abingdon: Routledge).

Ferguson, Leonard W. (1939) 'Primary social attitudes', *Journal of Psychology* 8/2, 217–23.

Ferguson, Leonard W. (1940) 'The measurement of primary social attitudes', *Journal of Psychology* 10/1, 199–205.

Ferguson, Leonard W. (1941) 'The stability of the primary social

attitudes, I: Religionism and humanitarianism', *Journal of Psychology* 12/2, 283–8.
Ferguson, Leonard W. (1942) 'The isolation and measurement of nationalism', *Journal of Social Psychology* 16/2, 215–28.
Feuerbach, Ludwig (1841) *Das Wesen des Christentums* (Leipzig: Otto Wigand).
Finlayson, Alan (2007) 'From beliefs to arguments: interpretive methodology and rhetorical political analysis', *British Journal of Politics and International Relations* 9/4, 545–63.
Finlayson, Alan (2012) 'Rhetoric and the political theory of ideologies', *Political Studies* 60/4, 751–67.
Finlayson, Alan (2013) 'Ideology and political rhetoric', in Michael Freeden, Lyman Tower Sargent, and Marc Stears (eds), *The Oxford Handbook of Political Ideologies* (Oxford: Oxford University Press), 197–213.
Finlayson, James Gordon (2014) 'Hegel, Adorno and the origins of immanent criticism', *British Journal for the History of Philosophy* 22/6, 1142–66.
Firestone, Shulamith (1970) *The Dialectic of Sex: The Case for Feminist Revolution* (New York: William Morrow).
Fisher, Mark (2009) *Capitalist Realism: Is There No Alternative?* (London: Zero Books).
Fisher, Mark (2017) *The Weird and the Eerie* (London: Repeater Books).
Foucault, Michel (1977 [1975]) *Discipline and Punish: The Birth of the Prison* (New York: Pantheon).
Foucault, Michel (1980) *Power/Knowledge: Selected Interviews and Other Writings, 1972–77*, ed. Colin Gordon (London: Penguin).
Foucault, Michel (1982a [1969]) *The Archaeology of Knowledge* (New York: Vintage).
Foucault, Michel (1982b) 'The subject and power', in H. L. Dreyfus and P. Rabinow (eds), *Michel Foucault: Beyond Hermeneutics and Structuralism* (Brighton: Harvester), 208–26.
Foucault, Michel (1988 [1961]) *Madness and Civilization: A History of Insanity in the Age of Reason* (New York: Vintage).
Foucault, Michel (1994 [1966]) *The Order of Things* (New York: Vintage).
Foucault, Michel (1996 [1963]) *The Birth of the Clinic: An Archaeology of Medical Perception* (New York: Vintage).

Foucault, Michel (2000) *Power: Essential Works of Foucault, 1954–1984*, ed. James D. Faubion (New York: Free Press).

Foucault, Michel (2007) *Security, Territory, Population: Lectures at the Collège de France 1977–78* (New York: St Martin's Press).

Freeden, Michael (1996) *Ideologies and Political Theory: A Conceptual Approach* (Oxford: Oxford University Press).

Freeden, Michael (2003) *Ideology: A Very Short Introduction* (Oxford: Oxford University Press).

Freeden, Michael (2013) 'The morphological analysis of ideology', in Michael Freeden, Lyman Tower Sargent, and Marc Stears (eds), *The Oxford Handbook of Political Ideologies* (Oxford: Oxford University Press), 115–37.

Freeden, Michael (2015) *The Political Theory of Political Thinking: The Anatomy of a Practice* (Oxford: Oxford University Press).

Freire, André (2015) 'Left–right ideology as a dimension of identification and of competition', *Journal of Political Ideologies* 20/1, 43–68.

Gadamer, Hans-Georg (2013 [1960]) *Truth and Method* (London: Bloomsbury).

Geertz, Clifford (1973) *The Interpretation of Cultures: Selected Essays* (New York: Basic Books).

Gelhorn, Heather L., Michael C. Stallings, Susan E. Young, Robin P. Corley, Soo Hyun Rhee, and John J. Hewitt (2005) 'Genetic and environmental influences on conduct disorder: symptom, domain and full-scale analyses', *Journal of Child Psychology and Psychiatry* 46/6, 580–91.

Gellner, Ernest (1988) *Plough, Sword and Book: The Structure of Human History* (London: Collins Harvill).

Gentile, Emilio (2013) 'Total and totalitarian ideologies', in Michael Freeden, Lyman Tower Sargent, and Marc Stears (eds), *The Oxford Handbook of Political Ideologies* (Oxford: Oxford University Press), 56–72.

Gerber, Alan S., Gregory A. Huber, David Doherty, Conor M. Dowling, and Shang E. Ha (2010) 'Personality and political attitudes: relationships across issue domains and political contexts', *American Political Science Review* 104/1, 111–33.

Geuss, Raymond (1981) *The Idea of a Critical Theory* (Cambridge: Cambridge University Press).

Giddens, Anthony (1984) *The Constitution of Society: Outline of the Theory of Structuration* (Cambridge: Polity).

Giddens, Anthony (1985) *A Contemporary Critique of Historical Materialism*, vol. 2: *The Nation-State and Violence* (Cambridge: Polity).
Gilligan, Carol (1982) *In a Different Voice: Psychological Theory and Women's Development* (Cambridge, MA: Harvard University Press).
Glynos, Jason (2008) 'Ideological fantasy at work', *Journal of Political Ideologies* 13/3, 275–96.
Goertz, Gary (2006) *Concept Formation* (Princeton, NJ: Princeton University Press).
Goldmann, Lucien (1964 [1955]) *The Hidden God: A Study of Tragic Vision in the Pensées of Pascal and the Tragedies of Racine*, trans. Philip Thody (London: Routledge).
Goldthorpe, John H. (2005) *Social Mobility and Class Structure in Modern Britain* (Oxford: Oxford University Press).
Gramsci, Antonio (2011 [1929–35]) *Prison Notebooks*, 3 vols (New York: Columbia University Press).
Gregg, Melissa, and Gregory J. Seigworth (eds) (2010) *The Affect Theory Reader* (Durham, NC: Duke University Press).
Habermas, Jürgen (1975) *Legitimation Crisis* (Boston: Beacon Press).
Habermas, Jürgen (1984, 1987) *The Theory of Communicative Action*, 2 vols (Boston: Beacon Press).
Habermas, Jürgen (ed.) (1990) *Moral Consciousness and Communicative Action* (Cambridge, MA: MIT Press).
Hall, Stuart (1973) *Encoding and Decoding in the Television Discourse* (Birmingham: Centre for Contemporary Cultural Studies).
Hall, Stuart (1980) 'Encoding/decoding', in Stuart Hall, Dorothy Hobson, Andrew Lowe, and Paul Willis (eds), *Culture, Media, Language: Working Papers in Cultural Studies, 1972–79* (London: Hutchinson), 128–38.
Halle, Louis J. (1972) *The Ideological Imagination: Ideological Conflict in Our Time and its Roots in Hobbes, Rousseau, and Marx* (London: Chatto & Windus).
Harvey, David (2007) *A Brief History of Neoliberalism* (Oxford: Oxford University Press).
Hausman, Daniel M., and Brynn Welch (2010) 'Debate: to nudge or not to nudge', *Journal of Political Philosophy* 18/1, 123–36.
Heidegger, Martin (1962 [1927]) *Being and Time*, trans. John Macquarrie and Edward Robinson (Oxford: Blackwell).

Heidegger, Martin (1977 [1954]) *The Question Concerning Technology and Other Essays* (New York: Garland).
Hochschild, Arlie Russell (1983) *The Managed Heart: Commercialization of Human Feeling* (Berkeley: University of California Press).
Honneth, Axel (2008) *Reification: A New Look* (Oxford: Oxford University Press).
hooks, bell (1981) *Ain't I a Woman? Black Women and Feminism* (Boston: South End Press).
hooks, bell (2003 [1992]) 'The oppositional gaze: black female spectator', in Amelia Jones (ed.), *The Feminism and Visual Cultural Reader* (New York: Routledge), 94–105.
Horkheimer, Max, and Theodor Adorno (1972 [1947]) *Dialectic of Enlightenment*, trans. John Cumming (New York: Herder & Herder).
Hosti, Ole R. (1969) *Content Analysis for the Social Sciences and Humanities* (Reading, MA: Addison-Wesley).
Howarth, David, Aletta J. Norval, and Yannis Stavrakakis (eds) (2000) *Discourse Theory and Political Analysis: Identities, Hegemonies, and Social Change* (Manchester: Manchester University Press).
Huizinga, Johan (2016) *Homo Ludens: A Study of the Play-Element in Culture* (London: Angelico).
Huntington, Samuel P. (1996) *The Clash of Civilizations and the Remaking of World Order* (New York: Simon & Schuster).
Inglehart, Ronald (1977) *The Silent Revolution* (Princeton, NJ: Princeton University Press).
Inglehart, Ronald (1990) *Culture Shift in Advanced Industrial Society* (Princeton, NJ: Princeton University Press).
Inglehart, Ronald (2018) *Cultural Evolution: People's Motivations are Changing, and Reshaping the World* (Cambridge: Cambridge University Press).
Inglehart, Ronald, and Christian Welzel (2005) *Modernization, Cultural Change, and Democracy: The Human Development Sequence* (Cambridge: Cambridge University Press).
Jaeggi, Rahel (2008) 'Rethinking ideology', in Boudewijn de Bruin and Christopher Zurn (eds), *New Waves in Political Philosophy* (Basingstoke: Palgrave Macmillan), 63–86.
Jäger, Siegfried (2009) 'Discourse and knowledge: theoretical and methodological aspects of a critical discourse and dispositive analysis', in Ruth Wodak and Michael Meyer (eds), *Methods of Critical Discourse Analysis* (London: Sage), 32–62.

Jameson, Fredric (1981) *The Political Unconscious: Narrative as a Socially Symbolic Act* (Ithaca, NY: Cornell University Press).
Jost, John T., Christopher M. Federico, and Jamie L. Napier (2009) 'Political ideology: its structure, functions, and elective affinities', *Annual Review of Psychology* 60, 307–37.
Jost, John T., Christopher M. Federico, and Jamie L. Napier (2013) 'Political ideologies and their social psychological functions', in Michael Freeden, Lyman Tower Sargent, and Marc Stears (eds), *The Oxford Handbook of Political Ideologies* (Oxford: Oxford University Press), 232–50.
Kadushin, Charles (2012) *Understanding Social Networks: Theories, Concepts, and Findings* (Oxford: Oxford University Press).
Kirchheimer, Otto (1969) *Politics, Law, and Social Change: Selected Essays of Otto Kirchheimer* (New York: Columbia University Press).
Kitschelt, Herbert (2010) *The Transformation of European Social Democracy* (Cambridge: Cambridge University Press).
Kojève, Alexandre (1947) *Introduction à la lecture de Hegel* (Paris: Gallimard).
Koselleck, Reinhart (2002) *The Practice of Conceptual History: Timing History, Spacing Concepts*, trans. Todd Samuel Presner (Stanford, CA: Stanford University Press).
Koselleck, Reinhart (2004) *Futures Past: On the Semantics of Historical Time*, trans. Keith Tribe (New York: Columbia University Press).
Koselleck, Reinhart (2018) *Sediments of Time: On Possible Histories*, ed. and trans. Sean Franzel and Stefan-Ludwig Hoffmann (Stanford, CA: Stanford University Press).
Kosters, Mark, and Jeroen van der Heijden (2015) 'From mechanism to virtue: evaluating nudge theory', *Evaluation* 21/3, 276–91.
Kracauer, Siegfried (1952) 'The challenge of qualitative content analysis', *Public Opinion Quarterly* 16/4, 631–42.
Kriesi, Hanspeter, Edgar Grande, Romain Lachat, Martin Dolezal, Simon Bornschier, and Timotheos Frey (2008) *West European Politics in the Age of Globalization* (Cambridge: Cambridge University Press).
Krippendorff, Klaus (2004) *Content Analysis: An Introduction to its Methodology* (London: Sage).

Krippendorff, Klaus, and Mary Angela Bock (eds) (2008) *The Content Analysis Reader* (London: Sage).

Kristeva, Julia (1980) *Desire in Language: A Semiotic Approach to Literature and Art* (New York: Columbia University Press).

Kristeva, Julia (1982 [1980]) *Powers of Horror: An Essay on Abjection* (New York: Columbia University Press).

Künzler, Jan (1989) *Medien und Gesellschaft: Die Medienkonzepte von Talcott Parsons, Jürgen Habermas und Niklas Luhmann* (Stuttgart: Enke).

Labriola, Antonio (1907 [1897]) *Socialism and Philosophy*, trans. Ernest Untermann (Chicago: C. H. Kerr).

Lacan, Jacques (1994) *The Four Fundamental Concepts of Psychoanalysis* (London: Penguin).

Lacan, Jacques (2006) *Écrits: The First Complete Edition in English*, trans. Bruce Fink (New York: W. W. Norton).

Laclau, Ernesto (1997) 'The death and resurrection of the theory of ideology', *MLN* 112/3, 297–321.

Laclau, Ernesto, and Chantal Mouffe (1985) *Hegemony and Socialist Strategy: Towards a Radical Democratic Politics* (London: Verso).

Lane, Robert E. (1962) *Political Ideology: Why the American Common Man Believes What He Does* (New York: Free Press).

Lane, Robert E., and David O. Sears (1964) *Public Opinion* (New York: Prentice Hall).

Langton, Rae (2009) *Sexual Solipsism: Philosophical Essays on Pornography and Objectification* (Oxford: Oxford University Press).

Larraín, Jorge (1979) *The Concept of Ideology* (London: Hutchinson).

Larraín, Jorge (1994) 'The postmodern critique of ideology', *Sociological Review* 42/2, 289–314.

Lasswell, Harold Dwight (1948) *Power and Personality* (London: Chapman & Hall).

Latimer, Karen, Philip Wilson, J. Kemp, L. Thompson, F. Sim, C. Gillberg, C. Puckering, and H. Minnis (2012) 'Disruptive behaviour disorders: a systematic review of environmental antenatal and early years risk factors', *Child: Care, Health, and Development* 38/5, 611–28.

Leader Maynard, Jonathan (2013) 'A map of the field of ideological analysis', *Journal of Political Ideologies* 18/3, 299–327.

Lenin, Vladimir (1961 [1902]) *What is to be Done?*, in *Collected Works*, vol. 5 (Moscow: Foreign Languages Publishing House), 347–530.
Lepenies, Robert, and Magdalena Małecka (2015) 'The institutional consequences of nudging – nudges, politics, and the law', *Review of Philosophy and Psychology* 6/3, 427–37.
Levinas, Emmanuel (1969 [1961]) *Totality and Infinity: An Essay on Exteriority* (Philadelphia: Duquesne University Press).
Leys, Ruth (2011) 'The turn to affect: a critique', *Critical Inquiry* 37/3, 434–72.
Lippmann, Walter (1922) *Public Opinion* (New York: Harcourt, Brace).
Lipset, Seymour Martin, and Stein Rokkan (eds) (1969) *Party Systems and Voter Alignments: Cross-National Perspectives* (New York: Free Press).
Luhmann, Niklas (1995 [1984]) *Social Systems*, trans. John Bednarz and Dirk Baecker (Stanford, CA: Stanford University Press).
Luhmann, Niklas (2012–13 [1997]) *Theory of Society*, 2 vols (Stanford, CA: Stanford University Press).
Luhmann, Niklas, Stephen Holmes, and Charles Larmore (1982) *The Differentiation of Society* (New York: Columbia University Press).
Lukács, György (1923) *Geschichte und Klassenbewusstsein* (Berlin: Malik).
Luxemburg, Rosa (1976 [1909]) *The National Question: Selected Writings by Rosa Luxemburg*, ed. Horace B. Davis (New York: Monthly Review Press).
Lyotard, Jean-François (1984 [1979]) *The Postmodern Condition: A Report on Knowledge* (Minneapolis: University of Minnesota Press).
Lyotard, Jean-François (1988 [1983]) *The Differend: Phrases in Dispute* (Minneapolis: University of Minnesota Press).
Lyotard, Jean-François (1992) 'Mainmise', *Philosophy Today* 36/4, 419–27.
Lyotard, Jean-François (1993 [1986]) *The Postmodern Explained: Correspondence, 1982–1985*, ed. Julian Pefanis and Morgan Thomas (Minneapolis: University of Minnesota Press).
Lyotard, Jean-François (1994 [1991]) *Lessons on the Analytic of the Sublime* (Stanford, CA: Stanford University Press).

MacKinnon, Catharine A. (1989) *Toward a Feminist Theory of the State* (Cambridge, MA: Harvard University Press).
McLellan, David (1995) *Ideology* (Minneapolis: University of Minnesota Press).
McLuhan, Marshall (1951) *The Mechanical Bride: Folklore of Industrial Man* (New York: Vanguard).
McLuhan, Marshall (1962) *The Gutenberg Galaxy: The Making of Typographic Man* (Toronto: University of Toronto Press).
McLuhan, Marshall (1964) *Understanding Media: The Extensions of Man* (New York: McGraw-Hill).
Malešević, Siniša, and Iain MacKenzie (eds) (2002) *Ideology after Poststructuralism* (London: Pluto Press).
Mann, Michael (1986–2012) *The Sources of Social Power*, 4 vols (Cambridge: Cambridge University Press).
Mannheim, Karl (1936) *Ideology and Utopia: An Introduction to the Sociology of Knowledge*, trans. Louis Wirth and Edward Shils (New York: Harcourt, Brace).
Manning, David John (1980) *The Form of Ideology* (London: Allen & Unwin).
Marcus, George E., W. Russell Neuman, and Michael MacKuen (2000) *Affective Intelligence and Political Judgment* (Chicago: University of Chicago Press).
Marcus, George E., John Sullivan, Elizabeth Theiss-Morse, and Daniel Stevens (2005) 'The emotional foundations of political cognition', *Political Psychology* 26/6, 949–63.
Marcuse, Herbert (1964) *One-Dimensional Man: Studies in the Ideology of Advanced Industrial Society* (Boston: Beacon Press).
Marx, Karl (1975 [1843]) *Contribution to the Critique of Hegel's Philosophy of Law*, in Marx and Engels, *Collected Works*, vol. 3: *1843–44* (London: Lawrence & Wishart), 175–87.
Marx, Karl, and Friedrich Engels (1976 [1845]) *The German Ideology*, in Marx and Engels, *Collected Works*, vol. 5: *1845–47* (London: Lawrence & Wishart), 19–539.
Mauss, Marcel (1934) 'Les Techniques du corps', *Journal de Psychologie* 32/3–4.
Meiksins Wood, Ellen (1986) *The Retreat from Class* (London: Verso).
Merton, Robert K. (ed.) (1968) *Social Theory and Social Structure* (New York: Free Press).
Michels, Robert (1911) *Zur Soziologie des Parteiwesens in*

der modernen Demokratie: Untersuchungen über die oligarchischen Tendenzen des Gruppenlebens (Leipzig: Werner Klinkhardt).
Mills, C. Wright (2000) *The Power Elite* (Oxford: Oxford University Press).
Minogue, Kenneth (1985) *Alien Powers: The Pure Theory of Ideology* (London: Weidenfeld & Nicolson).
Mols, Frank, S. Alexander Haslam, Jolanda Jetten, and Niklas K. Steffens (2015) 'Why a nudge is not enough: a social identity critique of governance by stealth', *European Journal of Political Research* 54/1, 81–98.
Mondak, Jeffery J. (2010) *Personality and the Foundations of Political Behavior* (Cambridge: Cambridge University Press).
Mondak, Jeffery J., and Matthew V. Hibbing (2012) 'Personality and public opinion', in Adam J. Berinsky (ed.), *New Directions in Public Opinion* (Abingdon: Routledge), 217–38.
Mouffe, Chantal (2000) *The Democratic Paradox* (London: Verso).
Mouffe, Chantal (2005) *On the Political* (Abingdon: Routledge).
Murray, Joseph, and David P. Farrington (2010) 'Risk factors for conduct disorder and delinquency: key findings from longitudinal studies', *Canadian Journal of Psychiatry* 55/10, 633–42.
Nartey, Mark, and Isaac N. Mwinlaaru (2019) 'Towards a decade of synergising corpus linguistics and critical discourse analysis: a meta-analysis', *Corpora* 14/2, 203–35.
Noelle-Neumann, Elisabeth (1993 [1980]) *The Spiral of Silence: Public Opinion – Our Social Skin* (Chicago: University of Chicago Press).
Norris, Pippa, and Ronald Inglehart (2009) *Cosmopolitan Communications: Cultural Diversity in a Globalized World* (Cambridge: Cambridge University Press).
Norval, Aletta (2000) 'The things we do with words', *British Journal of Political Science* 30/2, 313–46.
Nucci, Larry (ed.) (2014) *Conflict, Contradiction, and Contrarian Elements in Moral Development and Education* (Abingdon: Routledge).
Nussbaum, Martha (1985) 'Objectification', *Philosophy and Public Affairs* 24/4, 249–91.
Nussbaum, Martha (2004) *Hiding from Humanity: Disgust, Shame, and the Law* (Princeton, NJ: Princeton University Press).

Oesch, Daniel (2006) *Redrawing the Class Map: Stratification and Institutions in Britain, Germany, Sweden, and Switzerland* (Basingstoke: Palgrave Macmillan).

Ostrowski, Marius S. (2021) 'You've got to ask the right expert: who gives political advice?', in Colin Kidd and Jacqueline Rose (eds), *Political Advice: Past, Present, and Future* (London: I. B. Tauris), 161–76.

Pareto, Vilfredo (1935 [1916]) *The Mind and Society* (New York: Harcourt, Brace).

Parsons, Talcott (1951) *The Social System* (London: Routledge & Kegan Paul).

Parsons, Talcott (1967 [1937]) *The Structure of Social Action*, 2 vols (Glencoe, IL: Free Press).

Paulus, Stefan (2015) 'Methodologische Überlegungen und methodisches Vorgehen bei einer intersektionalen Dispositivanalyse', *Forum: Qualitative Social Research* 16/1.

Pêcheux, Michel (1969) *Analyse automatique du discours* (Paris: Dunod).

Phillips, Anne (2010) 'What's wrong with essentialism?', *Distinktion: Journal of Social Theory* 11/1, 47–60.

Piketty, Thomas (2020) *Capital and Ideology*, trans. Arthur Goldhammer (Cambridge, MA: Harvard University Press).

Plamenatz, John (1970) *Ideology* (New York: Praeger).

Pocock, John Greville Agard (1972) *Politics, Language, and Time: Essays on Political Thought and History* (Chicago: University of Chicago Press).

Pocock, John Greville Agard (2009) *Political Thought and History: Essays on Theory and Method* (Cambridge: Cambridge University Press).

Poulantzas, Nicos (1975 [1968]) *Political Power and Social Classes* (London: NLB and Sheed & Ward).

Price, Vincent (1992) *Public Opinion* (London: Sage).

Purvis, Trevor, and Alan Hunt (1993) 'Discourse, ideology, discourse, ideology, discourse, ideology ...', *British Journal of Sociology* 44/3, 473–99.

Raftopoulos, Athanassios (2007) *Cognition and Perception* (Oxford: Oxford University Press).

Rawls, John (1971) *A Theory of Justice* (Cambridge, MA: Belknap Press).

Reddy, William (2001) *The Navigation of Feeling: A Framework for the History of Emotions* (Cambridge: Cambridge University Press).

Ricœur, Paul (1974 [1969]) *The Conflict of Interpretations: Essays in Hermeneutics*, trans. Willis Domingo et al. (Evanston, IL: Northwestern University Press).
Ricœur, Paul (1976) *Interpretation Theory: Discourse and the Surplus of Meaning* (Fort Worth: Texas Christian Press).
Ricœur, Paul (1985) *Lectures on Ideology and Utopia*, trans. George H. Taylor (New York: Columbia University Press).
Rokeach, Milton (1973) *The Nature of Human Values* (Glencoe, IL: Free Press).
Rorty, Richard (1984) 'Deconstruction and circumvention', *Critical Inquiry* 11/1, 1–23.
Roth, Steffen, and Anton Schütz (2015) 'Ten systems: toward a canon of function systems', *Cybernetics and Human Knowing* 22/4, 11–31.
Sartori, Giovanni (1969) 'Politics, ideology, and belief systems', *American Political Science Review* 63/2, 398–411.
Sartori, Giovanni (1970) 'Concept misformation in comparative politics', *American Political Science Review* 64/4, 1033–53.
Sartori, Giovanni (1976) *Parties and Party Systems: A Framework for Analysis* (Cambridge: Cambridge University Press).
Schmitt, Carl (1996 [1932]) *The Concept of the Political*, trans. George Schwab (Chicago: University of Chicago Press).
Schopenhauer, Arthur (1819) *Die Welt als Wille und Vorstellung* (Leipzig: Brockhaus).
Schwarzmantel, John (2008) *Ideology and Politics* (London: Sage).
Seliger, Martin (1976) *Ideology and Politics* (London: Allen & Unwin).
Sewell, William H. (1992) 'A theory of structure: duality, agency, and transformation', *American Journal of Sociology* 98/1, 1–29.
Shils, Edward (1968) 'The concept and function of ideology', in David L. Sills (ed.), *International Encyclopedia of the Social Sciences*, vol. 7 (New York: Macmillan), 66–76.
Shklar, Judith (1964) *Legalism: An Essay on Law, Morals, and Politics* (Cambridge, MA: Harvard University Press).
Silva, Sónia (2013) 'Reification and fetishism: processes of transformation', *Theory, Culture & Society* 30/1, 79–98.
Skinner, Quentin (1969) 'Meaning and understanding in the history of ideas', *History and Theory* 8/1, 3–53.
Skinner, Quentin (1978) *The Foundations of Modern Political Thought*, 2 vols (Cambridge: Cambridge University Press).

Skinner, Quentin (2002) *Visions of Politics*, vol. 1: *Regarding Method* (Cambridge: Cambridge University Press).
Smith, Merritt Roe, and Leo Marx (eds) (1994) *Does Technology Drive History? The Dilemma of Technological Determinism* (Cambridge, MA: MIT Press).
Sorel, Georges (1912 [1908]) *Reflections on Violence* (New York: B. W. Huebsch).
Specht, Jule, Boris Egloff, and Stefan C. Schmukle (2011) 'Stability and change of personality across the life course: the impact of age and major life events on mean-level and rank-order stability of the big five', *Journal of Personality and Social Psychology* 101/4, 862–82.
Spivak, Gayatri Chakravorty (1988) 'Can the subaltern speak?', in Larry Grossberg and Cary Nelson (eds), *Marxism and the Interpretation of Culture* (Basingstoke: Macmillan), 66–111.
Spivak, Gayatri Chakravorty (1996) 'Subaltern studies: deconstructing historiography?', in Donna Landry and Gerald MacLean (eds), *The Spivak Reader* (London: Routledge), 203–37.
Stahl, Titus (2017) 'Immanent critique and particular moral experience', *Critical Horizons*, https://doi.org/10.1080/14409917.2017.1376939.
Stråth, Bo (2013) 'Ideology and conceptual history', in Michael Freeden, Lyman Tower Sargent, and Marc Stears (eds), *The Oxford Handbook of Political Ideologies* (Oxford: Oxford University Press), 3–19.
Strauss, Leo (1952) *Persecution and the Art of Writing* (Glencoe, IL: Free Press).
Strauss, Leo (1964) *The City and Man* (Chicago: Rand McNally).
Tawney, Richard Henry (1931) *Equality* (London: Allen & Unwin).
Thagard, Paul (2006) *Hot Thought: Mechanisms and Applications of Emotional Cognition* (Cambridge, MA: MIT Press).
Therborn, Göran (1980) *The Ideology of Power and the Power of Ideology* (London: Verso).
Therborn, Göran (2008) *What Does the Ruling Class Do When it Rules? State Apparatuses and State Power under Feudalism, Capitalism, and Socialism* (London: Verso).
Thompson, John B. (1984) *Studies in the Theory of Ideology* (Cambridge: Polity).

Thompson, John B. (1990) *Ideology and Modern Culture* (Cambridge: Polity).
Thompson, John B. (1995) *The Media and Modernity: A Social Theory of the Media* (Cambridge: Polity).
Tomkins, Silvan S. (1962–3, 1991–2) *Affect Imagery Consciousness*, 4 vols (London: Tavistock / New York: Springer).
Tomkins, Silvan S. (1987) 'Script theory', in Joel Arnoff, A. I. Rabin, and Robert A. Zucker (eds), *The Emergence of Personality* (New York: Springer), 147–216.
Tönnies, Ferdinand (1922) *Kritik der öffentlichen Meinung* (Berlin: Springer).
van Dijk, Teun A. (1998) *Ideology: A Multidisciplinary Approach* (London: Sage).
van Dijk, Teun A. (2008) *Discourse and Power: Contributions to Critical Discourse Studies* (Basingstoke: Palgrave Macmillan).
van Dijk, Teun A. (2009) *Society and Discourse: How Social Contexts Control Text and Talk* (Cambridge: Cambridge University Press).
van Dijk, Teun A. (ed.) (2011) *Discourse Studies: A Multidisciplinary Introduction* (London: Sage).
van Dijk, Teun A. (2013) 'Ideology and discourse', in Michael Freeden, Lyman Tower Sargent, and Marc Stears (eds), *The Oxford Handbook of Political Ideologies* (Oxford: Oxford University Press), 175–96.
Vessey, Rachelle (2013) 'Challenges in cross-linguistic corpus-assisted discourse studies', *Corpora* 8/1, 1–26.
Vessey, Rachelle (2017) 'Corpus approaches to language ideology', *Applied Linguistics* 38/3, 277–96.
Villadsen, Kaspar (2021) '"The dispositive": Foucault's concept for organizational analysis?', *Organization Studies* 42/3, 473–94.
von Beyme, Klaus (1985 [1982]) *Political Parties in Western Democracies* (New York: St Martin's Press).
Wallerstein, Immanuel (2004) *World-Systems Analysis: An Introduction* (Durham, NC: Duke University Press).
Wallerstein, Immanuel (2011) *The Modern World-System*, 4 vols (Berkeley: University of California Press).
Weber, Max (1978 [1922]) *Economy and Society: An Outline of Interpretive Sociology*, ed. Guenther Roth and Claus Wittich (Berkeley: University of California Press).
Weiss, Gilbert, and Ruth Wodak (eds) (2003) *Critical Discourse*

Analysis: Theory and Interdisciplinarity (Basingstoke: Palgrave Macmillan).

White, Jonathan (2011) 'Left and right as political resources', *Journal of Political Ideologies* 16/2, 123–44.

White, Rachel, and Kimberly Renk (2012) 'Externalizing behavior problems during adolescence: an ecological perspective', *Journal of Child and Family Studies* 21/1, 158–71.

Williams, Howard (1988) *Concepts of Ideology* (New York: Wheatsheaf).

Wittgenstein, Ludwig (1973 [1953]) *Philosophical Investigations*, trans. G. E. M. Anscombe (Oxford: Wiley-Blackwell).

Wodak, Ruth (1996) *Disorders of Discourse* (London: Longman).

Wodak, Ruth (ed.) (2013) *Critical Discourse Analysis*, 4 vols (London: Sage).

Wodak, Ruth, and Michael Meyer (eds) (2009) *Methods of Critical Discourse Analysis* (London: Sage).

Wolff, Jonathan, and Avner de-Shalit (2007) *Disadvantage* (Oxford: Oxford University Press).

Wright, Erik Olin (1998) *Classes* (London: Verso).

Wright, Erik Olin (ed.) (2008) *Approaches to Class Analysis* (Cambridge: Cambridge University Press).

Wright, Richard D., and Lawrence M. Ward (2008) *Orienting of Attention* (Oxford: Oxford University Press).

Zaller, John R. (1992) *The Nature and Origins of Mass Opinion* (Cambridge: Cambridge University Press).

Žižek, Slavoj (1989) *The Sublime Object of Ideology* (London: Verso).

Žižek, Slavoj (ed.) (1994) *Mapping Ideology* (London: Verso).

Žižek, Slavoj (1996) 'Fantasy as a political category: a Lacanian approach', *Journal for the Psychoanalysis of Culture and Society* 1/2, 77–85.

Žižek, Slavoj (1999) *The Ticklish Subject: The Absent Centre of Political Ontology* (London: Verso).

Žižek, Slavoj (2002) *Welcome to the Desert of the Real: Five Essays on September 11 and Related Dates* (London: Verso).

Žižek, Slavoj (2006) *The Parallax View* (Cambridge, MA: MIT Press).

Žižek, Slavoj (2010) *Living in the End Times* (London: Verso).

Index

Page numbers in *italic* refer to figures and tables

Abercrombie, Nicholas 34
absolutism 28, 77
Adorno, Theodor 31
advocacy 1
affect theory *21*, 40, 157–9
agency 45, 53, 56–7
agonism and antagonism 80–1
Ahmed, Sara 40
Allerweltspartei 33, 130
allocation, ideological 114, 115
Althusser, Louis 18, 19, 34, 79, 116, 123, 144, 165
alt-right 73
anarcha-feminism 78
anarchism 11, 29, 72, 83, 88, 90, 96, 104, 105, 125
anarcho-primitivism 75
anomie 140, 167
anthropology 23, 33, 143
anti-absolutism 87
anti-capitalism 90, *95*, *96*, *97*, 101
anticolonialism 87, 88, 92, 98
antiracism 38, 74, 92, 98

anti-statism *95*, *96*, *97*
anti-technocracy 102
anti-vaxxer ideology 64
'applied' ideology 8, 48, 58–9, 61, 63, 64, 66, 70, 93
archaeology of knowledge 35
Arendt, Hannah 31, 142, 166
aristocratic-bourgeois struggle 24, 29, 83
Aron, Raymond 32, 166
authoritarian populism 73, 85
authoritarianism 71, 72, 77, 78, 88, 91, 103
autonomisation of ideology 38

Barbalet, Jack 40
Barth, Hans 12
Barthes, Roland 19, 36, 37
Bauer, Otto 29
behaviouralism 30, 33
Bell, Daniel 31, 166
Berlin, Isaiah vii
Bernays, Edward 26
Bernstein, Eduard 27–8
Beyme, Klaus von 33

Index

'Big Four' ideologies 11, 87–8, 92
  see also anarchism; conservatism; liberalism; socialism
Billig, Michael 40
Boudon, Raymond viii, 11, 166
Bourdieu, Pierre 19, 37, 59, 142, 166
bourgeoisie 6, 24–5, 27, 29, 38, 83
Brown, Wendy 39
bureaucracy 29, 32, 96, 97, *118*
Butler, Judith 39, 142, 144, 166

caesarism 73
Cambridge School 151
capitalism 6, 14, 24, 27, 30, 64, 71, 72, 77, 85, 87, 89, 90, 103, 104, 105, 147
  anti-capitalism 90, *95*, *96*, *97*, 101
'centre', 'centrism' *96*, 103
chauvinism 83, 98, 102
Christian democracy 11, 29, 60, 62, 64, 83, *88*, 90, 91, 93, *96*, 101, 104, 105
circulation, ideological 26, 34, 75, 114, 138, 140, 158
civil rights movements 37
civil society 26
class 14, 18, *21*, 30, 34, 37, 81, 85, 104
  consciousness 24, 29
  economic divisions 24, 29, 81
  intra-class factionalism 29
  'retreat from class' 29, 30, 38
  struggle 6, 24, 27, 28–9, 35, 80, 81, 101
  see also bourgeoisie; proletariat
climate activism 76
climate-change denialism 64
cliques 82–3
cognition 22–3, 44–5, 49, 119, 145, 158–9, 161
cognitive-affective maps 158
Cold War 34, 41, 72, 92, 104, 143
collective sentiments 7–8
Collins, Patricia Hill 38
communication studies 145
communism 11, 29, 30, 61, 62–3, 83, 85, *88*, 90, 91, 97, 100, 103, 105, 125, 147
  decline of 38, 77–8, 92–3
  see also Marxism
community 63
compatibilism 9, 32, 38, 166
complexity, ideological 60, *65*
conceptual decontestations 99–101, 137
conceptual history (*Begriffsgeschichte*) 12, 151–2
conceptual morphology 145–6, 155, 163
consciousness 110
  collective 76, 81
  false 25, 29
  practical 59
conservatism 11, 29, 47, 61, 62, 64, 71, 72, 77, *88*, 89, 90, 91, 92, 93, *95*, 101, 102, 103, 105
  liberal 78, 104
  national-conservatism 78
  neoconservatism *88*, 91
  paleoconservatism 91
consistency, ideological 63, *65*
constitutionalism 13
constructionism 73
consumerist society 32
content analysis 154–5, 163
contextualism 19, 83–4, 85, 123, 129, 135, 151, 152
contrarianism 137

cooperativism 64, 72, 96, 97
cosmopolitan liberalism 136
cosmopolitanism 130
countercultures 91, 132
Crenshaw, Kimberlé 39
critical discourse analysis (CDA) 9, 152–4, 163
critical race theory 142
crowd psychology 10
cues, ideological 8, 127–30, 132, 133, 134, 136, 138, 141
  frequent repetition principle 129, 135
  hinterland 129, 130
  macroscopic 127–8
  mesoscopic 128
  microscopic 128
  one-shot occurrences 128
  periodic 129
culture 6, 14, 36–7, 38
cultural turn 21, 38

de Man, Paul 36
Debray, Régis 41
decolonisation 3, 29, 37, 91, 104
deconstructionism 35–6, 149
deep ecology 75
defining ideology 3, 15, 42–69
  combinations and arrangements of ideas 15, 42–3, 65, 69
  habitus see habitus
  ideological characterisation 15, 58–65
  what is/is not ideology 65–9
definition, ideological 62, 65
deindustrialisation 38
Deleuze, Gilles 37, 39, 144
democracy 6, 61, 85, 89, 90, 93, 95, 97, 99, 103
  illiberal democracy 73
  liberal democracy vii, 6, 32, 85
  see also Christian democracy; social democracy
democratism 71, 72, 77, 89, 97, 102
demographic characteristics 74, 76, 77, 81, 83, 84, 136
density, ideological 60–2, 65, 155
Derrida, Jacques 35–6, 144
design plans, ideological 54, 56, 57, 111, 114, 126, 165
Destutt de Tracy, Antoine 18, 19, 164
diachronic differentiation 75–6, 77, 86, 105, 131
différance 36, 61
differentiation, ideological 15, 60, 65
  diachronic 75–6, 77, 86, 105, 131
  synchronic 73, 74, 76, 77, 86, 131
dirigisme 73
(dis)ability 11, 92, 93
discourse 6, 14, 35–6, 38, 65–9, 148
  biopolitical approach 35
  discursive turn 21, 39–40
  distinguishing ideology from 65–8
  semantics of 35
  see also ideological discourse
dispositifs 116, 122, 155
dispositions, ideological 49, 50, 58, 59, 114
dispositive analysis 155
dissemination, ideological 18, 26, 116, 119, 122, 123, 129, 135
  see also circulation, ideological
dogmatism 30
domination/subjection
  distinctions 81, 82, 84, 121, 146, 147, 148

doxa 37, 122
dualism 43
durability, ideological 64, *65*
Durkheim, Émile 19, 28

Eagleton, Terry viii, 12
ecofascism 78
ecologism (green ideology) 37, 47, 61, *88*, 92, 93, 97
economic ideologies 73
ecosocialism 78
electoral franchise 28, 29, 89
electoral ideologies 6, 14, 28–30, 33, 70, 82–3
  see also party politics
Elias, Norbert 59
elites 121, *124*, 135, 159
embodiment 44–5, 57, 74, 76, 80
'end of history' 3, 31, 167
'end of ideology' 3, 6, *21*, 31, 167
Engels, Friedrich 18, 19, 22, 23, 24, 25, 146, 164, 165
Enlightenment 10, 20, 22, 31, 79
environment 44, 57, 59, 61
epistemology 10, 20, 23
essential contestation and co-option 94, 99–101, 104, 113, 137
ethnography 10, 23
Eurocentrism 13, *98*
Evangelicalism 72
evolution of ideology theory 10–13, 14, 17–41, *21*, *88*, 165
  classical period (1800–1890) 14, 20–5, *21*
  core authors 18–19
  emergence of ideology studies (1980–now) 37–44
  four waves in 87–93
  new concerns and approaches (1890–1945) 25–30
  terminological and methodological challenges (1945–1980) 14, 30–7
existentialism 25
experiencing ideology 15, 109–40
  developmental stage 110–12
  early-years incomprehension 110–12
  ideological apparatuses 34, 115–25, *118*, *124*, 127, 131, 135, 136, 137, 138, 141
  ideological objectification 112–14
  ideological subjectification 15, 114–40
  individually/collectively 109–11
extremism 14, 30–1, 132

factionalism 15, 82, 83, 84, 85, 123, 129, 141
Fairclough, Norman 41
false consciousness 25, 29, 32
families and traditions, ideological 11, 15, 18, 19, 70–108, 141, 165, 167
familles spirituelles 33, 78, 105, 143
fanaticism 1, 30
fascism 11, 29, 30, 63–4, 72, 83, *88*, 90, 91, 93, *96*, 100, 101, 104, 105
  neofascism *88*
federalism 60, 62, 72, 78, 90, 96, 97
Federico, Christopher M. 39
feminism 11, 38, 74, 90, 93, *98*, 142, 144
  anarcha-feminism 78
feudalism 6, 24, 86, 104
Feuerbach, Ludwig 22, 164
Firestone, Shulamith 38
firmness, ideological 62–3, *65*

formalism 30
Foucault, Michel 18–19, 35, 144, 166
fragmentation, ideological 26, 37, 41, 89
Frankfurt School 19, 31, 32, 144, 146
free trade 83, 89
Freeden, Michael 40, 142, 166
freedom and liberty vii–viii, 25, 60, 64, 65, 89–92, 94, 95, 96, 97, 103, 105, 107, 145
negative/positive freedom vii, viii
republican freedom viii
French Revolution 31, 103
Freud, Sigmund 19, 34, 144
fringe groups 72
Fromm, Erich vii
futurism 75

Geertz, Clifford 19, 36
genocide 3, 30, 89, 91
geography 11, 23, 58, 75–7, 79, 157
Geuss, Raymond 12
Giddens, Anthony 59
Gilligan, Carol 40
global North and global South division 38, 85–6, 92
global village 75
glocalisation 76
Goldmann, Lucien 19, 34
Gramsci, Antonio 18, 19, 26, 27, 34, 36, 144, 165
grassroots activism 76, 145
green ideology (ecologism) 11, 37, 47, 61, 88, 92, 93, 97
group consciousness 76, 81
Guattari, Félix 37, 39, 144

Habermas, Jürgen 19, 32, 63
habitus 37, 59, 62, 63, 65, 69, 114, 115, 116, 117, 119, 122, 125, 127, 128, 130, 131, 132, 133, 134, 135, 137
dispositions 49, 50, 58, 59, 114
norms 15, 50–2, 58, 59, 114
perspectives 15, 57–8, 68, 114
practices 15, 52, 54, 58, 114
structures 15, 54, 58, 59, 114
systems 15, 55–6, 58, 59, 114
Hall, Stuart 36
haredim 72
hegemony, ideological 6, 27, 32, 34–5, 36–7, 39, 71, 73, 76, 82, 83, 84, 85, 123, 148, 159
Heidegger, Martin 33
here/there distinctions 84
hermeneutics 149–50
hierarchies 7, 15, 73, 77, 81, 82, 85, 123, 125, 129, 135, 136, 141
Hill, Stephen 34
Hindutva 72, 90
Hochschild, Arlie Russell 40
Holocaust 30
homophobia 74, 85, 147
hooks, bell 38–9
Horkheimer, Max 31
humanitarianism 107
hybridisation, ideological 78, 102, 105, 143, 144
hypermodernism 75

identity 7, 14, 21, 38–9, 74, 93, 95, 96, 97, 99, 113, 115
ideologies of 89, 92, 105
non-class 29
performativity 39
self-identification 38, 71, 81, 102
wounded attachments 39

identity/difference 81
ideological apparatuses 34,
    115–25, *118*, *124*, 127,
    131, 135, 136, 137, 138,
    141
  'averaging' tendency 133
  counter-apparatuses 123
  differentiation 125
  dysfunction 132
  life-cycle encounters with
    118–19, *120*
  'ploughing-ahead' tendency
    134
  running 121–2
ideological categorisation 15,
    102–8
  cultural dimension 104–6,
    107
  ideological compass 105,
    106–7, *106*, 108, 123, 130
  left–centre–right spectrum
    15, 102–8, 123, 130
  political-economic dimension
    104, 105, 106, 107
  universal criteria, attempts to
    find 108
ideological characterisation
    51–2, 58–65, 115
  density 60–2, *65*
  integrity 63–4, *65*
  robustness/fragility 62, 64,
    65, 65, 69, 70, 77, 79,
    131, 141
  size 59–60, *65*
  strength 62–3, 64–5, *65*
  thickness/thinness 62, 64, *65*,
    65, 69, 70, 77, 78, 79, 82,
    83, 84, 131, 141
ideological discourse 38, 66–9
  completeness, claims to
    67–8, 69, 70, 79–80, 86,
    87, 114, 128, 138
  comprehensiveness, claims to
    66–7, 69, 70, 79–80, 86,
    87, 114, 128, 138
  correctness, claims to 68, 69,
    70, 79–80, 86, 87, 114,
    128, 138
ideological state apparatuses
    (ISAs) 116, 123
ideologies *see* families and
    traditions, ideological
'ideologology' 3, 9, 14, 19,
    32, 41, 143, 144, 162–3,
    164–5
idéologues 3, 20, 22, 23, 157
ideology
  'applied' 8, 48, 58–9, 61, 63,
    64, 66, 70, 93
  central debates concerning
    4–9
  defining 3, 15, 42–69
  diverse connotations 1–2
  evolutionary trajectory 10–13,
    14, 17–41, *21*, *88*, 165
  explicitness or implicitness of
    8, 167
  families and traditions 11,
    15, 18, 19, 70–108, 141,
    165, 167
  first use of the term 10, 18,
    79
  individuality or collectiveness
    of 7, 167
  limitations of 130–40
  necessity or unnecessity of
    5, 166
  pejorative/non-pejorative
    understandings of 3, 4, 14,
    20, 25, 30, 38, 42, 142
  preconditions 78–86
  premodern existence of 86,
    87
  'pure' 34, 48, 58, 59, 61, 64,
    65, 66, 70, 93
  semantic roots 2
  singular or plural conception
    of 6–7, 28, 122–3
  temporariness or permanence
    of 5–6, *9*, 166

truth or falsity of 4, 9, 166
'turn against' 30–1, 35, 37, 41, 65
'what counts as' 40, 78
ideology studies 15–16, 141–63
  analytical focus 160–1, 162
  analytical methodology 161–2
  comparative political science approach 159–60, 163
  conceptual morphology 145–6, 163
  content analysis 154–5, 163
  critical discourse analysis (CDA) 152–4, 163
  emergence as autonomous subdiscipline 15, 37–44, 143, 160
  emotion and affect theory 157–9, 163
  epicentre 16, 145–51
  hermeneutic approach 149–50, 163
  ideology critique 146–7, 163
  ideology studies compass 160–3, *162*
  inputs from other disciplines 143–5
  methodological fiefdoms 142–3
  opinion research 160, 259
  penumbra 16, 151–60
  poststructuralist approach 147–9, 163
  qualitative/quantitative analysis 163
  renaissance in 17, 38, 143, 164
  rhetorical analysis 8, 150–1, 153, 158, 163
  semiotic analysis 155–6, 158, 163
  social- and political-theoretical analysis 144, 145–51, 152

social-psychological analysis 145, 156–7, 163
social-scientific and humanistic analysis 142, 151–60
illiberal democracy 73
illusion, ideological 14, 19, 20, 22, 26, 148
immanence 114
imperialism 25, 83, 87, 91, 104
'imperialist white-supremacist capitalist heteropatriarchy' 82
in-group/out-group distinctions 82, 83, 84, 85, 123, 125
incorporation, ideological 60, 65
indigeneity 92, 93
individuation 76, 83, 84
industrialisation 87
Inglehart, Ronald 38
integrity, ideological 63–4, *65*
intellectual history 144, 152, 155
intelligentsia 14, 26–7, 28, 121, *124*, 135, 137, 145
internationalism 73, 93, 103
interpellation 34, 115, 116
intersectionality 39, 74, 82, *98*, 99, 147
interventionism 104, 105, 106, *106*
Islamism 72, 90
'ism'(s) 2, 47, 48, 59, 65, 69, 79, 86, 129

Jakobson, Roman 33
jihadism 72
Jost, John T. 39
journals 12

Khālistānism 72
Kirchheimer, Otto 33
knowledge-production 26
knowledge workers 26

194 Index

Kojève, Alexandre 31
Kristeva, Julia 39

labelling, ideological 47
Labriola, Antonio 27–8
Lacan, Jacques 34, 39, 144
Laclau, Ernesto 39, 142, 144
laissez-faire 89, 104, 105, 106, 106
Lane, Robert E. 33
Larraín, Jorge 12
latifundism 24, 104
'left', 'left-wing', 'leftism' 102–3
left–centre–right spectrum 15, 102–8, 123, 130
legal ideologies 73
Lenin, Vladimir 27–8, 34
Leninism 60, 100
lenses, ideological 49, 50, 114, 126, 165
Lévi-Strauss, Claude 19, 33
LGBTQQIP2SAAK* 92
liberal conservatism 78, 104
liberal democracy vii, 6, 32, 85
liberal socialism 78
liberalism 11, 29, 32, 34, 47, 60, 61, 63, 64, 71, 72, 87, 88, 89–90, 95, 101, 103–4, 105, 125
  classical liberalism 87, 88, 89, 91
  cosmopolitan liberalism 146
  high liberalism 88, 91, 92, 93
  national-liberalism 78
  neoliberalism 13, 85, 88, 91, 92, 93, 100, 102
  social liberalism 88, 89–91, 100
libertarianism 11, 60, 65, 88, 91, 93, 97, 104, 105, 125
  national-libertarianism 73
like/other distinctions 80, 81, 83, 85, 123, 125

linguistics 33, 35, 144, 153–4, 155
Lippmann, Walter 26, 44, 166
literalism 73
longue-durée ideological families 77–8, 108, 143
Lukács, György 18, 19, 27, 34, 146
Luxemburg, Rosa 29
Lyotard, Jean-François 36

MacCallum, Gerald vii–viii
MacKinnon, Catharine A. 38
McLellan, David 12
McLuhan, Marshall 36–7
macro-ideologies 71–2, 76, 77, 78, 87, 105
  see also 'Big Four' ideologies
Mannheim, Karl 18, 19, 27, 28
Manning, David viii, 12
maps, ideological 48, 49, 50, 54, 56, 58, 114, 115, 116, 117, 119, 122, 125, 127, 128, 130, 131, 132, 133, 134, 135, 137, 139, 141, 146, 165
Marcuse, Herbert 31–2
Marx, Karl 18, 19, 22, 23, 24, 25, 144, 146, 164, 165
Marxism–Marxisantism 3, 10, 18, 19, 22, 27, 29, 31, 32, 79, 136, 143
  base and superstructure theory 23, 24, 28, 34
  economic turn 23–4
  ideological analysis 9, 25, 27, 28, 41, 70, 142, 146–7, 167
  social analysis 23–4, 30
  structuralist Marxism 34
Mauss, Marcel 59
media 10, 41
media analysis 143, 154
Meiksins Wood, Ellen 38
mental models 34, 39

mercantilism 73
meso-ideologies 72–3, 76, 77, 78, 90, 91–2, 105
metalanguage 36
metanarratives 76
Michels, Robert 29
micro-ideologies 72, 76, 77, 78, 89, 90, 91–2, 93, 105
micronarratives 76
militarism 73, 82, 91, *95*, 96
Minogue, Kenneth 12, 166
mirror stage 111
modernism 25, 30
modernity 5–6, 79, 86
monarchism 77, *88*, 103
monism 60, 105, 106, *106*
moral panics 7, 135
morphology, ideological 15, 43, 48–9, 59, 59–65, *65*, 70, 71, 78, 86–102, *95–9*, 108, 125, 127, 141, 144, 165, 166
  conceptual morphology 145–6, 155, 163
  social morphology 59, 70, 71, 93, *95–9*
Mouffe, Chantal 39, 142, 144
multiculturalism 13, 37, 93

Napier, Jamie L. 39
national-conservatism 78
national-liberalism 78
national-libertarianism 73
nationalism 11, 64, *88*, 89, 90, *96*, *98*, 102, 103, 107, 125, 142
Nazism 30, 31
neoconservatism *88*, 91
neofascism *88*
neoliberalism 13, 85, *88*, 91, 92, 93, 100, 102
(neo)Luddism 75
nihilism 25
Noelle-Neumann, Eliabeth 33, 166

norm-giver and norm-taker societies 85
norms, ideological 15, 50–2, 58, 59, 114
Nussbaum, Martha 40

objectification, ideological 112–14
ontology 45, 149
opinion research 159, 160
ordinary thinking and expression *21*, 39–40
originalism 73
overload, ideological 132
'ownership disputes', ideological 100

paleoconservatism 91
Pareto, Vilfredo 19, 26
parliamentarism 24, 61, 90, *95*, *96*, *97*, 99
partisanship 1, 29, 30, 70, 82
party politics 6, 14, 28–30, 33, 70, 80, 81, 87, 159
patriotism 13
Pêcheux, Michel 35
peer groups 122, *124*
performative (self-) contradiction 63
permeation between ideologies 71, 78, 91, 94, 100, 143–4
Peronism 60
personality traits, ideologies and 39, 157
perspectives, ideological 15, 57–8, 68, 114
phenomenology 33, 46, 149
  see also social phenomena
Plamenatz, John 12
plebiscitarism 61, *97*, 102
pluralism 60, 105, 106, *106*, 142, 143, 166–7
points of contact with other ideologies 78, 85, 94

polarisation, ideological 13, 106, 136, 137
political ideologies 14, 73
  see also specific index entries
political religions 88, 90, 98
political science 12, 21, 33, 41, 142, 143, 145, 159–60
populism 11, 64, 73, 85, 88, 93, 102, 142
post-material values 38, 105–6
postcolonial studies 142
postcolonialism 38
posthumanism 75
postmodernism 30
poststructuralism 11, 147–9, 153, 166
postwar consensus 72, 91
Poulantzas, Nicos 19, 34, 38
practices, ideological 15, 52, 54, 58, 114
preconditions for ideology emergence 78–86
  chronological starting point 79
  contextual belonging, '*Volk*' 83–4, 85
  factionalism, 'party' 82, 83, 84, 85
  social hierarchies, 'class' 81, 82, 85
pre-ideological psychology and behaviours 114, 126
premodern existence of ideology 86, 87
primers, ideological 51, 59, 111, 114, 126, 165
priority, ideological 61, 65
progressivism 13, 87, 102, 166
proletariat 6, 24, 25, 27, 29, 38, 83
propaganda 1, 10, 31
proportionality, ideological 61–2, 65
protectionism 83, 102
proximity, ideological 61, 65

pseudo-environment 44
psychoanalysis 34, 39
psychoanalytic semiology 155
public opinion theory 7, 14, 21, 26, 29–30, 33
'pure' ideology 48, 58, 59, 61, 64, 65, 66, 70, 93

queer ideology 11, 38, 47, 74, 88, 92, 93, 99
queer studies 142

racism 13, 74, 96, 147
radicalism 1, 7, 13, 87, 88, 90, 96, 100, 102, 103–4
rationalism–irrationalism binary 39
reactionarism 7, 37, 82, 87, 88, 90, 95, 96, 100, 103
realism 30
reality
  chaotic and self-contradictory 5, 43, 45, 53, 117, 130
  early-years incomprehension 112
  engaging with and making sense of 43, 48–58, 59, 60, 72, 93, 114, 133–4, 165
  ideology and 4–5, 15, 20, 22, 23, 39, 48–58, 167
  ideology–reality gap 46, 53
  masking/unmasking 4, 25, 138, 138–40
  'multiplicity' 43–4
  overwhelming experience of 45, 59
  'pure' 43, 63, 139
  social reality 43
  'steering' 56, 59, 87, 123, 131, 138, 139
  unfiltered 112
'red scares' 102
Reddy, William 40
religiosity 104, 107

religious associations of ideology 1
religious fundamentalisms 72
religious ideologies 11, 73
religious tolerance 87, 89
religious traditionalism 77, 91, 93, 107
republicanism 11, 60, 88, 89, 97
restorationism 73
rhetorical analysis 8, 150–1, 153, 158, 163
'right', 'right-wing', 'rightism' 103
robustness/fragility, ideological 62, 64, 65, 65, 69, 70, 77, 79, 131, 141
Rorty, Richard 36

Salafism 73
Saussure, Ferdinand de 33
schemata 39, 49, 119, 157, 161
Schopenhauer, Arthur 19, 22, 164
science, ideology and 14, 22–4, 33, 79
scientism 25, 30
scripts, ideological 39, 52–3, 56, 111, 114, 126, 165
Second International 19
sectarianism 83
secularism 60, 104, 107
self-identification 38, 71, 81, 102
self-interest 2, 29
Seliger, Martin viii, 12
semantic roots of ideology 2
semiotics 36–7, 39, 155–6
sexism 13, 74, 85
Shils, Edward 32
Shklar, Judith 32
simulations, ideological 56, 57, 59, 111, 114, 126, 165
'single-issue' ideologies 60, 64, 107
size, ideological 59–60, 65

slavery and serfdom 87
social and political theory 16, 144, 151
social democracy 11, 29, 61, 64, 72, 83, 88, 90, 91, 92, 96, 101, 104, 105
social domains 6, 73, 74, 76, 77, 81, 82, 117, 118, 121, 123, 136
social groups 80–1, 82, 83
social market economy 90–1, 102
social morphology 59, 70, 71, 93, 95–9
social phenomena viii, 8, 13, 42, 49, 50, 51, 52, 54, 55, 56, 57, 66–7, 68, 76, 113, 134, 138, 148, 155
social psychology 9, 39, 145, 156–7, 158, 159
socialisation, ideological 15, 117, 131
early-years socialisation 119, 126, 132
see also ideological apparatuses
socialism 11, 29, 30, 47, 61–2, 64, 71, 72, 78, 83, 88, 89, 91, 93, 95, 103, 105, 125, 147
ecosocialism 78
liberal socialism 78
societal development 74, 75, 79, 81–2, 83, 87, 102, 135
'milestones' 79, 87
sociology of knowledge 18
solidarity 7, 38, 57, 76, 89, 97, 98, 103, 115
Sorel, Georges 19, 26, 29
'source' ideologies 78, 105, 143
stability, ideological 64, 65
Stalinism 30, 100
stereotypes 51, 99, 113
strain, ideological 63, 65
strategic essentialism 101

strength, ideological 62–3, 65
structural divisions within
  society 79, 80
structuralism 10, 19, 34, 166
structures, ideological 15, 54,
  58, 59, 114
subalternity, ideological 72, 76,
  82–4, 114, 123
subjectification, ideological 15,
  114–40
  cues 8, 127–30, 132, 136, 141
  failure of 131–40
  self-subjectification 127
Sun Yat-Sen 100
sustainability 37, 61, 97
symbolic commodification and
  exchange 41
symbols and symbolism 8,
  36–7, 39, 41
synchronic differentiation 73,
  74, 76, 77, 86, 131
syncretism 12, 14, 41, 163, 166
syndicalism 73, 95, 96
systems, ideological 15, 55–6,
  58, 59, 114

technological development
  74–5
tension, ideological 4, 64,
  113–14, 132–3
terminological (de)contestation
  of ideology 13, 142
textualism 73
theocracy 28, 98, 103, 107
Therborn, Göran 12
thickness/thinness, ideological
  62, 64, 65, 65, 69, 70, 77,
  78, 79, 82, 83, 84, 131,
  141
Third Way 72, 88, 92
Thompson, John B. viii, 12, 41
'time-sliced' ideological families
  77–8

Tönnies, Ferdinand 26–7
totalitarianism vii, 14, 30,
  31–2, 104
traditions, ideological *see*
  families and traditions,
  ideological
transgender ideology 92, 93
transphobia 74
'turn against ideology' 30–1,
  35, 37, 41, 65
Turner, Bryan S. 34

unconscious and subconscious
  7, 37, 39
unconscious manifestations of
  ideology 37
universalisation 75, 83, 84
university centres for the
  studies of ideology 12
urbanisation 24, 87

van Dijk, Teun A. 39
vantage-points, ideological 58,
  59, 114, 126, 165
Volkspartei 33, 102
voluntarism 104

welfare-statism 31, 61, 89, 90,
  91, 100, 101
'what counts as' an ideology
  40, 78
Williams, Howard 12
Wodak, Ruth 41
world-systems division of the
  globe 85
'world values' clusters 38, 85,
  107
worldviews 1, 27, 34, 58, 76,
  131, 137, 146

Zaller, John R. 39
Zionism 72, 90
Žižek, Slavoj 39, 45, 142, 144